YOUTHFUL

EXPLORERS

—IN—

BIBLE LANDS:

A FAITHFUL ACCOUNT OF THE
SCENERY, RUINS, PRODUCTIONS, CUSTOMS, ANTIQUITIES
AND TRADITIONS OF SCRIPTURAL COUNTRIES;
AS YOUTHFUL PENS WOULD DESCRIBE THEM.

JOPPA AND JERUSALEM.

PREPARED AND PUBLISHED UNDER THE AUSPICES OF "THE SCHOLARS HOLY LAND EXPLORATION" OF THE UNITED STATES,

BY ROBERT MORRIS, LL. D.,
SECRETARY.

CHICAGO:
HAZLITT & REED, PRINTERS, 90 WASHINGTON STREET.
1870.

PREFACE.

Walking the shell-paved beach of Joppa, on May-day, 1868, we pondered this question: How can we best interest the general mind in this Bible-hallowed land? The present volume has grown out of the reflections of that hour.

The *plan* of this work, patent upon its face, was so to write each chapter that *youngest* readers would be allured to peruse *a part*, and older ones *the whole* of the book. Having been accustomed ever since we were twelve years of age to keep a diary, we felt at home in this style of literature. We have intentionally given to little Elliot a predominating share in the task, and a pleasant confidence is felt that boys and girls of not more than twelve years of age, will follow with delight the clever little fellow in his daily "researches," and so secure their part of that knowledge which it is the sole purpose of this book to communicate.

We feel it due to gratitude and friendship to make acknowledgements here for the personal favors extended to us, both during our tour in the Orient in 1868 and since, to H. E. Mohammed Raschid, Pasha General of Syria, resident at Damascus. This noble ruler has been placed by a favoring providence in a field, where his generous spirit can have full sway. Happy for the Land of Inspired Truth, if such men can always be found to occupy its high places. Coupled with his name, that of Noureddin Effendi, Kaimakam of Joppa, merits grateful notice.

Among the Christian friends whose counsel and aid have

contributed the most to enliven these pages, it is proper to name Mr. Samuel Hallock, of the American Protestant Mission, Beyrout; Mr. Serapion J. Murad, of the Prussian Consulate, Jerusalem; Lieut. Charles Warren, of the London, Palestine Fund; and Hon. E. T. Rogers, H. B. M. Consul, at Cairo, Egypt.

It was thought appropriate that this volume,—the first of a series of six preparing on the same plan,—should be the initial publication of "The Scholars Holy Land Exploration," of the United States, now in its second year of existence. To reach the minds of the young by lectures and specimens was the first step in the labors of that institution; to publish the results of recent researches in Palestine in a style adapted to youth, is an object worthy of untiring endeavors.

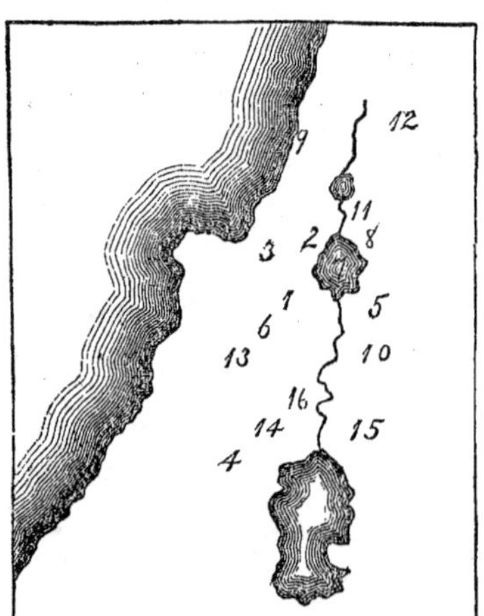

Miniature Map of the Holy Land.

The figures, 1 to 16, refer to the Sixteen Miracle-localities in the life of our Lord, viz.:

1. Cana of Galilee.
2. Capernaum.
3. Galilee.
4. Jerusalem.
5. Gadara.
6. Nain.
7. Sea of Galilee.
8. Meadow Place.
9. Sarepta.
10. Decapolis.
11. Bethsaida Julias.
12. Mount Hermon.
13. Samaria.
14. Bethany.
15. Peræa.
16. Jericho.

TO THE READER.

Elliot, John and Harriet Morrell are the only children of Mr. Ebenezer Morrell, a wealthy and pious merchant of New York. This gentleman has taken great pains to interest his children in Bible knowledge; and he promised them several years ago, that if they made good proficiency in the geography and history of the Holy Land, they should some day pay a visit there, and see that memorable country for themselves. In February, 1869, they started.

He put them under charge of Mr. Richard Fountain, a well educated and religious gentleman, nearly fifty years of age, who has already made a visit to the Lands of the Bible. It was a very fortunate thing that the young people had so good and kind a guardian, entirely competent to advise them, and devoted to their improvement and happiness. Mr. Fountain has for a long time been Superintendent of the Sunday School of which Elliot, John and Harriet are members.

Elliot is only twelve years of age, but he can read and write well, can sketch with his pencil, can write short hand, and knows a very large number of Bible verses by heart. He is well grown for his age and thinks himself almost a man. You will be pleased at what the brave boy says, and sees, and does. He is the very soul of truth and honor, and will not tell you anything but what he believes to be true.

John is seventeen, and a good student. Harriet is twenty, and has a polished education. Both of them are first-class Bible scholars, and professors of religion. They desire nothing more earnestly than to become useful Christians. It is their diaries which make up this book.

Such is our simple fiction. In its use we promise to give our readers fresh and abounding information upon the Scenery, Ruins, Productions, Customs, Antiquities and Traditions of Scriptural countries, written in styles adapted to all classes of readers.

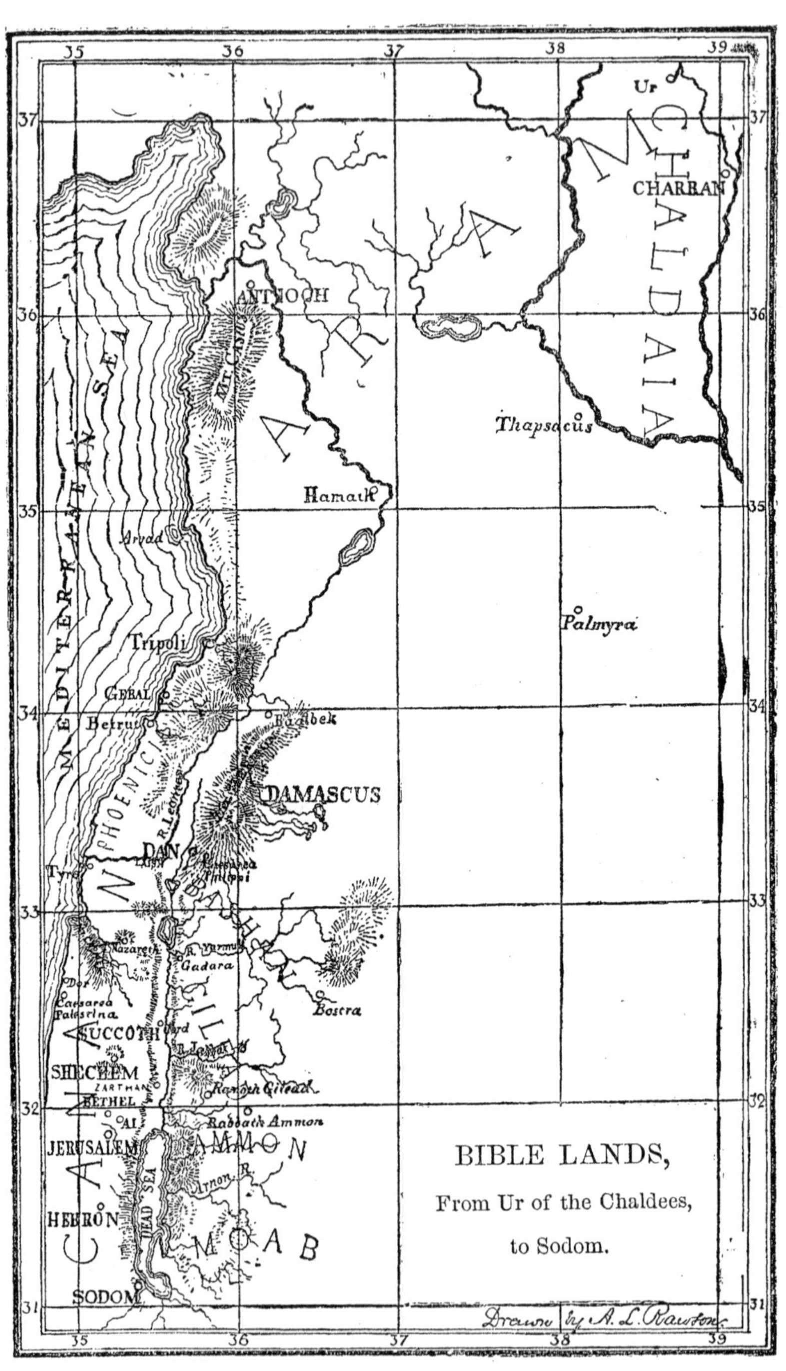

BIBLE LANDS,
From Ur of the Chaldees,
to Sodom.

YOUTHFUL

Explorers in Bible Lands.

CHAPTER I.

SETTING FOOT ON HOLY LAND.

Midnight view of Joppa—Glories of the Starry World—Going on shore—Uproar at Landing—Custom House customs—Streets narrow, steep and foul—Curious arches—Hotel—Call on the Governor—First breakfast in Holy Land—Collecting shells—The donkey Tyeeb—Camp o umbrellas—Scare from Bedouins—Telegraph line—Climbing palm-tree—Arab fight—Strolls through Joppa—Mosks—Schools—Dinner with the Governor—Mr. Floyd—Andromeda and Perseus—Saracenic Fountain—Pilgrim Mission—Music to Stabat Mater—Description of Joppa—Description of our three youthful explorers.

ELLIOT'S DIARY.

STEAMER L'AMERIQUE, Midnight, Monday, March 15, 1869.

I WAS twelve years old January 3d. When I left New York, five weeks ago, I promised father and mother I would keep a diary every day while in the Holy Land, and now I begin.

As I come on deck at this midnight hour, Mr. Fountain turns my face towards the south, and says, "Open your eyes wide, my lad, for yonder is Joppa!" My first thought is, shall I ever reach that shore? Somehow I feel as if I never shall step upon the Holy Land. It seems all a dream to me; like those dreams in which I reach, and reach, and reach after something and never reach it.

The city of Joppa sprawls all over a round hill, and the stars shine so bright I can almost count the houses in it. Now I wonder which one belonged to Simon, the tanner, where Peter boarded when he had his vision? (Acts x: 9-16.) I can fancy how the cannon of Napoleon roared through this bay, and how the victorious shouts of his troops sounded when he captured Joppa, March 3d, 1799. It must be the orange trees yonder that smell so deliciously on this midnight air. I see a palm tree on the top of that hill in the middle the town. I guess it is as tall as any of them, and I intend to climb it, as told the boys I would when I left home. And now Mr. Fountain says I must go to bed again, for at 9 o'clock this morning we are to set foot on the Holy Land.

STEAMER L'AMERIQUE, 9 A. M.

We are ready to push off from the ship and go ashore, and the next entry in my diary will be *in the Holy Land.* Captain Le Maitre, who has treated me very kindly all the way from Marseilles, has kissed me and given me his photograph. I have promised to send him mine when I go home. This captain is a real clever fellow, and I wish he would come to New York instead of confining himself to the Mediterranean Sea. A sea that has no tides in it is no sea at all to my notion, and so I told him. I notice that he calls this town Jaffa, and so it is printed on the advertisements. But I shall always call it as the Bible does, Joppa, and nothing else. (2 Chr. ii: 16; Ezra iii: 7; Jonah i: 3; Acts ix: 36; x: 5, 32; xi: 5.)

BLATTNER'S HOTEL, at Joppa, 11 A. M.

Here we are at the "English Hotel" in Joppa. All my superstitions fancy that I should never set foot on the shore of the Holy Land proves foolish. When we left the steamer *L'Amerique*, more than fifty rowboats were round the ship, greedy for passengers. Such scrambling, such screaming, such howling! The boatmen fight like dogs. One of them was knocked overboard with a valise in his hand. He came up again, valise and all, and crawled back into the boat, and all the others laughed at him. He had a turban on his head and lost it in the water. Then I saw that his head was shaved smooth as a pumpkin, all but a top-knot, like a Pawnee Indian's. This was funny.

Our boatman was a Greek named Caracoussi. He wore petticoats, and they tripped him up as he stepped along the seats. He had four other Greeks to row the boat, and they all wore petticoats, too. This makes them look queer. Their oars are made different from ours. In the middle they begin to bulge out large, so as to have the upper end the heaviest, so the weight of the oar lifts itself out of the water. This suits these lazy Greeks, who don't like hard work. The boatmen stand up while rowing, and push their oars from them. They face the same way they row.

As our boat rushed along, the water looked as blue as mother's indigo tub on washing day. A reef of rocks was lying between us and the shore, having a passage-way through it. This is pointed out by a tall granite column that stands as a guide on the right hand of the entrance. Our boat went through that opening like a shot. There were a great many small sail vessels inside of the reef loading with oranges for Egypt; an English brig was there, taking in a cargo of bones for England.

When we got near the shore, we saw a perfect jam of people waiting for us. They held out their hands as the hackmen do in New York, but they screamed worse than a thousand hackmen, and kept their arms going like windmills. Mr. Fountain bade us pay no attention to them, but to follow him right along. He took a heavy carpet-bag, when the boat grounded, and jumped into the crowd without saying a word. I don't know how many of the Arabs were knocked down, but he made as big a gap as Arnold Winkelried did among the Austrians, and we followed him post-haste. And so it came to pass that we all came safe to land. (Acts xxvii: 44.)

But oh, the racket those rowdies made! One man who had been pushed into the water got so mad he picked up a stone and hit himself with it on the head. We followed our leaders, as Peter followed the angel (Acts xii: 7—10), first through a gate in the city wall, then up a good many flights of stairways, then along steep, narrow lanes, dreadfully filthy, and so on, until we saw the sign, "English Hotel," in a dirty little street, upon the second story of a stone house. This is our present lodgings. It is kept by some brothers, named Blattner, who used to be guides for travelers, and when they had made money enough, they opened this hotel. One of the Blattners came out this morning to our steamer, and engaged to board us for ten francs a day apiece; that is two dollars. A dead cat was lying near the foot of the steps, right in front of the hotel, and it smelt bad. I couldn't make the servant see it, so I picked up the cat by the leg and dragged it to the foot of somebody else's steps, more used to such things than we are, and there I left it.

Breakfast was almost ready when we came in. There was a fine large fish caught this morning in Joppa bay, in a hand-net. It cost eight piastres. A piastre is four cents. Mr. Fountain says the principal kinds of fish caught off this coast are of the families Sparidæ, Percidæ, Scomberidæ, Rariadæ and Pleuronectidæ; but I think the fish are not so ugly as their names.

I couldn't learn the Arabic name of our fish. The Bible says the Jews must not eat any fish that hasn't scales or fins and so they won't eat cat-fish or oysters. (Deut. xiv: 9.) The Egyptians only eat fish that have scales on them. Our bread is made of wheat flour. It is good enough, but it tastes as though it had mill-stones in it. Mr. Fountain says it has. He says it is owing to the way the millers let the stones run on one another while grinding their grain. Those millstones are made of basaltic rock that comes from near the Sea of Galilee. I shall see piles of them when I get to Tyre. We had French coffee, and the most splendid oranges. I ate oranges, chiefly, for my breakfast. I am going to put up a few of them in a jar of alcohol, and send them to mother for curiosities. I never saw such large oranges before.

An English party took breakfast with us. They call their baggage *luggage*, but the French call it *baggage*, just as we do, and I think *they* are right. I got a scolding from Aunt Liddy for telling them that Bonaparte was a much better man than ever *they* had for a general. They had better read their own war history before they abuse Bonaparte so much for his doings here in 1799. But how they do hate the French! And the French hate them too. Our pilot on board *L'Amerique* was always telling me how mean John Bull was. He called him *Jeen Bull.*

BLATTNER'S HOTEL, 3 P. M.

We have been taking an excursion along the sea beach south of Joppa, gathering shells. This is the best place in the world for shells. I felt like singing the song, about gathering shells, "One summer eve," all the way. There is a million wagon loads of shells here, of a thousand sorts. I saw a pomegranate tree and chewed some of the leaves as it is related in Lalla Rookh the Fire Worshipers did, "to cleanse their mouths from inward uncleanliness."

We had a donkey to carry our baskets for us. His name is Tyeeb; that means a *good one.* His ears are heavier than his legs. Every once in a while he throws up his head and tail and brays. Oh, such braying! It sounds like sawing loose boards.

From this side of town, Joppa looks like a hill so crowded with buildings as almost to push one another off. It has less vacant lots than any town I ever saw.

There is a telegraph line that runs past Joppa to Egypt. It is connected with the line that goes to New York. Only think, we are going to send a dispatch home to-morrow and get an answer back again. I kissed a telegraph pole, and whispered to it what I wanted dear father and mother to know. The wind whistled through the glass insulators just as it does at home, sounding like some one playing a flute.

I had rare fun chasing the land-crabs into their holes. I rode Tyeeb on a gallop and he stepped on some loose earth and threw me head first into the sand. Where *his* head struck, there was a hole big enough to bury him in. But I was not hurt, nor he either. We got more than five bushels of shells here.

As we came back along the beach a party of wild Arabs galloped on us from behind some sand-hills. At first it looked as though they would ride us down with their long spears. But there was no danger. Mr. Fountain spoke to them in Arabic, and they answered very kindly. I hallooed *Owafy* to them as they passed. I had heard somebody say it on board the steamer. They looked back and laughed and answered, *Allah yafik*. *Owafy* means "good luck to you." *Allah yafik* means, "May God give you good luck." Their chief was a tall, thin, gaunt, time-worn ruffian. He had a gray beard, a bright, flashing eye and very white teeth. By riding so much in the sun he was tanned to the color of sole leather. Their horses were poor and bony, but rode swift as the wind.

BLATTNER'S HOTEL, 5 P. M.

I have been out by myself climbing the palm tree that I saw last night in the middle of the town. It is about sixty feet high, straight as an arrow and not a limb on it. Every foot or so there is a kind of natural ring round it, exactly like a cabbage stalk, and this makes it as easy to climb as a ladder. I went clean to the top as I promised the New York boys. I picked a bunch of the flowers and one of the great leaves, longer than my body. These I will take home to mother. From the top I saw all the town of Joppa, and a great ways to the east over the orange groves, and clear out to sea. Our steamer, *L'Amerique*, was just starting out for Egypt. I waved a good bye to her with one of my suspenders, for I had tied the flowers up in my handkerchief, so I couldn't wave that. As I came down the tree, some rascally boys who had been bawling at me all the time, though I didn't understand them, began to throw stones at me. This made me mad. I dropped my bundle, grabbed the biggest one by the neck and shook the stones out of his hand. Then the crowd scattered. Not a stone went amiss. The biggest fellow ran at me with a stick, and I was obliged to hit him with a stone on the forehead, where David smote Goliath. He tumbled down like an ox, and then I was scared. But he came to again and went home howling dismally. Mr. Fountain advised me not to climb trees anymore in this country, unless I have somebody to watch at the foot of the tree, for the boys stole my boots while I was up there. He says the Arab boys were only doing as their Bible commands them, throwing stones at Satan. Their bible is called the *Koran.* He says the boys halloed at me, *Leish tasyad ila harthar ashajerar?* That means, "What are you climbing that tree for?" but I couldn't understand such lingo as that.

I have dedicated that noble palm tree to Rev. J. H. Vincent, of New York, whose lectures on the Holy Land were the first ones I ever heard that I could understand. His language is as graceful and sweet as the blossoms I picked from the top of that palm tree. Mr. Fountain says that *the Turks* practice civility and acts of endearment as well as any other people. It is only the lower classes, *these Arabs*, that insult travelers, and they not so often as they used to.

Next I got a man to take me to the place where they say Jonah was thrown on shore by the whale. It is near a hole in the city wall. Of course the story is a hum, but I am going to enter in my diary all the stories I hear in this country. As we came down the coast last week on the steamer, Mr. Fountain showed me two places where they say Jonah came on shore; one was at Issus near an old gray stone tower, the other a few miles north of Sidon. Of course the whale couldn't have landed at all these places. I asked my guide how he knew that Jonah came ashore here, and he answered, *backsheesh.*

BLATTNER'S HOTEL, 8 P. M.

We have had dinner and the Governor of Joppa dined with us. Also Mr. Rolla Floyd, an American gentleman who has lived here for several years. The Governor is a good looking man, about fifty years old, very pleasant. He kissed me. Everybody kisses everybody in this country. He talked to me in French while Harriet interpreted. He said he means to go to the United States some day and is trying now to get appointed consul at an American port. I gave him the presents I had brought for him. He was delighted with them. But Mr. Floyd was the man I liked best. He has promised to spend to-morrow with us and show us the splendid orange-groves of Joppa and the other sights. He has been collecting bones for the English brig in the harbor. All around Joppa, he says, the ground is white with bones of cattle, camels, horses and dead men, and sometimes he can hardly tell them apart. The brig is taking a load of bones to England to be ground up into bonedust. Mr. Floyd has a wagon and team and is the first man who has taken a wagon to Jerusalem for many hundred years. The Governor has promised to have his soldiers find my boots for me. He thinks Bonaparte did nothing here but what any military man would have done. So ends my first day in the Holy Land, and now I am going to bed.

JOHN'S DIARY.

STEAMER L'AMERIQUE, Monday, March 15th, 1869. Midnight.

My age is 17. I am pledged to my dear parents to keep a diary for them all the time I stay in the Holy Land, and thus I commence it.

My first sight of Joppa, by midnight, will never be forgotten. It is sublime. We cast anchor north-west of the city, and as I come through the gangway and look south-east, the great constellation *Scorpio*, with its forty-four stars, hangs right over it, and sparkles with a brilliancy that is startling. Its principal star, Antares, always exhibiting a remarkably blood red appearance, seems exactly in the range of the expanded tuft of a palm tree that crowns the hill in the centre of Joppa. I shall never look on that starry group again without associating it with the tree, the town, and this glorious midnight hour. It is a strange coincidence that the Jewish astrologers, when they divided out the twelve constellations among the twelve tribes of Israel, gave *Scorpio* to Dan, and the town of Joppa yonder *was a part of Dan.*

I wonder whether Jonah, when he fled from the face of the Lord, from Joppa toward Tarshish, did not see that crimson star Antares. It must have followed the guilty renegade like an avenging meteor. And yet had he seen it he would certainly have turned back and gone to Nineveh, as the Lord had commanded him.

BLATTNER'S HOTEL, 10 A. M.

We are at our hotel now, and in the Holy Land. At half past nine we set foot on the shelly beach of Joppa, treading into powder those frail gems of pearl, and rose and lovely brown. The crowd was so great that at first I could not see how we were to get on shore. But Mr. Fountain has been to Joppa before, and understands the people. Coolly taking a piece of baggage in each hand, as soon as the boat's keel grated on the sand, he jumped into the thickest of them, making an opening in their ranks like a stone from a catapult, and we all followed him. Mr. Fountain's idea is that the only way to deal with these people is to show them you are their master. As the Arabs stood on the shore in solid phalanx, determined to fleece us handsomely for handling our baggage and showing us the way to the hotel, had we tried to conciliate them at all, the more determined they would have been to prey upon us. But we showed no signs of hesitation and got pleasantly through, while the passengers in the other boats were horribly cheated.

The boatmen who had rowed us ashore took our baggage on their shoulders and followed us into town. At the gate, some fifty steps from the shore, a custom house officer stopped us, but Mr. Fountain quietly handed him a five franc piece, and he stepped aside. The officer placed his right hand on his left breast and said *Salaam Aleikam*, that is, peace be with you, and Mr. Fountain did the same. This is their manner of expressing good will.

We mounted the steep hill of Joppa, a city of five thousand inhabitants, sometimes by stairways, sometimes by precipitous alleys, over dungheaps and under arches, till we reached the "English Hotel," and so settled down to our first Oriental lodging place, glad to be on solid land again. While waiting for breakfast I wrote this "Story of a Shell," that I picked up on the spot where my foot first struck the shore:

STORY OF THE SHELL.

"I was washed up from the bottom of yonder blue sea, in the days when Adam was young. I lay here unnoticed when the warriors of Dan took Joppa at the edge of the sword. I was here four hundred and fifty years afterwards, when the temple-builders came from Tyre with cedars and firs and a freightage of marble and precious metals, on the way to Jerusalem. I was here two hundred years after that, when the foolish Jonah came to Joppa seeking to escape from under the all-seeing eye of God. I was here three hundred years after that, when the builders of the second temple brought materials from Mt. Lebanon. I was here five hundred years after that, when the apostle Peter had his vision on the house top. I was here one thousand years after that, when the Crusaders came down the coast and took possession of the country in the name of Jesus. And I am here now, nine hundred years after that, when a New Yorker picks me up and makes me tell him this *Story of the Shell!*"

Although this is called "the English Hotel," the owners are not English people, nor is there anything English about the house except the name. All the books and newspapers that lie around on the table and seats are French, German or Hebrew, and as Mr. Fountain advises us not to go out until he returns from calling on the Governor, we amuse ourselves looking into the Visitor's Book. It is the custom for travelers in this country, when they write their names in the Hotel Register, to add some account of themselves; where they traveled last; what they think of the hotel, etc. Most of the entries are silly enough. Some are good. I copy a few.

"Very Comfortable." "Satisfied with the evident desire of the landlord to make us comfortable." "Very fair." "Lord Seymour was highly satisfied." "Existence here will be found supportable by those who are profoundly resigned to their fate, if detained any time waiting for a steamer." "We have, greatly daring, dined." Our old friend Col. Sandford, of the 47th Iowa, writes: "I am much surprised to find the accommodations so good. Paul and Herman are both dragomans and I recommend them, not only as good and obliging, but also intelligent and well-posted in regard to the history of Palestine."

BLATTNER'S HOTEL, 11 A. M.

Mr. Fountain has returned and says the Governor promises to dine with us at the hotel at six o'clock. This will be quite a treat; for we have long heard of Noureddin Effendi as a pleasant gentleman, who was very kind to Mr. Fountain last year, and we hope he will be our friend also. Harriet is uneasy lest she should not know how to conduct herself in the Governor's society, but Mr. Fountain assures her that he is one of the plainest of men, and puts on no style whatever.

We had breakfast with some English travelers who were fellow-passengers with us on *L'Amerique*. They are friendly but not very sociable. Their conversation consisted mostly in abusing Bonaparte for his cruelty while here sixty-nine years ago. This is rather a dry subject for a social party, and I paid little attention to it. Elliot, however, flared up at something they said, for he is a great admirer of Bonaparte, and used words so saucy that Aunt Liddy was obliged to scold him severely.

BLATTNER'S HOTEL, 3 P. M.

After breakfast we started out for a stroll. We hired a man with a donkey to take the basket of provisions and some boxes for specimens. We went out at the east gate, the only gate there is on the land side of Joppa, and turned to the right, taking the caravan road that goes to Egypt. On our left hand we passed gardens and groves of oranges, lemons, citrons, pomegranates and other trees deliciously fragrant and prolific. Reaching the beach I was astonished to see the quantities of oranges collected here in baskets, for shipment. They are brought here on donkeys, mules, horses and camels, from the orchards around the city. A basket is slung on each side of the animal. At the shore these baskets are loaded into rowboats, taken out to the sail vessels that cannot get nearer the beach on account of shoal water, and so emptied into the holds to ship abroad. These are said to be the largest and sweetest oranges in the world. The camels with that wise gravity and intelligence peculiar to their race, kneel down at the word of command to permit the loaded baskets to be removed from them.

On the beach, are found numerous shells of different kinds, but Mr. Fountain advised that a mile or two down the coast they are far more abundant and in greater varieties. So turning south, we walked, ran and skipped along the smooth, sand beach, so hard that our donkey's feet scarcely made a mark on it. As we went, we picked up the rarer objects, as Mr. Fountain named them for us, the cuttle-fish, sponges, crabs-claws, oyster-shells, jelly-fish, &c., with *Serpulæ* attached, until, in a half hour, we had one box full of specimens.

Then we came to shells indeed. In places the beach was almost a solid layer of white, brown, purple and red ones. In other places piled two or three feet high, they lay in long windrows as wave and wind heaped them. The blue, gelatinous sea-nettles were also abundant. We took our choice of shells freely, and soon gathered ten species. No doubt we could collect three times as many by more diligent search. As we walked southward, the long lines of telegraph posts stretched out before us, as far as the eye can reach, the wires glistening in the sunbeams like bright cobwebs. This telegraph line runs from Constantinople to Alexandria, more than eight hundred miles. It is affecting to think that by this line, continued through Europe and under the Atlantic to New York, we can, in a few hours, send messages directly to our dear parents in New York. Mr. Fountain has promised us that we shall do it to-morrow.

By two o'clock we got all the shells we could carry on the donkey, Mr. Fountain thinks as many as ten thousand specimens, and setting our umbrellas around a telegraph pole, we made a hasty camping place, and ate our luncheon. The view of the Mediterranean Sea, before us, was grand. The heavy strokes of the waves moving inward, steadily as a pendulum, beat along the shore; the water becoming thinner and thinner as it rushed up the beach, until its force was spent; then, pausing a moment and gathering itself for a recoil, roaring seaward it hastened, as though impatient to join the mighty flood from which it had been separated;

"And rolling far along the gloomy shore,
The voice of days of old, and days to be."

But King David has described this beautiful phenomenon much better than I can. "He gathereth the waters of the sea together as a heap: He layeth up the depth in storehouses." (Ps. xxxiii : 6.)

Some vessels far out, sailing towards the south, were orange boats, bound, as Mr. Fountain informed us, for Egypt.

Turning back to Joppa, we were overtaken by four desert Arabs or *Bedouins*, who had come up the coast from Gaza, on business with the Governor of Joppa. They answered our salutation politely, looking with special interest as I could see, towards Harriet. It is a rare thing to them to be allowed to see the face of a strange woman.

BLATTNER'S HOTEL, 5 P. M.

Resting a little at the hotel, we started out again under the guidance of a native, who could talk some English, and strolled leisurely through the city. It is curious to see the variety of arches used in the doorways of these houses. As there is no wood here for building materials, the houses of course are all of stone; but I was not prepared to see the ingenuity with which the workmen have constructed arches.

We visited several of the mosks, a school room, the court room of the Governor, the Saracenic Fountain, and other places, then returned to the hotel to prepare for dinner and write up our diaries.

Elliot went out by himself, to climb a palm tree, which he saw from the ship's deck last night, and got into a row with some Arab boys, who stole his boots, and undertook to stone him. But they found their match; for there is not a boy in his class who can throw stones with Elliot. He knocked one of them down with a stone in the forehead, and we were afraid at first had killed him; but he recovered his senses and went home, crying loudly. Near the foot of this palm tree is located the scene of that ancient fable of Andromeda and Perseus, which is still represented in the constellation of Taurus. Pliny says that here at Joppa, Andromeda was tied to a rock and exposed to a sea-monster. As she was about to be devoured, she was released by Perseus, who undertook the dangerous exploit, under promise from her father, that she should become his wife. He turned the monster into stone by showing it the head of Medusa. Then Perseus unbound the lately-despairing maiden and married her. Pliny, furthermore, says that the bones of this monster were brought to Rome during the government of Pompey, by Scaurus, (about B. C. 63) and were there carefully preserved. As this is the first mythological story I ever have located, I feel quite interested in it. But I am more skeptical than Sir John Maunderville, who was here five hundred years ago, and stated that the bones were still here at Joppa. There are bones enough lying round the streets, but none of them of such gigantic dimensions.

Ovid, in his "Metamorphoses," gives the whole story in immortal verse:

Hic immeritam maternæ pendere linguæ
Andromedam pœnas iniustus jusserat Ammon:
Quam simul ad duras religatum brachia cautes
Vidit Abantiades, nisi quod levis aura capillos
Monerat, et tepido manabant lumina fletu
Marmoreum ratus esset opus: trabit inscius
Et stupet: eximeæ correptus imagine formæ inges;
Pene suas quatere est oblitus in ære pennas. *Book* 50.

The beauty of Andromeda and the surprise of Perseus when he beheld her, are prettily described in these lines.

Every starry night we may see the constellation of Perseus and Andromeda in Taurus, just as the poet sung long ago:

"Still in the heaven, her captive form remains,
And on her wrists still hang the galling chains."

BLATTNER'S HOTEL, 8 P. M.

Our dinner, with Noureddin Effendi, Governor of Joppa, was very agreeable to us all. We presented him the things we had brought from home for him. I think he prized the photographs of the Presidents the most of any. I could talk a little with him in French; and Harriet, who is an excellent French scholar, helped me out whenever I broke down for a word. The Governor told me many things in answer to my questions, which surprised me. Amongst others, he said he had never known a regular *Bedouin*, or desert Arab, who could read or write. Indeed, they are taught to believe it is a disgrace to have any book learning. He told me that every tribe in the desert has a peculiar mark with which they designate their camels. When he asked me what were our plans of travel, in this country, I answered we had resolved to shape our own course as independent Americans, little heeding advice; to go where we will, and to undertake whatever we think expedient. He laughed heartily at this, and said it was the right way to travel in the East. He thinks we shall make a successful tour, and offers us any advice or assistance we may need. This is the right time of year, he says, for our journey, and there is not the least danger in visiting any place west of the Jordan. I knew it was improper to ask a Turkish gentleman any questions about his family, but I did venture to enquire of the Effendi how many children he had? He sighed, smiled, made a queer grimace in French style, and said--none, for he had never been married! He had heard that Admiral Farragut was in the Mediterranean Sea last year, and very much regretted that he did not come to Joppa.

The Governor told me that the yearly taxes in this part of the Holy Land are one piaster (four cents) for every she goat; ten for a donkey; twenty for a horse or mule, and thirty for a camel.

I showed him a piece of fossil salt I had bought of an Arab, and he says, when I go to the Dead Sea, I shall find a mountain of it, seven miles long, and that Lot's wife is there.

In my intercourse with the natives he advises me never to joke with them, never to seem afraid of them. I must always pay them a just price, he says, for what I purchase, and no more, and never appear very rich or very poor, while dealing with them. He was full of frankness and good will to us. Noureddin is a good man. When the "Adams' Colony" came here in 1865, the Governor so ordered matters at the Custom House as to save the "Colony" five hundred dollars in duties. He says that an American who expects to travel with Arabs, must sleep on the ground, drink only water, sit cross-legged and use the short stirrup to the saddle, which at first is very hard to learn. He seemed pleased when I told him I had seen his name, Noureddin, in the Arabian Nights Entertainment. It is an established custom in the Holy Land, from the days of Abraham, never to appear before a superior without a gift, and I had read the story of a Noureddin who was Turkish King in 1163. The name is pronounced *Nou-red-deen*—drawing out the last syllable. As soon as dinner was over I retired to my room, and having written up my diary, I shall now go to bed.

HARRIET'S DIARY.

STEAMER L'AMERIQUE, Midnight, Monday, March 15, 1869.

When Mr. Fountain awoke me at mignight, as he had promised, and said, "Come, Harriet, we are in Jonah's Bay; we have cast anchor in the harbor of

Joppa," I was revelling in a sweet dream of home and friends; and much as I desired to secure the earliest glimpse of the everlasting hills of the Holy Land, yet, for the moment, I was sorry to be roused from the vision. But this feeling was instantly dispelled, for as I stepped upon the deck, I discovered myself under a concave of celestial imagery, such as American skies can never exhibit. The stars in innmerable hosts and brightest radience were out, and illumined the long, low line of the Palestine coast. Stephen, at his martyrdom, "looked steadfastly into heaven." So, for a few minutes, did I, awe-struck, yet delighted, at the view. No wonder the Easterns worshiped these skies before they knew God. What a meaning that promise to Abraham expresses to me now: "Look now toward heaven and tell the stars if thou be able to number them. And He said unto him, so shall thy seed be."

The word *Joppa*, anciently signified "the watchtower of joy and beauty." It is in such sweet connection I shall ever recall it.

And now, our country's passion for pilgrimage which has carried the adventurous steps of Americans into every corner of the earth, has brought *me* here. Old Joppa rests under these older skies. The deep azure of the heavens, studded with the very dust of stars, and most brilliant constellations, is a picture never to be forgotten. These orbs witnessed the events of Bible history from Abraham to Jesus. The journeys of Peter from Lydda to Joppa, and from Joppa to Cæsaraea; his vision of tolerance, and the flight of Jonah from this very harbor, are associated with the glitter of these diamond-sparks flashing above me. Oh, transcendently beautiful! And with this I commence my diary, which I have promised my dear parents to keep regularly all the time I am in the Holy Land.

STEAMER L'AMERIQUE, 6 A. M.

After a few hours' sleep, I have taken an early watch upon the deck of *L'Amerique*, which we are to leave at nine. The noble vessel lies at anchor almost steady, though I perceive, by the motion of the small boats around us, that the sea rolls quite heavily. The foam upon the reef of rocks between us and the shore, betokens the same agitation; the roar of the surf can easily be heard, although it is nearly two miles off. Captain LeMaitre says he never dares take his vessel nearer than we are now, on account of the rocks. He has shown me in a French copy of the Travels of Saewulf, an account of a storm in the sea of Joppa, in the year 1102. The ships were driven from their anchors by the violence of the waves which first threw them aloft and then below, until they were aground or upon the rocks, and there beaten backward and forward and crushed to pieces. The violence of the wind would not allow them to put out to sea, while the character of the coast forbade their putting in to shore. Thirty very large ships were destroyed. More than one thousand lives were lost. As I look over the bay and think of the awful scene, I shudder at the recital.

Captain LeMaitre informs us that in stormy weather his steamer passes this place without stopping. In such cases he carries his passengers on to *Caiffa*, if he is going north, or *Alexandria*, if he is going south. This is very much to their dissatisfaction.

Joppa looks from this distance exceedingly picturesque. It covers a small

2

hill about five hundred feet high, shaped like a hemisphere,—the sea being on three sides of it. The hill is entirely covered with houses as thickly as they can be built, and the fortified wall that encircles it, runs close under the base of the hill. Beyond the town I can catch tantalizing glimpses of the unparalleled orange groves of Joppa which I so much long to see.

BLATTNER'S HOTEL, 10 A. M.

About 9 o'clock I played my last tune upon the ship's piano, Captain LeMaitre's favorite piece, "Home, Sweet Home." Then I said adieu, and we left *L'Amerique*, perhaps never to see the good ship again. A dreadful squabble was going on among the boatmen who thronged the waters around us, in their tub-like crafts; and I was distressed to see one poor fellow knocked overboard. But he soon came to the surface, none the worse, but rather the cleaner for his submersion. We passed into our boats, a current of sailors, Turks, Arabs, passengers, carpet-bags, dragomans and travelers.

From the grand, swelling billows, we passed directly between dark, jagged reefs that front the town. Over these the creamy surf dashed in romantic agitation.

We landed safely, crushing the beautiful shells with which the shore is covered, and went directly through streets narrow, dirty and badly paved, to the English Hotel, where we are to remain until Wednesday. And now we join in congratulations and thanksgivings to God that we have reached the desired haven. Five weeks and two days was the length of our journey from New York. Already we inhale the rich aroma from orange groves and other odoriferous trees.

While Mr. Fountain goes to the office of the Governor I will make my first attempt at describing objects in the Holy Land. This hotel of Blattner's, three stories high, is built entirely of stone from foundation to roof. The steps, the lintels, the floor, the ceiling, all are of stone or cement. Owing to the scarcity of the timber here, the builder is compelled to adopt the arch for supporting floors and roofs. Over each small room, one arched dome is raised; over a larger one like this are eight resting on four pillars, a central dome crowning the whole. This style is very graceful to the eye, and it makes a strong and durable building. The housekeeping is horrid. The common hall or passage way is really filthy; three sets of noisy, dirty children were playing there together. In an opposite room, with an open door, a woman was dressing. The dinner table is of the cheapest material—a mere frame of rude plank—but the table cloth is the costliest damask. Several divans or sofas are ranged round the room covered with the same material. Yet, the carpet is a coarse cotton one, full of holes, and dirty. A splendid grand piano in one corner is used as a side board for the breakfast table. There are three large and costly clocks, all out of repair and useless; one a musical clock. Common colored lithographs of the Emperor and Empress of Austria, hang on the walls. There is absolutely nothing *English* about the house except the name.

The breakfast came none too soon for our hungry party, up at four and so busy. This French style of *dejeuner* at ten is not adapted to plain Americans, and we ate voraciously. This is evidently a continuation of the ancient Roman custom of taking a little food early, to stay the appetite. There the *prandium* at noon was the real breakfast. On the steamer we were allowed a little cup of black coffee, with a crust of bread, on rising. Then breakfast came at ten —always late for our appetites. Elliot used to say that if a man would experiment on the utmost pangs of hunger, without quite reaching starvation, he can do it to perfection on these French steamers.

At breakfast, Elliot illustrated his idea of "first fruits," (Numbers xviii: 12) by giving the first orange offered him, to a beggar boy who was watching and waiting at the door. So the ancient Hebrews gave the first-fruits of vintage, harvest, threshing-floor, wine-press, oil-press, fleece and bread-baking, of the new crops.

After breakfast we left the city through the heavily-arched and towered gateway, on the land side, the *Jerusalem Gate* of Joppa. We passed hedges of prickly pear (*cactus*) that defy all human approach with their density and armature, the stems being as thick, as a naval officer remarked to us, "as the mainmast of a man-of-war." We sauntered on to the beach, south of town. Along its smooth, hard sand, paved with countless millions of shells, we walked for an hour, the boys happy at their release from the confinement of the steamer, gathering, and all of us sketching the various objects discovered:

"While over them the sea-wind sang
Shrill, chill with flakes of foam!"

The most common shell is the famous *Pilgrim shell*, with its five spines denoting the birth, life, death, resurrection and ascension of our Lord Jesus Christ. Another shell quite plenty, is the *Cypræa*, which the Arabs fasten to the bridle of their horses and camels, and even wear around their own necks. A species of *Conus* is also common. Also more or less of the beautiful purple *Murex*, an elegant violet-tinted *Donax*, and a lovely purple *Haliotis*. How I wish I had given more attention to conchology, while at school, that I might describe them all.

We took lunch in a romantic way. Mr. Fountain set up our five umbrellas around a telegraph pole, making a queer sort of tent, and there we had our first camping place in Palestine. The grand old Main, blazing like a sea of sapphire, heaved before us; the Plain of Sharon was at our back. Wild flowers struggled through the sandy soil on every hand. The land-crabs chased each other merrily along the beach, where—

"Wet, glistening shells of every die
Along the margin of the water lie."

And the great sea-gulls winged fitfully overhead as though expressing their impatience at our tarrying. Sauntering back, we found the skeleton of a monstrous shark, more than six feet long, that had been dragged from the water's edge by the jackals. The tracks of a troop of them had trampled the earth—

"Harder and drier than a fountain-bed
In summer."

John measured the width of his jaws and the length of his teeth, and quietly remarked that he should confine his sea-bathing inside the reefs. As the shark abounds in the Mediterranean Sea, why may not the theory be correct that it was one of this species which the Lord prepared as the instrument of His designs concerning Jonah?

I am reminded, in examining the many varieties of shells collected, that we shall find this Scollop-shell carved upon the ruins at Balbek, a month hence.

As we walked back to Joppa, a company of Bedouins rode by, somewhat alarming Elliot, who was not looking for the sight. They appeared surprised to see a lady with her face uncovered; for their women never appear in public without a veil; at least this is the custom of the better class. They rode good horses. Each had a long spear in his hand, a pair of large pistols in his belt, and a gun strung across his shoulders. They were very polite in their way, and answered Mr. Fountain's greeting very courteously. The Arabic *Salaam* is extremely graceful. He puts his right hand on his left breast, with a slight bow; then raises it to his lips and then to his forehead, repeating the words *Salaam aleikam*, (peace be with you) in a deep, gutteral tone.

BLATTNER'S HOTEL, 5 P. M.

After a short stay at the hotel, we again sallied forth and rambled through the city. The place is so hilly that you may look directly down from one house upon the top of another. As the people sleep on the house tops in sultry weather, they make screens by building walls of earthern cylinders resembling jars with the bottom removed, all around the sides of the roof, and so they enjoy the breeze while they are concealed from the eyes of their neighbors.

Although the native women rarely or never go into the Turkish mosks (churches), yet I felt safe in doing so and visited all three of them. They are large empty rooms without carpets, seats or pulpits; no paintings or ornaments of any kind are allowed in them. The floors are covered with mats, rusty and ragged. People are very quiet and solemn in the mosks; they do not smoke or even speak above a whisper. That part of the building which is in the direction of Mecca (south-east) has a small niche in the wall just like those made to contain small statues, and it is towards this the people bow when praying. This niche they call *Kiblah*. I was not at all interrupted or even noticed by the people when entering the mosks, yet the Holy Land, that brought forth fruit through which every one is saved unless it is his own fault, is a wretched place for woman. No provision is made for her religious instruction, for they scarcely believe that a woman has a soul to be saved. The old *mollah*, or Mohammedan priest, whom I talked with in the French language, Abdallah was his name, while he evidently had the Mohammedan views on this subject, assured me that *after all God made women as well as men*. I asked him if God did not make Christians as well as Mohammedans, but he did not answer that. He said, however, that he believed in God, or as they call him, *Allah*, and that there was only one God.

These people are far from entering into their closets when they pray; they rather court publicity in their worship. One of the priests wore a green turban. He has been to Mecca where Mohammed is buried and is called a *Hadji*. They believe that a man who visits Mecca is sure of heaven. In former years these Hadjis would sometimes put out their own eyes, because, after seeing the tomb of Mohammed, they thought *nothing else worth looking at*. At the entrance of every mosk is a cistern of water, in which the worshipers wash their feet, hands, arms, neck and head before going to prayer. This part of their service I thought praiseworthy. Every one must leave his shoes outside the door of a mosk, so all our party went in stocking feet

Around the coffee houses and mosks we saw numbers of Turkish soldiers and officers. To an officer who opened a door for me and brought me a stool, I offered *backsheesh*, that is a piece of money, but he declined it with a gesture that showed my offer ill-timed. I asked his pardon in French. All the Turkish officers, I am told, talk French, some of them fluently. I observe a native dignity in the dress and deportment even of the poorest of these Orientals, that we do not find among our own countrymen. I notice also that the military salute here is very different from the American. A Turkish soldier brings his hand first to the lips and then to the forehead with a quick, graceful motion.

We visited several native schools during the afternoon stroll. One was a *kuttab* or child's school. The teacher told me that his wages for each child are only a piastre (four cents) a week and an annual present of a turban cloth and a pair of slippers for each child. This would hardly satisfy one of our American teachers. His only business, however, is to teach the boys to say their prayers (*suras*) in unison with the Moslem worshipers. In another school, the teacher, who aspires to something better, is a sort of under priest among the Mohammedans, and he engages to turn out *good scholars* for one hundred and fifty piastres each, but this only means to teach them to read the Koran and write Arabic. His employers board him from house to house as people board their teachers in our western settlements. I heard Stephen A. Douglas once relate at our house, in his inimitable way, his teaching school in Illinois, some forty years ago, and "boarding round." The Joppa Academy is nothing but a room twelve feet by twenty and five feet high, made by hanging mats around and with a mat roof. There his seventeen students squatted on the ground and read at the top of their voices from manuscript Korans. The boys had for their raiment nothing but blue cotton shirts. I hope they prove apt scholars.

I was much interested in the old fountain near the east gate of Joppa. It is highly ornamented in the arabesque Saracenic style with an Arabic inscription. This sort of ornamentation looks like honey combs or stalactites. It cannot be durable, even in this climate. In ours it would not stand ten winters.

I was warmly interested in calling at the house of Mr. Meitzler, missionary of "The Pilgrim Mission" at St. Chriscona, near Basle, in Prussia. This is one of the zealous but humble movements, prompted by God's spirit, that is to evangelize the world. I had never heard of it until Mr. Meitzler described it to me. It was called into life in 1840. Its purpose is "to prepare and send forth youths who love the Lord Jesus Christ, and desire to serve Him in the building up of His church throughout the earth." They have now more than sixty young men receiving a three years' course, including the German, English, Arabic and French languages, and a simple practical knowledge of the Bible which is carefully taught in the College. The students exercise their gifts and acquire facility and experience of utterance in the sixty villages and towns around the Seminary. Manual labor is combined with study. A considerable farm of meadows and field is cultivated by the students. All the shoes and clothes for the students are made by their own hands. They also manage their own kitchens, gardens and stables. They pursue the callings of carpenter, blacksmith, wagon-makers, etc., thus qualifying themselves in all respects for usefulness in heathen lands. A good printing establishment and book-bindery are attached and a periodical is published by them.

The whole institution is animated by the free spirit of the Gospel. Neither teachers nor students receive compensation. Already one hundred and twenty pastors have been furnished by this Seminary; nineteen are engaged in missionary labors; many are colporteurs; one is a Bible pedlar through Egypt and Arabia Petræa; six or seven are at work in Palestine, under the superintendence of Bishop Gobat of Jerusalem. The plan in this country is this: a mercantile business is conducted by C. F. Spittler & Co., with a branch at Joppa. These entirely support themselves by their own earnings and promote the Mission free of charge. In Jerusalem they have an Asylum for fifty-five Syrian orphan boys, who, after their studies are completed, are taught trades.

Passing the Roman Catholic Convent we stepped in a moment to hear the music. It was the *Stabat Mater*. I do not know who composed the music, but never before was I so impressed with the inimitable words of the old Latin hymn.

Stabat mater dolorosa,
Juxta crucem lacrymosa,
    Dum pendebat filius;
Cujus animam gementem,
Contristatem et dolentem,
    Per transivit gladius.

O quam tristis et afflicta,
Fuit illa benedicta
    Mater unigeniti!
Quæ mœrebat, et dolebat,
Pia mater dum videbat,
    Nati pœnas inclyte.

Quis est homo qui non fleret,
Christi matrem si videret,
    In tanto supplicio?
Quis posset non contristari;
Piam matrem contemplari,
    Dolentem cum filio?

Pro peccatis suæ gentis,
Vidit Jesum in tormentis
    Et flagellis subditum!
Vidit suum dulcem natum.
Morientum, desolatum,
    Dum emisit spiritum.

BLATTNER'S HOTEL, 8 P. M.

The Governor came in at 6 o'clock, attended by two of his Secretaries, and dined with us as he had promised. He has a pleasant face. Is about fifty years of age. He wears the *tarboush*, the common headgear, I am told, of all Turkish officers. He has lived much among Europeans, at Corfu, for instance, where he was stationed a long time, and in Paris, and elsewhere, so that his command of the French language is perfect. His manners are unexceptionable. He thinks he shall be removed to some other city before long. It is not the policy of the Turkish government, I am told, to keep an officer long in the same place. By his permission I make a pen-and-ink sketch of him. His dress is the semi-European costume now adopted by Turkish officers, in place of the old Oriental garb.

Our dinner was in the French style, not very well cooked nor served. I think an *imitation* French dinner is always a failure. One thing they have here for which we are not indebted to the cook, that is *the oranges.* These are splendid to the eye and delicious to the palate.

BLATTNER'S HOTEL, 9 P. M.

All above as well as below is symbol and dream. Let me turn for a parting moment to that which is real. "The Lord reigneth; the Lord is great in Zion; the Lord our God is holy; bless the Lord, oh my soul, and all that is within me, bless his holy name."

As pants the wearied hart for cooling springs
That sinks exhausted in the summer chase,
So pants my soul for Thee, thou King of Kings,
So thirsts to reach thy sacred dwelling-place!

A few minutes upon the flat house top before I retire to bed. The stars are scintillating in the calm brilliancy of an Eastern night. The deep silence of this Oriental town is broken only by the sea which comes booming in low, hollow sounds, from the shore "Along the many-sounding ocean tide." And now with heartfelt thanksgiving to God and a prayer for dear friends many thousand miles away, I go to rest. Should I live upon this anniversary day, how affecting it will be to remember that at such an hour, I (like Peter in Acts xi: 5) was "in Joppa praying."

RICHARD FOUNTAIN'S DIARY.

STEAMER L'AMERIQUE, Midnight, Monday, March 15th, 1869.

As the great anchor drops at this midnight hour, and I recognize that we are off the port of Joppa, I offer my grateful acknowledgements to Almighty God that he has safely brought us through the first stage of our journey. I awake my little party as I promised them when they retired to their rooms and we all go upon deck, note books in hand, *to see and to describe.* The city of Jonah and of Peter, of Andromeda and of Noah, shows at this quiet hour in its most attractive features. Like all other Oriental towns, it appears best *at night* and *at a distance.* My young friends are astonished at the glorious magnificence of the stars.

8 A. M.

We are ready to go ashore. I have bargained with one of the boatmen to land our party, and carry the baggage to the hotel for two dollars and a half. In dealing with these people my invariable rule is to make my contracts in advance, and have the price exactly understood. As I pay them honestly, according to my agreement, I compel them honestly to fulfill theirs. Our baggage was all ready packed on Saturday, and we had no occasion for delay. But before leaving this good steamer *L'Amerique*, which has brought us so pleasantly from Marseilles, a two weeks' journey, our party gathers together in my state room, Bibles in hand, to acknowledge the mercies of Him who "hath ruled the raging of the sea; when the waves thereof arose he stilled them." (Ps. lxxxix : 9.) We read, alternately, the 107th Psalm, and Matthew, chapters i to iv. We sang—

"Nearer my God to thee,"

those sweet lines. We join hands affectionately in that little apartment, and ask the Great Giver to fill the coming months with good things, and to restore us in due time to our own happy land. AMEN.

BLATTNER'S HOTEL, 9 A. M.

We have set foot upon the Holy Land, and are safely ensconced in my old quarters at Blattner's Hotel. Our party consists of the following persons: Elliot, 12 years; John, his brother, 17; Harriet, their sister, 20; Mrs. Lydia Mason, their aunt, an elderly lady who accompanies us as companion to Harriet. With myself we number five. These young people are all Christian youths, educated in a pure faith, having invigorated understandings through the influence of good parents and preceptors, and coming from a nation, of all others, whose adventurous steps are searching every corner of the earth for knowledge. The single aim that moves us to make this excursion is to secure light upon Bible lands and Bible countries. Neither of the boys uses tobacco or is addicted to any gross vice. Their memories are thoroughly charged with Scriptural quotations. For several years their parents have been qualifying them for this journey by such branches of practical knowledge as will be most in demand here, and I do not see how it is possible we can fail in accomplishing our wishes.

Elliot is expert in arithmetic, geography, astronomy and history. His memory of Bible passages is something remarkable. He knows hundreds of verses and even whole chapters by heart. He is also expert in the use of the gun, athletic in climbing, and a good swimmer and horseman.

John has the common branches well, and is fairly up in the Latin and Greek classics. He plays the flute well. He has given much attention to the use of minerals, and their modes of application, and the arts; the value of ores in mining; the modes of reduction; the yield of mines in various countries, etc. He has visited the zinc mines of New Jersey; the copper mines of Lake Superior; the iron mines of Pennsylvania; salt mines of Virginia; lead mines of Iowa, and many other mines, quarries, manufactories, etc., etc.

Harriet is not deficient in any lady-like accomplishment. In music, the French and Italian languages, botany, and other branches of polite knowledge, she has made thorough proficiency. She is extremely fond of poetry, and writes in easy measure.

They all draw well and sing. They all write readily in the phonetic character. And best of all, they are devoted students in Scripture knowledge.

Their pledges to their parents are that they will note down, in phonographic character, daily, what attracts their attention, which they think could amuse or instruct their friends at home. For this purpose their note-books are to be always ready for instant use. Three or four times a day, at the various halting-places, they are to draw off, in their diaries, in legible character, and with full comments, what they have thus hastily noted. Once a week these diaries are to be transcribed, with full references, quotations and corrections upon sheets of French paper, and sent home by mail.

The only part I have to perform in the preparation of their elaborated diaries is to correct what errors, if any are made; and when needed, furnish explanatory notes from my own experience, in this country. Thus, I hope our reports will prove true, wide awake, practical and entertaining papers.

BLATTNER'S HOTEL, 9 P. M.

It is one of the mysteries of American politics, that while almost every civilized nation has a Consul at Joppa, for the information and protection of its countrymen, ours has none. Mr. Murad, the native Syrian, who served us here for forty years in that capacity, became too infirm for further duty, and the situation is not profitable enough for an American citizen to settle here. So, instead of making my first call upon an officer of my own government, I went to the Council Chamber, and paid my respects to the Kaimakam, or Governor, of Joppa, Noureddin Effendi, whose friendship I formed when here last year. He was pleased to meet me again, and adjourned his Court, although in the very midst of a criminal case, to take me to the *Serai*, or Governor's house. There we spent a social hour and talked over the past. When I told him that I had bronght a party of young persons to Palestine, and they wished to present him some pictures and other trifles they had brought him from America, he consented to dine with us at six this afternoon. The rest of the day's proceedings are recorded in the diaries of the party, to whom I venture to apply the words of Isaiah :

" Bring my sons from afar, and my daughters from the ends of the earth. And all thy children shall be taught of the Lord, and great shall be the peace of thy children. Behold I and the children whom the Lord hath given me."

NOTE.—The map that precedes this chapter, represents the lands of the Bible from Ur, of the Chaldees to Sodom. Joppa may be marked with a pencil point on the coast line north-west of Jerusalem.

NOUREDDIN EFFENDI, GOVERNOR OF JOPPA 1864–9.

CHAPTER II.

ALL AROUND JOPPA.

Familiar sounds—Tarboush—A Yankee harvester—Native plow—Goad—Women carrying wood—All sorts of noises—The judge in the gate—The golden orange groves—Lepers—Kerosene lamps—The Governor in Court—Dressed for Palestine—Rules of the youthful explorers—School—Sending telegram home—The way it went—Almond trees—Sailing through the harbor—Building stone—Private houses—The Bazaars, or markets—History of Joppa—Palestine model farms—American colony—Manufactures of Joppa—Sparrows—Morning views from housetops—American photographs—Dorcas—Tamarinds—Citrons—Wells—House of Simon the tanner—Convents—Jews—Vegetables—Tents—Djereed—Collecting specimens.

ELLIOT'S DIARY.

JOPPA, Tuesday, March 16th, 1869. 10 P. M.

WHEN I woke up this morning, I heard a baby crying, a rooster crowing, a dog barking, and a lamb bleating,—all four in as plain American as ever was. So, if I ever get tired of hearing Arabic talked, I shall always have these old fashioned noises to fall back upon.

I have learned these ten words of Arabic already: *bate* means a house; *bint* means a girl; *kitarb* a book; *libbarn*, milk; *tyeeb*, good; *narm*, yes; *lar*, no; *hassarn*, a horse; *yad*, a hand; *barood*, powder; *sin*, a tooth. Aunt Liddy thinks I have made a good beginning. I am going to learn the whole of the "Lord's Prayer," this week in Arabic.

Before I got up this morning, one of the Governor's soldiers brought my boots that the boys stole yesterday from under the palm tree. How kind that was in the Governor. Mr. Fountain gave the soldier a *bishlik*, that is thirty cents.

As soon as I got up, I went out to the *bazaars* or markets and bought me a *tarboush*. They called it a *fez* in Smyrna. Mr. Fountain says the Orientals generally are laying aside the old fashioned *turbans*, and wearing this sort of *tarboush* in place of it. I gave five francs ($1.00) for the *tarboush* and two francs more for the silk tassels, which they weighed and sold me by weight. The *tarboush* is made of felt. It is thick and heavy and lasts a great while. I intend to wear mine all the time I am in this country. It is the same red cap that the New York zouaves wear. I asked the merchant if he knew the name of the Turkish Sultan. That is the President of this country. He said he didn't. I told him the name was Abd-el Asiz. He looked surprised but said it made no difference to him. He doesn't seem to care enough to talk about it.

After buying the *tarboush*, I walked by myself to see Mr. Rolla Floyd, who was so kind to me yesterday. The atmosphere was delicious, the sky cloudless. As I passed the Jerusalem gate, I noticed its huge old valves and mighty hinges.

Mr. Floyd lives at the American settlement, half a mile north of Jpppa. Here is where Bishop G. J. Adams built his town a few years ago. But it all fell through. The village has eight frame houses and a church, all built of timber brought from the State of Maine. One hundred and eighty-five people came with Adams, but nobody has stayed except Floyd. He owns a reaper and two horses. In harvest time he cuts wheat and barley for the people at a *medigia* an hour. That is ninety-five cents. He can cut more grain in a day with his reaper than fifty native men. The people here, when they harvest wheat, *sit down* in the field and smoke all the time. They reap with a sickle not bigger than a case knife. The fences here are all hedges of prickly pear from three to ten inches thick and fifteen feet high. It is called *opuntia.* When Mr. Floyd first brought his wagon to Joppa, he was afraid he couldn't get it through these narrow lanes. Then the Governor told him that the soldiers should cut down the hedges for him on one side of the streets and let the wagon pass. That is the way Turkish officers deal with these Arabs. The prickly pear has great soft fibrous stems, fringed with leaves that look like thick green cakes. Neither man nor beast can get through it. The ground all around Mr. Floyd's house is white with sea shells like those we saw yesterday. Mrs. Floyd is a very nice woman. She showed me the photograph of her little boy she lost ten years ago, the only child she had. She never expects to go to America again. Says she is contented here.

As I went back to town, I saw a man going out to plow. His team was two little cows not bigger than the yearling calves on father's New Jersey farm. I have read somewhere that in the fourteenth century they plowed here with cows, just as they do now. The yoke is six feet long and so heavy that the cows' necks bend under it. It is so rough, too, that it chafes deep creases in their hide. If Titus plowed up the foundations of Jerusalem he must have had a stronger implement than this. The man had a goad on his shoulders as heavy as the plow itself. It was a pole eight feet long and two inches in diameter at the butt-end where I measured it. It was pointed with iron, to punch the legs of the cows with. At the large end this goad had a sort of a chisel to clean the plow with. The fellow jabbed one of his cows while I was looking on, and she kicked back at him. Then I understood the words that Christ spoke to St. Paul, "it is hard for thee to kick against the pricks." (Acts ix: 5.) I could see, too, how Shamgar could slay of the Philistines six hundred men with an ox goad. (Judges iii: 31.)

Next I met a lazy fellow jogging along, smoking a pipe with a cocoanut bowl, while behind him walked his wife carrying a heavy load of thorn bushes on her back. This was like our Savior's charge against the scribes and pharisees, who loaded men with burdens grievous to be borne, while they themselves touched not the burdens with one of their fingers. (Matt. xxiii: 4.) I shall never forget the richness and orchard-beauty of my morning's walk.

Mr. William C. Prime was here thirteen years ago. When I saw him last summer he got me to promise to bring him a pound of the seeds of these large oranges, when he knows very well that *they have no seeds.* This was his joke. Mr. Prime wrote a book once called "Tent Life in the Holy Land;" which mother used to read to us out of *Harper's Magazine.*

At one point north of town I could see clear around the water side of Joppa. "Although Joppa has always been a sea gate of Jerusalem it has no docks, no quays, no jetties, no landing stairs and no lights." So says a man who was here some time ago, and he says true. Josephus wrote long ago that Joppa was not fit to be a harbor. As I got near the city, I wrote down the different noises that I could hear in the crowd around me. The snarl and yelps of a mob of cur dogs; the wild, sweet notes of birds; the cries of men (muezzins) high up the church steeples; the chatter of the Arabs, who gabble like parrots; the shrieks of the camels and the tinkle of their bells; the snort and tramp of horses; the swearing of a party of sailors who are quarrelling over a bottle; the awful bray of donkeys; the laughter of some sportive boys—all these and I don't know how many more sounds were going on at once. Hundreds of dogs were lying asleep in the deep military ditch that is dug round the town. A judge, (called the *kadi*) was sitting in the gateway of the city holding court. I stopped to see a man flogged who had been caught stealing a knife. From the time the soldier brought him to the *kadi*, to the time he was kicked out the gate, was less than five minutes, including a bastinado of thirteen strokes, well laid on. The *kadi* only listened for a second or two to the evidence and then gave sentence. How the miserable wretch howled, but everybody else laughed. They enjoyed it. The *kadi* didn't laugh but he didn't look sorry either.

BLATTNER'S HOTEL, 5 P. M.

We have had a glorious time among the orange groves, this morning. Mr. Floyd has been with us all day, as he promised. I never supposed there were such oranges in the world. They looked like pumpkins on the trees and hung as thick as apples. I ate and ate and ate. They don't cost anything hardly. For one piastre I got twelve oranges and had to leave most of them behind me for they made so heavy a bundle. The lemons are as large as the oranges, and what is queer they are *sweet* instead of *sour!* How deliciously an orange grove does smell. Curious that the word "orange" is not found in the Bible; neither is the word "shell" nor "prickly pear." Eight millions of oranges were grown last year around Joppa. Wearing my *tarboush* this morning almost blinded me and I have packed it away. I shall wear it no more. It has no rim and doesn't suit an American boy at all.

The English party have been very kind to me to-day and I am sorry I insulted them yesterday. One of the ladies asked leave to let her read my yesterday's diary. She actually copied a part of it to send to her little nephew in Sheffield. She told me to write down these words: "The child's views of Oriental scenes and customs are both original and instructive." And yet the English dislike the French so that I heard her say she wanted to get away from this soil, "desecrated by Bonaparte's murder of his helpless prisoners!" When they say a person is *clever*, they mean *smart*.

A Jewish rabbi at our hotel asked me a thousand questions about the United States, which he says is "the Canaan of his people," whatever that means. His name is Jonah, which I thought curious, but he tells me that Jonah in Hebrew means a dove. He says "the Turks abhor Israel;" but if they abhor Israel worse than Israel abhors the Turks, it is hard on the Turks. In looking at this venerable old man, I thought of King Solomon's expression, "the beauty of old men is the gray head." (Prov. xx: 29.)

All the well dressed women that you meet here keep a veil on, so you can't see their faces. They call the veil a *yashmak*. But I met one coming from the Saracenic Fountain, to-day, with a jar of water on her head, and she stumbled and dropped her veil, so I saw her face. It was so homely that I couldn't help telling her that if I had such a face as that, I would keep mine covered, too. As she couldn't understand English, she thought I was complimenting her, so she smiled and said, *tyeeb*, which means that's so. Then she walked away giggling. That is just like girls.

We saw a lot of lepers sitting under the orange trees by the roadside. One of them had a tin cup fastened to the end of his arm; his arm was nothing but a black bone, the hand having rotted off. I never saw any thing so dreadful in all my life. One of them was white as this sheet of paper.

In the house where we called I was surprised to see a kerosene lamp, just like ours at home. Then Mr. Fountain told me that all the better classes of people here use kerosene now. There were three ship loads of kerosene oil sent to this country from the United States last year. One kerosene lamp gives more light than ten olive oil lamps, such as they always used before. This kerosene comes from the United States and the lamps from Austria. "Hurra for Uncle Sam," I halloed when I saw it. The man, when he heard that answered *tyeeb*.

We called on the Governor at his Court room. He was sitting on some cushions, cross legged, smoking. Every body in the Court room was smoking. He was very kind to us and made us sit by him. A prisoner was standing before him, hand-cuffed, and he was smoking, too. While Harriet was talking with the Governor in French, there came in a ragged, dirty fellow who walked right up to the Governor and showed a dreadful sore he had on his left arm. The Governor said *ruak;* that means get out; but he gave the fellow a present of a clean shirt, which was the thing most needed. Every body has the right to approach a Turkish ruler in this way, even the Sultan himself, who is the head Governor of them all. The Governor doesn't use any law book. He told me the Koran was law book enough for him. He seemed surprised when I told him I had read the Koran through. No lawyers practice in the Courts here. Everybody talks up his own case—and oh, how loud they do talk! It seems to me the man who yells the loudest wins the suit. I think our New York lawyers would have gay times over the Koran for their law book. It proves anything you want to. The Governor invited us to dine with him this evening, but Mr. Fountain said as we are to leave to-morrow, we must decline. I should like to have taken dinner at a Governor's palace. Harriet has made a good likeness of the Governor.*

To-day I have put on the dress and rigging made for me in New York expressly for our trip. A white hat, shaped like a fireman's helmet; a coat, vest and pantaloons all white; white shoes and a white umbrella. This is because the *color white* is cooler than any other color. Mr. Fountain and John are dressed exactly the same way.

Mr. Fountain tells me to write these rules in my diary. They are the rules we are going to keep:

---

* See the engraving facing the Second Chapter.

First.—We must begin every day with singing a hymn, Bible reading and prayer. We are to read the whole Bible through while in Bible countries.

Second.—We are never to speak unfriendly to each other.

Third.—Our diary *must* be made up *everyday*, unless we are sick.

Fourth.—We are *never* to travel Sunday.

Fifth.—If any hard thoughts towards each other arise in our minds, they are *always* to be forgiven and forgotten, before we go to sleep.

As I was passing by the orange bazaar, to-day, I stumbled over a rope, and fell. All the men near me bawled out *Allah, Allah*, as loud as they could. When I asked why they did this, they said it was a part of their religious faith. They believe when a horse stumbles, or a man is in any danger, if you say *Allay, Allah*, pretty loud, you will be saved from harm. The word Allah, means *God*. They use it very often. It sounds to me very much like swearing, the way they use it: may be not. This is a yelling people. They say *yellah* to a horse to make him move, and they are always yelling when they talk. They think us Americans are not in earnest because we don't talk loud, and swing our hands about, and stamp and keep everything in motion.

One of my nine heroes landed here in 1844. This was Constantine Tischendorf, the great Bible scholar. And Aunt Liddy tells me to be sure to say something about him in my diary. Tischendorf came to this far-off land looking for old Bibles. Infidels, who are as thick in Prussia as fleas are here, had told him that the Bible is a modern book. Tischendorf has spent his life proving that they lie when they say it. Satan lied no worse than that to Eve. Tischendorf came here with the Grand Duke Constantine, of Russia, and visited the ancient libraries in Jerusalem, at San Saba, Beyrout, Ladikia and other places, and found a great many old manuscript Bibles. I hope we shall call on him as we go home. I thought of him just now when I read this passage: "Righteousness shall go before him; and shall set us in the way of His steps." (Ps. lxxxv.: 13.)

My list of nine heroes is George Washington, Bonaparte, Judas Machabeus, Garibaldi, Saladin, Abd-el-Kader, Godfrey de Boullion, Oliver Cromwell and Constantine Tischendorf. Five of these were either born in this country or they have lived here.

My list of *scallawags* only has four names: Benedict Arnold, Judas Iscariot, Absalom and Aaron Burr. Two of these were Holy-landers and I shall have a good time at Jerusalem throwing stones at Absalom's monumuent, and spitting upon Judas' grave.

I noticed in Court, to-day, that when Governor Noureddin writes an order of any kind, he doesn't sign his name to it, as officers do in our country, but he takes some ink upon a pen, rubs a little of it on a seal which he carries in his pocket, and then presses the seal down upon the paper. Then he sprinkles colored sand on the paper to keep the ink from blotting.

The town of Joppa is wretchedly dirty. We visited a school this afternoon that we missed yesterday, Such a school! A sort of alley with matting over it for shade. No floor but the ground; thirty-four boys but no girls. The Mohammedan girls never go to school. A man told me a girl has got no more soul than a cat. All the boys were sitting cross legged on the ground. There was a sort of blackboard on a frame. The teacher would write something on it, with chalk, and tell them the name. Then they would all hallo out the word a hundred times over at the top of their voices. It was the *loudest* school I ever saw. A boy with but one eye who sat near where I stood, pretended to be listening to the teacher. But he was cursing me in some slang he had learned of the sailors. I told Mr. Fountain and he told the teacher. How mad the teacher was. He said something in Arabic. Then four boys grabbed the little rascal and turned him upside down. The schoolmaster then lashed him with a rattan, on the soles of his bare feet, about twenty times. Of all the screaming. But the rest of the scholars laughed so you could hardly hear him. I hope it will prove a lesson to them. Out of the thirty-four boys I counted ten who had only one eye apiece. Nearly all of them had sore eyes. Mr. Fountain says this is the case with the children in this country, generally. They live so mean and dirty, no wonder.

We sent a telegraph home, to-day, to dear father and mother, and I expect we shall get an answer to-morrow.

At dinner, Rolla Floyd and his wife dined with us. It is a wonder such nice people ever could believe in Bishop Adams.

Harriet and John have written so much in their diaries about oranges, that I will only make two or three notes of things they did not observe. The orange farmers graft orange slips on lemon stocks, because they think the lemon is a hardier tree than the orange. The Joppa orange has a skin nearly half an inch thick. They produce few or no seeds. The merchants sell them by *weight* as they do everything else here. Every other day the farmers dig the dirt away from around the tree, and let water in upon them—quite a puddle. These oranges and lemons are the largest in the known world. The groves have no equal upon earth. I tried my best to get a big orange in my pocket, to-day, but failed, it was so enormous. The farming here is rude and wasteful. They draw water for the gardens by wheels that scream awfully for want of grease. More than half the mechanical power is lost in friction. I told one fellow he ought to build a windmill. He answered, *bishmillah*, and then asked me for *bachsheesh*. He gave me a stalk of sugar cane to eat. It was insipid but refreshing. The Christian soldiers, during the Crusades, when they were short of provisions, used to chew sugar cane and live on the sweet juice. We shall see some ruins of their sugar mills near Jericho. Mr. Floyd says that a steam engine has been recently brought there and set up. What an advance over the day when the sinews of the great army of Solomon's workmen could hardly cut and move one of these great stones that the steam engine will shape and lift as easily as the mother lifts her child.

Mixed in with the orange groves were tall, waving cypresses. The cypress is the most enduring wood they have here. Formerly they made *idols* of it. Now they plant it at the head of graves. The *cactus* is what they make their fences of, and it is impenetrable. It is now nearly in fruit. A sort of fig grows on it which they say is palatable, but not delicious. The birds were singing very sweetly in the groves as we passed. At every garden I came to they would say, *tesherbetoo moyar*. That is, will you drink water. Then I would take large and refreshing draughts. They also raise bananas in these gardens.

JOHN'S DIARY.

MARCH 16, 1869. 8 P. M.

This has been indeed a busy day with us all. At 9 o'clock we prepared a telegraphic despatch and sent it to New York. It read, in English as we wrote it, this way: "Ebenezer Morrell, New York:—Landed yesterday. All well. We love you dearly. Holy Land is beautiful. Answer immediately." Mr. Fountain wrote the first three words; Harriet the next four; then I wrote four, and Elliot the other six. It was 9 A. M. here when this despatch was sent and this made it about one hour after midnight in New York—for the difference in time between Joppa and New York is about eight hours. So if the despatch went right through, father got it some time before it was sent! The cost of this despatch was three hundred francs in gold, which is about eighty dollars in American currency. Pretty expensive. Before he handed it in at the office, Mr. Fountain turned it into French, like this:

JAFFA, Syrie, 9 matin 16 Mars.

A Ebenezer Morrell, New York:—Debarques hier. Tous bien. Nous vous aimons tendrement. La Terre Sainte est bien belle. Repondez immediatement.

To reach New York this telegram will have to go up the coast, between Mt. Lebanon and the Sea; through Asia Minor; through Constantinople; through Vienna, Berlin, Paris and London; under the Irish Channel; through Newfoundland and the New England States, and so on to New York—as much as six thousand miles. We expect an answer to it to-morrow. What a wonderful discovery was the telegraph! Governor Noureddin told me, at dinner, yesterday, that the name of Sydney F. Morse would be remembered when that of Alexander the Great is forgotten! How proud I was to inform him that we are acquainted with Mr. Morse, for he had often called at our house in New York. I noticed in the telegraph office that none of the operators read *by sound;* all use paper machines. These make noises like small grist mills. Our American operators would laugh at such.

To-day I was particularly struck with the almond tree in the hedges around Joppa. It is now in fullest bloom, recalling Moore's lines—

"The silvery almond flower,
That blooms on a leafless bough,"

for the almond tree, with white flowers, blossoms on the bare branches. The almond ripens here in the month of April. In the Hebrew the name is *luz* and *shared.* This tree, conspicuous for its early flowering, showy appearance and useful fruit, is found all through the East. Our pastor preached a beautiful discourse not long ago from "the almond tree shall flourish," (Eccl. xii: 5,) and alluded to the hoary hairs of age. The four bowls of Moses' candlesticks were made in the shape of this beautiful flower. (Ex. xxv: 33.)

My explorations will be directed to harvesting new facts to illustrate the taste, the antiquities and the geological history of the Holy Land.

I have been around the city, to-day, and across it in various directions. The best point of view of this landing place of pilgrims for more than ten centuries, is from the reef, an eighth of a mile out in the bay. So I got on a polacre, one of the squabby boats they use here, and went out there and wrote my notes, leaning against the granite column that stands there. The water in the bay is only about three feet deep. I dedicated that stray, granite column to our dear friend, the enthusiastic Sunday school worker, Mr. E. C. Wilder, of New York. May he live to point erring souls safely into the port of truth, even as this stone pillar has guided weary pilgrims to the landing place of Joppa.

I took a delightful bath in the cool brine, on the inside of the reef.

Joppa stands on a little romantic hill of oblong shape. It has about five thousand inhabitants. Its houses and streets rise regularly above each other in tiers. If the tradition could probably be true that Noah's ark was built and launched here, as the natives say it was, what a view the unbelieving heathen had of the process, from that fine slope! One writer correctly describes Joppa as rising in the form of an amphitheatre, surrounded on the top by a round castle. It used to be claimed that from the top of that hill Jerusalem could be seen. Of course, however, that is all nonsense. Its latitude is 32 degrees 2 minutes north; longitude 34 degrees 47 minutes east of Greenwich.

It is plain to me that the old harbor of Joppa, into which the small shipping of ancient times could run and be secure from storms and pirates, lay in a swampy place in the rear of the present city. There is a kind of circular plain considerably lower than the sea level. When Lieutenant Lynch was here in 1848, he make a calculation that for one hundred thousand dollars this morass could be dug out and a canal made to connect it with the sea.

The building stone of Joppa is very poor, being nothing more than coral rock or a scaly, friable limestone. We have boxed up some pretty large pieces of it to send home for specimens. As it is nearly twelve miles to the stone quarries in the hills, these indolent people prefer to use this, rather than go so far for a much better article.

Every one says that the sea sand is encroaching upon the shore, year by year, along this coast, and already much of the beautiful Plain of Sharon has been turned into swamps by the sand damming up the water courses, and so preventing the outlet.

At the arched entrance of some of the larger houses, may be noticed fragments of granite columns, marbles bases, carved capitals and cornices, used now as steps to the buildings and lying along the sea-wall of Joppa, showing that, in olden times in this only port of the Hebrews, splendid architecture was practiced.

The best buildings and stores of the merchants are on the west side of the city, under protection of the cannon, of which there are two batteries.

We visited two or three houses occupied by the native Christians. Their rooms are high, pierced with numerous windows, very fresh and well aired. They have attempted to ornament them with paintings of landscapes and animals, but these are only detestable daubs. The Mohammedans are not allowed, by their religious creed, to do this, and I admire their taste. The Joppa mehanics certainly have special skill in the construction of arches.

The country Arabs we met to-day, remind me forcibly of the description given of them in the fourteenth century, "they wrap their heads and necks with a great quantity of linen cloth, and they are right ferocious and foul, and of a cursed nature!"

The most characteristic place around Joppa is the open space outside the east gate. It is crowded through the day with the venders of oranges, vegetables, meats and all the varieties of eatables used here. The space within the walls of Joppa is so circumscribed that the markets are necessarily held outside. Every tradesman has a little booth shaded with matting, and there he sits from day light till dark, patiently waiting for customers. When I purchased a blank book of one of them he sold it to me *by weight*. It is useless for a foreigner like me to ask one of them the price of anything; his answer invariably is, *as much as you please*. Yet, he by no means intends to let me have the goods at my own price. The Orientals deal so largely in hyperbole, that they scatter numbers and values with reckless profusion. He only means that I must make him a bid and he is sure to refuse it and demand more. So I have already learned to offer considerably less than I expect to give them.

In the open space around the market-place stood all the idle and unemployed men of Joppa, waiting for work; as in the parable. (Matt. xx: 7.) In many of these booths that vile and poisonous stuff called *arrack* is sold, but this only to Christians. The Mohammedans won't drink it. The Turkish merchants don't look as if they cared whether they sell anything to you or not. In their lazy manner they seem to say: "Good people, I am willing to disturb myself to render you a service; but I beg of you to annoy me as little as possible." They use *stones* for weights, but whether they observe the injunction of Leviticus xix, I had no means of ascertaining. Some of the stones seem as if they might have been brought from Egypt, they were worn so smooth by age and long handling. In the vicinity of the town, the roads are numerous but narrow. They are shaded by the splendid fig—sycamore or sycamine—tree of scripture. I feel like calling it the *Zaccheus* tree, as it always calls *his climb* to my remembrance. (Luke xix.)

A traveler says of Joppa that the houses of grayish stone rise one above another with the castle like a crown at the top; huddled together in strange confusion without regard to comeliness or comfort. These descriptions, like the other one I copied, are good. Another says that Joppa is picturesquely placed on a slight promontory which has grown somewhat by the wreck of ages. That, too, is very likely. None of them say how high the hill is.

I had quite a romantic vision while standing by that granite column on the reef. I tried to imagine the Knights Templar arrayed on yonder plain. They were terrors to evil doers, a defense to women and orphans, the poor and distressed, and the monks, the servants of God.

I also recalled the beautiful description of old Sandys, who was here in 1610. He is describing the stormy character of this port and says: "The fury of the north wind driving the waves against the rugged cliffs, do make them more turbulent and the place less safe than the open sea incensed with tempests." This is true to the present hour. And yonder city has been three times sacked; first by Arabs in 1722, then by the Mamelukes in 1775; finally by Bonaparte in 1799. The Machabees took it and burned it up in punishment for the gross barbarity of its people. (2 Macc. xii: 6.) Godfrey took it at the head of the Crusaders, in 1099, just before the capture of Jerusalem in July of that year. King Richard of England long lay sick here in 1192. King Louis of France took it in 1253, and fortified it with twenty-four towers and three gates. And as it depends entirely upon Christian commerce for its feeble existence, we, *the American party* have taken it and sacked it and raised our flag over it! Hurrah for the United States! Dr. J. T. Barclay thinks the town used to extend a good ways to the north-east of its present location, and so it seems to me.

I was sorry to find that the "Palestine Model Farm and Industrial Institute for Jewish Converts," to which father contributed one hundred dollars, and of which we used to read such hopeful reports, is almost abandoned and deserted. The house is a large stone edifice finely built upon a healthy and commanding situation about two miles north-east of Joppa, and it is hard to tell why the enterprise failed so miserably.

There is but one family left of the "American Colony" or "Adams Colony" as it is generally called. The school-house is standing in which Bishop Adams used to preach and act plays. Its upper story was partially fitted up for a freemasons' lodge, but never used. Adams' dwelling house is still standing but occupied now by a native family. They permitted me to go up to the house top, from which a fine view is had of the plain, Joppa and the marsh that I think was the ancient port of Joppa. No doubt the wrecks of Phœnician, Grecian and Roman triremes might be found in that swampy, deep black mud. The flagstaff is still standing on which Adams used to raise the American flag every Sabbath morning and whenever one of his countrymen called on him. This colony, that originally consisted of nearly two hundred persons, came out here in 1865, full of hope that they should elevate old Canaan religiously, politically and agriculturally. Mr. Adams baptized his assistant bishop, Mr. Toombs, in the Jordan, built an altar at Bethel and set up his banner here with brilliant prospects. But it all failed. He has gone to England now, and the rest of his colonists, except Mr. and Mrs. Floyd, have returned to the United States.

The chief manufacture of Joppa is *soap*. It is shipped from here to Egypt. Large ash-heaps are found outside the town. Out of the five thousand population, more than three thousand are Christians.

Mr. Fountain is engaging servants to accompany us in our journey, which we commence to-morrow. The applicants are very numerous, ten times as many as we can employ. Most of them have written certificates from their former employers. As these are usually in French or English and the natives cannot read them, we have considerable amusement in examining them. One fellow shows this *certificate* signed by five jolly officers of a British party, which reads: "The bearer of this has a name nobody can pronounce. Whoever hires him had best call him *Jewsharp*." That is all there is, yet the poor fellow supposes the paper to be a high recommendation. I begged Mr. Fountain to give poor *Jewsharp* a trial and he said he would. Another one exhibits this frank certificate: "I have changed my servants four times in three weeks and the bearer is unquestionably the biggest scoundrel of the lot."

The *Outfit* upon which we commence our journey to-morrow, comprises a medicine chest with an assortment of well-selected drugs, instruments and appliances; one tent large enough to hold three iron bedsteads, a table and three chairs for Mr. Fountain, Elliot and myself; a second tent for Aunt Liddy and Harriet, made of double cloth, and very close and strong; and a small tent for the kitchen apparatus and the cook. Each of us has a thick, white umbrella, extra large; a gum poncho or cloak that covers a person; a field glass; a pocket compass; a sort of a helmet hat that protects both eyes and neck, and a satchel to hang at the saddle bow. For clothing, each has four pairs of thick socks; six pairs of cotton socks; one pair heavy boots; one pair heavy shoes; two dark woolen blankets; woolen gloves; cotton gloves; a mosquito net; a ten bladed, multiple knife; a pocket bible and memorandum book. We brought our saddles from London; two strong side saddles for Aunt Liddy and Harriet, with double girths as security in climbing hills; and three deep, well padded saddles for Mr. Fountain, Elliot and myself. A surveyor's compass and chain we have purchased here.

As apparatus for examining minerals, etc., we have a file, magnets, a small series of crystallized minerals, vials of acids, muriatic, nitric and sulphurous, a blowpipe, the common fluxes, (borax, salt of phosphorus and carbonate of soda,) charcoal, strips of mica, and lamp for blowpipe, platinum foil, wire and forceps; glass tubes; a goniometer; models of crystals; balances; hammers; small anvil; chisels; microscopes; magnetic needle and other obvious matters. They are all neatly packed in a strong chest, the whole weighing about fifty pounds. As a means of "astonishing the natives" we have a beautiful Swiss music box which plays twelve tunes of every variety from gay to severe. In the way of books and maps we have not brought many. Our parents insisted, before letting us sail that we should become well posted in most of the details of this country, both as to its present state and past history. We have Thomson's "Land and Book," a set of Smith's "Bible Dictionary," and the works of Robinson, Tristam, Reland, Josephus, Rollin and a few others.

The Syrian sparrows are extremely numerous in this noighborhood, not only in the groves, but also on the house-tops. (Ps. cii: 7.) Their twitterings contrasted strangely to me, this morning, with the brawling sound of the Mediterranean waves. I observed in the bazaars long strings of little birds for sale, such as sparrows, larks and wagtails, a dozen for a piastre. They recalled the words of our Lord: "Are not two sparrows sold for a farthing?" (Matt. x: 29.) "Are not five sparrows sold for two farthings?" (Luke xii: 6.) In some of the cook shops they had the little creatures ready cooked for sale, about a mouthful each.

To-morrow we set our face toward Jerusalem. (Ezekiel xxi: 2.)

HARRIET'S DIARY.

BLATTNER'S HOTEL, 5 A. M.

My room is one of those high chambers so agreeable in the East, especially in seaports like this. It is such an "upper chamber" as "the certain disciple named Tabitha" was laid in, in this very city, after the preparations for her burial had been completed. (Acts ix: 36.) Would that I could believe this the same chamber. But that is impossible. The numberless destructions and re-edifications of Joppa since her day, forbid it. But if it were so, here, too, might St. Peter have stood, "kneeled down and prayed." And in yonder corner the precious form of Dorcas (Tabitha) might have lain, to which he said, in imitation of Jesus at Bethany, "Tabitha, arise!"

I am surprised and delighted to find that one of these girls has a photograph likeness of Mrs. Emma Willard, of Troy, New York, my dear mother's old preceptress. She doesn't remember *where* she got it, or *when*. On the back of it is written, "Born February 23d, 1787." I kissed it for mother's sake, and told the girl what a good woman Mrs. Willard is. Oh, if she could educate a generation *here*, how she would revolutionize this miserable woman-degrading race. Then I showed the girl my own album of the noble American ladies among my mother's acquaintances: Mrs. Sigourney, Mrs. Osborn, Mrs Welby, Mrs. Lucretia Mott, Mrs. Margaret Fuller Ossoli, Mrs. Willard, Mrs. Stanton, Mrs. Livermore, Miss Hosmer, Miss Chesebro, Alice Cary, Mrs. Southworth, Mrs. Bradwell, and Mrs. Stowe.

I have risen early and climbed to the house top; flat as all the house tops in Joppa are, and surrounded by a parapet of earthen jars so arranged that I can see everything around me without any one seeing me. This serves in place of the battlements ordered by Moses in Deuteronomy xxii: 8. The morning star has burst, radiant with brightness, over the mountains of Judah. Be patient, bright glory! in a few days I shall see you from Bethlehem! Below me, on a house top, is a man performing his prayers according to the seven ceremonies of the Moslem code. May his *Allah* hear his supplications and give him that first of gifts, a new heart. In another direction I hear three native Christians singing a morning hymn. It sounds dissonant and coarse to me, accustomed to the sweet cadences of our choirs, but if the hearts of the singers are musical before God, their notes sound as melodiously in the Father's ears as the low crooning of a little child in the ears of its delighted mother. The twittering of sparrows, on the house tops, is all around me.

To the east, I look over the beautiful Plain of Sharon, which, to-morrow, if it please God, I am to cross. Its myrtles, oleanders, cyclamens, crocus, maiden's hair, tulips, holly hocks, and marigold, even now allure me thither, and I long to be botanizing among their glories. How much dear mother would enjoy it, with her exquisite taste in the culture and arrangement of flowers! The location of Joppa for a town is a fine one. In the days when the tribe of Dan was strong, and Sharon a cultivated field, Joppa must have been a pleasant habitation. It is well built, and the bay before it, a charming one.

As I go down to my room, the girls of the family, who seem quite attached to me already, come with refreshments. One brings a porringer of milk; one a cup of honey and some bread; the third a branch loaded with ripe oranges.

11 A. M.

Our English party have said good-bye, and gone on to Jerusalem, where we shall meet them next week. They seem almost too closely wedded to "Murray's Hand-Book" for pleasant company. They follow too literally his instructions. When I spoke to them of the shells, the "Adams' Colony," the new road to Jerusalem, and other things to which Murray has not alluded, they appeared quite indifferent.

Elliot is picking up Arab words rapidly. He stops everybody he meets and asks the names of places and things with boyish freedom. He verifies the adage that children's questions are always the hardest. By dint of repeating the same word a hundred times over, he gets it so well that he cannot forget it. His young, fresh face, extravagant waste of breath, and earnest and youthful manner, win all hearts, while his knowledge of things, so remarkable for one of his age, secures general respect.

5 P. M.

This has been a day among the groves. Such flowers! such orange-bordered roads! such fruits! such bird songs! such gushing fountains! and—alas, such objects of poverty, and victims of loathsome disease! The oranges of Joppa are of such great size, that Elliot declares they look more like *pumpkins* upon the trees than fruit. The trees themselves are so large and spreading, and all of so fine growth, both stem and head, that I cannot imagine anything more perfect. The branches are gilded with fruit as thick as the apple trees in father's New Jersey orchard, several hundreds being borne on a single tree. Watered as they are, from the abundant wells upon this plain, they recall the passage, from Ezekiel xix : 10: "Fruitful and full of branches by reason of many waters." An orange grove gives me a more vivid idea of rich, luxuriant fruitfulness, than any other object in nature.

How appropriate, already, I find Scriptural language to this country! To-day we have begun to read the Old and New Testament through, by topics, so as to complete it while we are in the country where it was written. The Elijahs, Ezekiels, and Malachis, of the old dispensation, in their deep-furrowed garments of trembling, their metaphorical speech and the hurrying movement of their thought and style, reminded me of an impatient eagle, I saw to-day, chained in a court yard. I can imagine him in his native home of Lebanon, flinging himself from side to side, from cliff to cliff.

I found to-day how useful it is to have a guide with us who has visited this country before. Mr. Fountain knows just *what* to look for; *where* to look, and *how* to find it. Mere curiosity in him being satiated, he is only anxious to give us the best views of Holy Land objects in the shortest possible space of time.

At our dinner, we had minced meat, wrapped in grape leaves and fried. Very good it is, cooked in that way. I remember reading, at the Minnesota massacres of 1862, that a poor woman lived for several days on *grape leaves alone.*

Among the rarer trees examined to-day, and noted in my memorandum book, are the *tamarind* and *almond.* The latter resembles a peach tree, but larger. The word means *a watcher*, in allusion to its early white blossom. They recall the appropriate stanza:

"Whose fruit and blossom, in the breeze
Were wantoning together free,
Like age at play with infancy."

Also, the *citron*, which is probably the apple of Canticles ii : 3 and viii : 5, and Joel i : 12. It is a fruit of rich color, fragrant odor and elegant appearance. But in fact there are endless groves of oranges and lemons, apricots pomegranates, figs and olives, with mulberry and acacia trees, the stately palm towering above them all. The number of gardens around Joppa is nearly four hundred, varying in size from three to twelve acres. One-third of these gardens have two wells each, the rest have one well. Each well employs three animals, working day and night to keep the ground irrigated, and each draws about one thousand cubic feet of water in twenty-four hours. Many of the oranges are four inches in diameter, not a few are six inches. Even the apricots are sometimes five inches in diameter (or fifteen inches round). To appreciate an orange, it must be eaten fresh from the tree. Thus, we enjoy the full aroma, treasured from sun and air.

Among the traditional places visited to-day, one is the house of " one Simon, a tanner," with whom Peter "tarried many days in Joppa." (Acts ix : 43.) It is by the sea side, and may, probably, be the same building, or standing upon the same spot. As the business of tanning was held in contempt by the Jews, this shows how little the apostle cared for their national prejudices. I imagined the water they gave me from the well in the yard, tasted of tan bark and leather. It was while boarding in Simon's house that Peter enjoyed the celestial vision which finally broke his shackles of Jewish exclusivism, and sent him out a missionary to the world. (Acts x.) I read a large part of the book of Acts while resting here. It is easy now to understand how he could have been in retirement and prayer on the house top.

I also visited the traditional tomb of Dorcas, the resting place of that noble creature, after death had finally claimed her for its own. The story believed here is that upon her first resurrection, she suffered great physical pain. Upon her second, all will be joy and gladness. Her tomb is a cave in a rock, descended by steps, twelve feet deep, a chamber eighteen feet long, having nine crypts, or burying places.

I also read here that other incident in the life of Peter, recorded in John xxi, and to which the poet has so beautifully alluded :—

'Tis long ago, yet faith in our souls
Is kindled just by that fire of coals
  That streamed o'er the mists of the sea :
While Peter, girding his fisher's coat,
Went over the nets and out of the boat
  To answer, Lov'st thou me ?
  Thrice over, Lov'st thou me ?

I also saw the place where some believe that the Jews put Lazarus and his sisters, Martha and Mary, into an open boat and forced them to go out upon the stormy sea. As there is not a particle of credibility in the tale, I didn't ask for the rest of it.

We visited the three Christian convents, but were very little interested in them. The Armenian convent, I noticed, was deliciously cool and clean. This building was used as a hospital by the French army, in 1799. The Roman Catholic convent belongs to the Franciscan denomination, whose beautiful emblem, cut over the doorway, is the two crossed and pierced hands of Jesus. This convent is small. The priests attend chiefly to Catholic pilgrims. The Greek convent is the smallest of the three. Here they brought some boiled eggs for our refreshment, but oh, how stony-hard they do boil eggs in this country!

I asked the Greek priest how many Jews there are in Joppa? He made a wry face as if the subject was unpleasant to speak of, but answered about one hundred and twenty. He says they are of the Sephardim sect, and have but one humble synagogue here. They are mostly merchants, carpenters and silk weavers.

The vegetables grown in this vicinity are numerous. They have squashes, watermelons (very large), muskmelons, peas, okra, eggplant, artichokes, which, like the French, they eat raw and without vinegar, Irish potatoes and many others. In a package of garden seeds I bought at the bazaar, I find the following varieties: cress, onions, beans, three sorts of peas, leaks, vegetable marrows, cucumbers, watermelons, Indian corn, parsley, ruzbra, radish, cauliflowers, cabbage, spinach, gourds, turnips, lettuce two kinds, endives, maach, mustard, carrots, peppergrass, etc., etc.

We have just returned from a visit to our tents, which Mr. Fountain set up to-day, that we might see the arrangements and be sure that nothing of importance has been omitted. The tents, three in number, are pitched on a piece of high ground just above the Greek convent, overlooking the sea. The largest is the one to be occupied by Mr. Fountain and my two brothers. It has the American flag floating over it. A smaller one is for Aunt Liddy and myself. The smallest is the kitchen-tent or *cuisine.* They seem comfortable and home-like after so much travel and confinement on ship-board, and I have no doubt we shall enjoy many happy hours in them.

From the doorway of my tent, the stony hillock of the town rises before me; behind me the grand towering chain of rocks, dark-swelling, ridge-like, flushing into pink and amber, is the mountain range which we are soon to penetrate, and in the heart of which lies *Jerusalem!*

As we return to the city we enjoyed the rare privilege of witnessing a game of *Djereed*, of which we have read so much. Two companies of horsemen formed lines facing each other, about five hundred feet apart. One cavalier would ride swiftly across the interval, turn to the left, pass along the line, and selecting his opponent, throw a short, blunt spear directly at him. The object was rarely hit. The challenger would then turn and gallop back, pursued at a furious pace by his opponent, who was almost certain to hit him as he fled. The horsemanship was magnificent. The riders would throw themselves almost to the ground, hanging by one stirrup, and dodging the blows, while the splendid horses seemed to devour the wind. I am told that many accidents happen at this manly and beautiful game, while

"The coursers' trampling feet
Rouse the thick dust to shadow all the plain."

Oh the groves and fountains of this delicious territory. Its flowers are such as Mohammed called "the tears of Eve." The pastures are covered with flocks, the valleys also are covered with corn; they shout for joy, they also ring. So wrote King David, long ago, of this very landscape. Samuel also described the tender grass, springing out of the earth, by clear shining after rain as it does to-day.

I had but little time to observe or inquire into the condition of women, while in Joppa, but it is plain to see that to the tenants of the harem, not a ray of light, religious or intellectual, can penetrate. The prince of darkness sits undisturbed in its dark chambers, pouring his poisonous precepts into the tender minds of the rising race. If ever his cruel empire over Palestine is to be broken, he must be assailed in the harem and driven thence. The richest women here, covered as they are with gold and embroidery, are as ignorant and foolish as children in everything except the simplest arts of life. Oh, what a field of female benevolence is here! But it would demand the first order of self-denial.

We see hundreds of pilgrims going to the celebration of Easter week at Jerusalem. Palm Sunday, or the Sunday before Easter, occurs this year next Sabbath, March 21st. EASTER SUNDAY being the first Sunday after the fourteenth day of the calendar-moon which happens on or next after March 21st, will occur this year March 28th. Good Friday is the Friday of Passion week, and Passion week is the week preceeding the Easter festival. There is so much said on this subject by every one I meet here that I thought it best to note these facts in my diary. These pilgrims are closely followed by hundreds of others who are hastening "to keep the feast in Jerusalem." Many on foot, some on horseback, others on mules and donkeys, whilst whole families nestled in cribs constructed like crates for merchandise and slung upon both sides the camel's tall back, pursue their journey all together, or as the Arabs say, *sava sava*. I saw the husband on one side, the wife on the other, and a brace of babies snugly cribbed with each, while the patient beast, with noiseless steps bore them onward and will carry them safely up the ruggedest ascent.

9 P. M.

And so closes an exhausting but most agreeable day of explorations in the Holy Land. This experience alone amply repays the traveler for his long journey from America. It has shown me traces of the footsteps of King Solomon, Hiram, Jonah, Zerubbabel, the Machabees, Peter, Dorcas, Richard of England, Saladin and Bonaparte. What a galaxy of names. How I wish we could add that the feet of Jesus have trodden here. But at no point in this week's journey shall we touch the footsteps of Christ. The only hope we have on that subject is based upon a very apocryphal tradition that when Joseph "took the young child and his mother and fled into Egypt," he came by way of Ramleh. But this is too unlikely for credence.

MR. FOUNTAIN'S DIARY.

March 16th, 1869. 8 P. M.

We began the day by assembling in the dining room, several strangers and members of the family meeting with us. Harriet read the book of Jonah: Elliot the tenth chapter of Acts. John selected that hymn of good Mr. Woodbury's, "Sweet Hour of Prayer," and we closed with prayer. We hope always to open every day's labors in this way.

"For so the whole round earth is everyway
Bound by gold chains about the feet of God."

At 9 o'clock we got off our first telegram to New York. Immediately after breakfast we struck out for a tour of observation through the orange groves and the opuntia hedges to the American colony and other places of interest, returning by dinner time. I have an experienced agent engaging horses and equipage for our journey, upon which we propose to set out, in the afternoon, to-morrow.

Our party is much looked at by those we meet; so young, so beautiful in the freshness and innocence of youth and clad in such good garments. Elliot's old nurse, Kathleen, a most credulous and simple-minded creature, gave him a list of inquiries, before leaving home, concerning the legends of this country and he has promised her to attend to them. This will impart a quaintness to his Diary at which his parents will smile. All three of them have fastened the "pilgrim's scollop shell" in hats and bonnet and set out, Bunyan-fashion, upon a pilgrimage. Heaven bless them in the undertaking.

We have collected here and prepared for shipment to the United States by way of Beyrout, the following objects illustrative of Bible story, viz: Of shells, five bushels; a trunk of each of the following trees, viz: palm, almond, citron, orange, lemon, olive, fig, sycamore, carob; more than fifty sorts of flower seeds and vegetable seeds; large pieces of rock peculiar to this locality; some curious carved fragments of marble, and other things of more or less interest in elucidation of Bible passages.

In making up their diaries to-day, the young people ran too much in the same channels. I have advised them, hereafter, to *divide their subjects* better, so that each can devote more space to fewer themes, and thus the *whole, united*, will be more interesting.

FOUNTAIN OF ABRAHAM, NEAR JOPPA.
(VIEWED FROM THE WEST.)

[The tufted tree in the centre is a *palm;* that on the right a sycamore. The shrubs to the left and in front are the *opuntia*, or prickly pear. The domes show the style of building described by Harriet in her diary of the first day.]

CHAPTER III.

OVER THE PLAIN OF SHARON.

Native wedding—Narghileh—Arab horse—Pilgrim's horses—Native cooking—Hassan—Camels and saddle—Donkey—The happy Arabs—Ancient spear—Drawing water—Native houses—Arabic words—Telegraph from home—The cross of Jesus—Going ahead—Abraham's Fountain—Olive tree—Tower at Ramleh—Catholic convents—Joseph of Arimathæa—Dogs Carod trees—Old church—Plain of Sharon—Picnic parties—Native music—Pendulum of history—Holy Grail—Condition of women—Lydda—Prevalence of blindness—Leprosy—Early Christian martyr—Renan's unfairness—Jackals at midnight—Camp Hazezon-tamar.

ELLIOT'S DIARY.

AT THE GATE OF JOPPA, Wednesday, March 17th, 1869. 1 P. M.

I SAW a wedding ceremony this morning; bride taken home to her husband. First came the happy fellow with a lot of his friends, walking two and two. Then came his spouse under a sort of tent held over her by other women. You couldn't see the bride at all. On each side of the tent was a man with a drawn sword. Then a row of women, filthy, haggard creatures, dressed as Harriet describes it "in unwomanly rags" of blue cotton. A great many musical instruments were in the crowd and all played together. There was no tune. The noise was dreadful.

I bought a *narghileh* this morning to send home to father who smokes. It is the water pipe of the Orientals. There is first a large glass decanter. Then a long brass tube that reaches nearly to the bottom of the decanter and fits tight in its mouth. The tobacco is first moistened with water, then placed in an earthen bowl at the top of this tube and a coal of fire laid on it. The decanter is filled with water, and a long snaky stem fitted in the side of the tube. So the smoke goes down through the brass tube, through the cold water and through the stem to the lips. The stem of my pipe is eight feet long. The *narghileh*, pipe and all, cost three dollars, but you have to have their kind of tobacco to smoke in it, and it is very different from ours. No more like our American tobacco than cabbage leaves.

We are through now at Joppa and ready to cross the sweet plain of Sharon, of which Harriet has talked ever since we left home. Governor Noureddin is going to ride a few miles with us. Such a beautiful horse as he has got. I asked him the cost. He said twenty thousand piastres. That is about seven hundred and fifty dollars. He is worth it. What a ridiculous sort of money it is that makes such big figures in counting a small sum. There are no bushes on the plain of Sharon any more than on the Iowa prairies, where I spent a month last summer. You can gallop your horse here as much as you want to.

I have just had a good laugh over a caravan of horses brought here to this gate by some pilgrims who have come from Jerusalem. Such a lot! They are of all colors, nations and tongues. White, brown, bay, gray and black; one-eyed, sore-eyed, no eyed; halt and lame; some of them wheeze with asthma; some of them snap at everything that goes by, like dogs with hydrophobia, but generally they are tame enough. The pilgrims don't seem to know one horse from another.

And here is a lot of natives just in from the country, wanting to hire out. Such dresses. They don't seem to care how naked they go, so they keep their heads covered. Such big, dirty bundles of turbans.

I saw a lot of them cooking. First they kindled a woodfire on the ground. When the ground is hot enough, they scoop away the ashes and dirt, six or eight inches deep and make a hole two feet square. The dough is fitted into that hole as carefully as a cook fits her pie crust into the plate. Then the coals are raked over the whole and presently the bread is baked. A pot of rice was boiled into which melted butter was poured. All being ready, they used pieces of bread for spoons, and scooped the rice out. The bread looked like a very smutty blacksmith's apron and nearly as tough. Lots of coal and ashes stick to it, but the people didn't care. May be 'tis all the healthier for that. They ate the rice scalding hot. Such mouthfuls. Our Newfoundland dog at home (old Lee, how I wish I could see him) never gobbled such mouthfuls as they do. As soon as they got through eating they went to sleep. I asked one of them if he knew the name of the Sultan of Turkey. He said, *lar*, *lar*. That means no, no. I asked him if he didn't want to know, and he said *backsheesh*.

Mr. Floyd and his wife are to travel a little ways out with us in their wagon. How they do like to meet American people. I wonder if I shall feel that way by the time I have been here four months. We got our telegram from New York this morning, and a rich treat it was to us all.

CAMP HAZEZOU TAMAR, at Lydda. 6 P. M.

We have launched out into the Holy Land and pitched our tents in the plain of Sharon, ten miles south of Joppa. Mr. Fountain hired a camel for me and a donkey. I insisted on having the camel, particularly; it is a she camel. We crossed a fruitful plain, abounding in corn, olives and vines. My camel has a long slow, rollicking gait, just like a rocking horse. The motion is very tiresome at first, but I shall get used to it. My camel is named *Jinn*, that means a *hobgoblin*. I shall call her *Jenny*. Her noise is so curious that no two of us are agreed what it sounds like. *I* say the hoarse squeal of a pig. *John* thinks the hollow bleating of a sheep; *Harriet* declares the lowing of a cow; Aunt Liddy says *all three mixed together*. I have got an Arab servant all to myself, named Hassan, a tall, homely, one-eyed fellow. Hassan has been a great traveler. He has been to Bagdad and Egypt, Damascus, Petra, Cyprus and Jerusalem. He says he means to go with me to New York. He is a kind-hearted fellow. He can read Arabic. He has read the "Arabian Nights" and the poem of "Antar" in Arabic. He says he don't believe much in Mohammed; but he shaves his head and I noticed before he left Joppa that he went to the mosk and performed his prayers. He wears a *cypræa* shell round his neck and something sewed up in a little bag which he won't let me see.

My saddle is a lot of crossticks like a double sawhorse, or as John says, "a

XX dollar greenback, with old General Spinner's name on it." It is made so that I can take any position while riding that I want to, except standing on my head. I can face to the right, face to the left and face to the rear, like the 43d New York. Or I can sit cross-legged like a tailor. This rests me. I hang a carpet-bag on one horn of the saddle, a bottle of water on the other. I fasten my gun and umbrella to some straps behind, whenever I choose. My water-bottle is the English military bottle, made of glass, covered with felt and black leather.

It is strange that the Romans never used the camel. Porus did when he fought Alexander, and the Parthenians did against Crœsus, but the Romans, never. May be it was owing to the hatred their horses had to camels. It is curious to see my camel eating prickly pear leaves. I should think they would be as bad as pin cushions stuck full of needles.

I call my donkey *Bob*. He looks like a great bundle of black coarse wool set upon four spindles. His ears are broad, unnatural flaps that stick out of the sides of his granite head as big as those that old Hannibal used to wear when Barnum showed him at 541 Broadway.

Hassan talks to the camel just as you would to a man. When he wants Jenny to stop he clucks like a biddy with chickens. If he wants her to kneel, he makes a sort of snore and down she comes. She has got great warts as big as my head where her legs and body touch the ground when kneeling. I practised on that *cluck* and that *snore* half the way from Joppa, but Jenny did not understand me. Hassan laughed at me. Now they have made Jenny kneel and tied a rope around her bent knees, so she can't get up again. She is cross to me, though I think she will get over that in a few days. She snarls when I go near her and screams when I mount her back. I handed her an orange and she spit at me, actually spit at me like a tobacco chewer. Then she blew something out of her mouth that looks like a dried bladder skin and I concluded to leave her awhile to herself.

Jenny has a young one about three months old. It is funny to observe the staid and sober demeanor of this baby camel. No frisky playfulness and grace like other young things, but cold gravity and awkwardness. They call the little fellow *Jereed*, but I shall name him Jerry. Hassan says camels' milk is as much better than goats' milk as goats' milk is better than cows' milk.

As we left Joppa our Arab servants broke out full of song and glee at the idea of being abroad on the free plains amidst the breezes, birds and flowers; but their music was no music to my ear.

These camels carry about three hundred pounds. The heavy camel of Egypt carries six hundred *ruttels*, that is four hundred and fifty pounds.

I found a large bronze spear head near *Abraham's Fountain*, as we stopped there at noon. Bronze is a mixed metal, two-thirds copper and one-third zinc; but in old times they used tin instead of zinc. The ancient Phœnicians carried on a very lucrative trade with Spain and Cornwall, for tin. My spear head is about three inches long and an inch wide. It reminded me that such a rude, sharp point as this was fastened to a pole and thrust into the Divine Heart upon the cross. (John xix: 34.) But the spear the Romans used was called a *pilum*. It was six and one-half to seven feet long with a staff large enough to fill the hand. The head of that spear was steel. The famous lance of King Arthur was named "Ron." It was a hand broad and fit for slaughter.

I saw a man drawing water from a deep well, near Ramleh. He fastened an ox to the rope and the ox walked off with it like a sailor on a ship's deck, till he got fifty steps, then stopped. The bucket was a goat skin open at the neck. It held about six pailsfull. The well must be one hundred and sixty feet deep. Jacob's well, at Shechem, is only one hundred. This place is called in the Bible *Lydda*, but the lazy people here pronounce it *Lidd.* I don't see why they do; for in pronouncing their own words they draw out the last syllable so long and accent it so strongly, that you can hardly hear any thing else. They say Kor-*arn* for their Bible; leb-*arn* for milk; kitt-*arb* for a book; Sult-*arn* for the Emperor of Turkey; firm-*arn* for his passport, and the like. But, for all that, they pronounce Lydda *Lidd*, Gibeon *Jib*, and many other of the old Bible words in the same short way. The name of Jerusalem in Arabic is *El-Koods.*

9 P. M.

We have had our first supper in a tent. Oh, how nice it is. I ate and ate, and when Mr. Fountain told me I was eating too much, I reminded him that the natives of this country make their principal meal *at night*, and I must begin to conform rigidly to their habits. I have just been peeping into some of the Arab houses. Such miserable places for human beings to live in. Everybody was asleep and their doors wide open. But there was nothing to steal. The only furniture I could see in the houses was a few water jars and some wooden vessels to hold milk. In some of them the sheep were lying down among the people. And oh, the bugs! the houses swarmed with them. Every house has a small lamp burning olive oil, which makes a very poor light. I remembered the Bible verse: "Oil in the dwelling of the wise."

The early Christians believed that every Mohammedan had a bad smell about him till he was baptised in the Christian faith. I don't know whether baptising them would make them smell better; but these lower classes do smell dreadfully, that's a fact. I read, once, the description of a place in these words: "Shoggle is a pretty large but exceedingly filthy place." So I should say of Lydda, "it is a pretty *small* but exceedingly filthy place."

To-day I have learned twenty more Arabic words—*Bordokarn*, means orange; *harmid*, sour; *jarie*, brave; *cobs*, bread; *wasick*, dirty; *battach*, a duck; *sharib*, to drink; *othen*, the ear; *farrig*, empty; *aksam*, to swear; *lyien*, soft; *saboon*, soap; *sin*, tooth; *sharb*, young; *shararb*, wine; *moyyah*, water; *mamarr*, path; *kalam*, pen; *dawar*, medicine; *cathrah*, plenty.

JOHN'S DIARY.

JOPPA, Wednesday, March 17, 1869. 10 A. M.

Just as we are about to sit down to breakfast, the telegraphic messenger brings us the fondly-anticipated despatch from home. It reads—

"NEW YORK, 8 A. M., March 16, 1869.

Richard Fountain, English Hotel, Joppa, Syria—We are all well. Dearest love to children and all the party. EBENEZER MORRELL."

The message made us all happy. Elliot went dancing round the room with the paper in his hand, like one distracted; while a pet deer, which belongs to the house, seemed as rejoiced as he. How wonderful, that we could send a message home and get an answer back within twenty-four hours. It is dated one hour earlier than the one we sent! This is for the reason that nine o'clock yesterday morning, at Joppa, was only *one* o'clock in the morning in New York. Father got our telegram in about six hours; that made it seven o'clock in the morning in New York, and he started his answer back at eight.

This is the French copy of father's telegram as it was handed to us—

"NEW YORK, 8 matin 16 Mars.
A Richard Fountain, Hotel Anglais, Joppa, Syria—Nous sommes tous bien. Notre amour aux enfants et a toute la compagnie. EBENEZER MORRELL."

As there is a telegraph office now at Jerusalem, it is no exaggeration to say that if our Lord Jesus should appear in that city, to-morrow, as he did there nineteen centuries ago, the whole Christian world would hear of it *before* the day is out—as it is connected by telegraph wires.

I have just made me a cross in imitation of the one on which our Saviour suffered, at Golgotha, thirty miles from here. As I am wearing a cockle shell on my hat, emblematic of pilgrimage, I suspend the cross upon my breast to denote that I fight under the banners of Prince Emmanuel. It is composed of four kinds of wood glued together. The bottom piece, or socket, is cedar of Lebanon; the upright post, cypress; the cross beam, palm; the tablet, on which the inscription was nailed, olive. The native Christians in this country believe that the cross on which Jesus suffered was composed of these four kinds of wood arranged in that order, and such was the Christian belief as early as the day of Chrysostom (A. D. 397). They used this Latin verse which my classical teacher directed me, last year, to get by heart. It expresses the idea very fully—

Quatuor ex lignis Domine crux dicitur esse;
Pes crucis est *cedrus;* corpus tenet alta *cupressus;*
Palma manus retinet: titula lætatur *oliva.*

They also taught, from traditions, that this cross was eight cubits high; the beam three and a half cubits long; the olive tablet one cubit long. A cubit, according to this reckoning, is eighteen inches.

In leaving Joppa, I leave one question unanswered; that is, how high is the hill of Joppa? Father told me particularly to find out; but neither man nor book informs me. This is a strange omission.

And now we start up to Jerusalem, the common centre to which Christians come from all parts of the earth, partly to behold the accomplishment of prophecy in the conquest and destruction of that city, and partly to pay their adoration at the sacred places. We are going right *eastward.* According to the Jewish notion, this is *forwards;* or, as we Americans say, *right ahead.* I was reminded of this by an Arab who was lying by the roadside, his hand shading his face, watching us keenly with one bright eye open. I asked him the way to Ramleh. He answered, as they always do, *doagry;* that is, right ahead. This is the sort of indefiniteness and want of precision interwoven with the very genius of Eastern character and language. The fellow would have said the same thing if I had been going directly the *other way.*

4

ABRAHAM'S FOUNTAIN, 2 P. M.

We came out here this morning through the beautiful and excellent gardens of Joppa, with their abundant supply of fruit. We are waiting here for some of our lagging servants. Mr. Fountain has gone back after them, and bade us stay for him here.

Our steady friend, Noureddin Effendi, Governor of Joppa, rode out several miles with us, and at parting, said *salaam aleikam*, with that peculiar grace native to a Turkish gentleman. He is a good and a friendly man. He rides a splendid Arab horse. The finest I ever saw. When he observed how much I admired the horse, he informed me that there is a strain of horses in possession of the great Sheikhs of the desert, of which a written genealogy has been preserved for two thousand years. It is called *kockland*, and the race is believed to have sprung from the celebrated horse of Solomon, of which so many extravagant stories are credited among the Orientals. But everything extraordinary in this country is attributed in some way to King Solomon, or as they call him *Suleyman*. The most celebrated horses of this country, the *Khamseen* stock, are descended from the five mares of Mohammed. The word *kamsa*, means five; wahid, ithnine, thalathah, arbah, khamsah,—one, two, three, four, five.

This old Arabesque fountain with its reservoir, is called "Abraham's Fountain," or as they call the name here *Ibraheem*. It has no inscription on it now, visible. I was in hopes to find one; for I have read of an Arabic fountain over which are these beautiful thoughts—"Many like me have viewed this fount. But they are gone. And their eyes are forever closed." I believe it is not known who was the builder of this structure. There is a *Nahr Ibraheem*, or River Abraham, twenty miles north of Beyrout, and there may be a connection between the two names. But Saladin was the great builder of khans and fountains in the middle ages. I have drawn a pencil sketch of this fountain.*

We three have agreed to dedicate this fountain to Rev. Edward Eggleston, editor of the *Sunday School Teacher*, which has proved to us all a fountain of religious refreshment ever since Mr. Eggleston has conducted it. May the good man live to pour out many a refreshing draught for the comfort of the generation yet to come. His initials, "E. E.," are lightly carved upon a retired corner of the wall.

A fine grove of olive trees, close by, has attracted my attention. The olive looks very much like the old apple trees of New Jersey, and I couldn't help feeling around in the hollow places of these trees for blue birds' eggs, just as I used to, among the apple trees, when a boy. The foliage of the olive tree, with its dull, grayish hue, scarcely deserves the name of *verdure*. The leaf is about the size and shape of the willow leaf. They say that some of these old trees will produce a hundred gallons of olive oil year by year. The older the tree, the more productive. The trunk is always hollow, and the limbs of the older trees are hollow. The natives fill the old trees full of stones packed closely together, to keep them from falling, and build stone walls to hold up he limbs. One of these trees, under which I am sitting, has three stone walls

* See the engraving facing the Third Chapter.

holding up its three principal branches. The fruit of the olive ripens in the month of June; it is a berry about as large as a wild plum.

RAMLEH, 4 P. M. On top of the Tower.

The rest of the party have gone on to Lydda, three miles to the northeast, while I spend an hour here making observations. There is a convent at Ramleh, of Roman Catholic priests. I had always supposed that *convent* meant a place for women, and *monastery* for men, but such is not the way they understand it in the Holy Land. Strictly speaking, however, the word convent may be applied to a house for either sex. There are also five mosks here, one of which has a fine white marble tomb with gilt inscriptions of Ayoub Bey, an Egyptian Mameluke officer, who died at Ramleh.

The priests of these convents are bound by their rules to accommodate all travelers, poor or rich, who are on their way to holy places, and entertain them for a certain length of time. At Ramleh the time is one day; at Bethlehem, three days; (the time in which Jesus remained under the power of death) at Jerusalem, thirty days.

Ramleh is surrounded by noble groves of olive trees. When Baldwin III. besieged a city of the Saracens, A. D. 1144, he began to cut down the olive trees, which were the principal support of the country. No sooner did the people see this, than they surrendered at discretion; for to destroy the olive trees is to destroy the land.

There is a noble old tower here that once belonged to a Christian church. An ornamental arch, near the top, is beautiful. There are five things to me most sad to contemplate—a stranded ship, a broken-winged eagle, a garden choked with weeds, a harp with broken strings, and a ruined church. This one affected me strangely. As I climb to the top of the tower, one hundred and twenty feet high, and, standing on the highest ridge of the plain, it seemed

"That all the old echoes hidden in the wall
Rang out, like hollow woods, at huntingtide."

The tower is ascended by steps from the inside, like the American light houses. A balustrade runs around it on the outside. The view from the top is truly extensive and interesting. Dr. Robinson describes this tower as unique for loftiness and elegance. It has an inscription over the doorway with the date of erection, 710—that is, A. D. 1310.

At the top, I found a party of travelers, some of them drinking pale ale, the others examining "Murray's Hand-Book," and identifying such of its statements as had truth enough to hold them together.

A poor, starved village, embowered in olive trees, was lying off to the eastward, which didn't happen to be mentioned in the "Hand-Book," and they appeared to take the omission as a personal offence. Formerly, all pilgrims got their stories of Holy Land from the *priests*, but now, from "Porter's" or "Murray's Hand-Book."

I have already said there is a commanding view from the top of this tower. A very ancient well lies on the south, called after Saint Helena. Great fields of wheat and barley extend over the plain in all directions. The gardens are fenced in like those of Joppa, with the giant cactus, now in bloom here. The dark foliage of the pomegranate treees, blazes with heavy scarlet flowers. The broad-armed sycamores strike my fancy. I can see Joppa very distinctly in the west, nine miles distant. In the south, my view extends nearly to Ascalon. The Plain of Sharon is a vast expanse of grain and grazing land. The long, white lines, yonder, are flocks of sheep, following their shepherd. Sometimes a black line appears,—that is the goats. On the north, there are no villages in sight; Lydda is a little east of north from me. All the villages in this plain seem to stand on elevated places. In coming here from Joppa, we passed the villages of Yazur, Kabab, Beit-Dejau, Safaryah, and Sarafand, all small hamlets, and none of them very near the road. These are marked on our map of the road.*

Everything around me blossoms as the rose. The country is dotted with dark, luxuriant olives. A company of Arabs is seated below by a hedge of clustering roses, waiting for us, and singing a rude chorus in which I distinguish the word *yokalay* repeated over and over again, with many a shake. The new road, built last year from Joppa to Jerusalem, goes winding up the hills yonder, crowded with travelers passing to and fro.

"Never yet
Has heaven appeared so blue nor earth so green,"

As they do from the summit of this tall tower.

Ramleh is supposed to be the ancient *Arimathæa* of the good Joseph who, by giving his Lord a death-home, has made himself to live forever. Perhaps, but for Joseph, the body of Jesus would have been thrown out to the dogs and wild beasts as I see them in every grave yard here. Noble man! how every Christian loves the memory of him who "went in boldly unto Pilate and craved the body of Jesus." (Mark xv : 43.) An English poet gives this tradition of the life of Joseph of Arimathæa:

"After the day of darkness when the dead
Went wandering o'er Moriah, the good saint,
Arimathæan Joseph, journeying, brought
To Glastonbury, where the winter thorn
Blossoms at Christmas, mindful of our Lord."

Referring to the cup, called *Holy Grail*, which, it is said, was used at the Last Supper by our Lord.

The streets of Ramleh are crooked, narrow and filthy. The houses have low domes and flat roofs. Many of them are substantial and commanding like those of Joppa. Hyssop grows abundantly in the crevices of the walls. Orchards of ancient olive trees are in the suburbs. At a distance it appears a stately village, but not so on close inspection. The tobacco raised around here is considered very fine.

As I came down from the tower, I glanced over the ruined mosk which lies around it. It was once a large and splendid edifice. The cisterns underneath are twenty-four feet deep, and covered with twenty-four vaulted ceilings, each twelve feet square, supported by massive pillars. As no Mohammedan can go into his church (mosk) without washing his feet, hands, arms, head and neck,

---

* See the map facing Chapter Seventh.

a cistern of water is always found close by. But what a dirty set these must have been to need so much water, especially here, where it is so easy to dig wells. But I believe they would rather drink rain water in this country than any other kind. They collect it from the roofs of their houses, and horrid stuff it is.

When I came out of Ramleh, I felt like quoting the words of David, for "dogs encompassed me." So many and such dogs! I counted four whole ears and a tail on three dogs. Such mangy, scurvy creatures. And such shameful attempts to imitate the true sound of dogs. Very much such barks as these Arabs talk like civilized Americans. When David wrote that sentence I guess he had been flying from his pursuers by night, and camping near some Philistine village where the dogs got after him.

Just outside the town, I saw a fellow lying asleep, with his back to me. As he heard me coming, he rolled over to look through his sore eyes. I said to him, in the words of Micah, "In the house of Aphrah roll thyself in the dust." He only answered, *bachsheesh*.

The fine carob trees out here remind me that the long, sweet pods of the carob are supposed to be the *husks* that the swine in the parable did eat. (Luke xv : 16.) But now there are no swine on all the plain of Sharon to eat them. Mr. Fountain says, in his last year's travels in this country, he only saw one small group of pigs, and that was a litter of wild swine near Gebal. He thinks if a person were to attempt to raise hogs here, the people would kill the *hogs*, and perhaps *him*, also—they abhor pork so earnestly.

The carob (pronounced *karoob*) is the *ceratonia siliqua* of botanists. The pods are often called St. John's bread, from a tradition that the Baptist lived upon its fruit in the wilderness. I often see them for sale in New York. This sweet pod tastes much like the pod of the honey locust. The people here often grind it and make a syrup out of the juice, which they call dibs. We have purchased some of it to send home.

An American writer says "it is a luguminous tree, an evergreen growing in hedges, a native of Spain, Italy and the Levant. It produces long, flat, brown colored pods filled with a mealy, succulent pulp, of a sweetish taste, which, in times of scarcity, have been used for food, and are called St. John's bread.

Dr. W. M. Thomson says that the leaves of the carob are of a deep, rich green color, and united to the stems in the same manner as the leaves of the locust. The fruit is a large, dark, red-colored pod, the seeds are red and very hard. The tree, seen at a distance, resembles in size and shape the apple tree.

The history of Ramleh is curious. The name means *sandy*, and alludes, probably, to the sandy soil of the plain around the town. The latitude is 31 degrees 59 minutes; longitude 35 degrees 28 minutes east from Greenwich. The population is three thousand; one-third of which are Christians. Formerly, it was no doubt much larger. The Crusaders took it, on their way to Jerusalem, A. D. 1099, and probably got the timbers here of which they formed their military engines for the siege. De Vogue, in his "Churches in the Holy Land," has the following account of a Christian church at Ramleh, which I translated a few weeks since as I crossed the sea :

"The city of Ramleh, according to Eusebius, and St. Jerome, the ancient

Arimathæa, contains a beautiful church of the time of the Crusades. The Musselmans have made a mosk of it, and have forbidden the Christians from visiting it. I regret that I was not able to draw it, for it seems to be entirely preserved with its three vaulted naves, its three apsides, and its complete arrangement of the twelfth century.

"At going out of the city, on the side of Joppa, are seen considerable ruins known under the name of 'Church of the Templars,' 'Cistern of St. Helena,' with a tower styled the 'Tower of the Forty Martyrs.' All these names seem to me erroneous. I think the entire collection is the remains of a grand Musselman establishment of the thirteenth, fourteenth and fifteenth centuries. The tower is an Arabic minaret, built by the Sultan Nasr-Mohammed-Ibn-Kaloun, and finished in 1318. Evident reminiscences of Gothic architecture are recovered here. So, also, the disposition of the platform and the windows, the form of the centre forts are imitations of the steeples of the Crusaders, without being exactly copies. The construction and the apparel are Arabic, and so are the moultures that encircle the upper windows, and the very characteristic *contour* of the gate.

"The Franciscan convent, whose hospitality has so often been precious to pilgrims, was founded in the fifteenth century, by Philip the Good, Duke of Bourbon. It is occupied by Spanish monks."

CAMP HAZEZON-TAMAR, near Lydda, 9 P. M.

We have camped, eaten supper, though our dragoman persists in calling it *dinner*, and I am scribbling my last notes for the day. The Arabs are chanting dolorously of love, war and religion and a miserable noise they make of it. *Corona Borealis* is over me, just fifty minutes behind *Scorpio*, as usual, and now I will try the virtues of my iron bedstead for the first time.

HARRIET'S DIARY.

AT ABRAHAM'S FOUNTAIN, WEDNESDAY, March 17th, 1869. 2 P. M.

We have stopped here for half an hour to wait for some of our baggage, and I take the opportunity to make my diary up to this moment.

All the way from Joppa, we have seen native picnic parties enjoying themselves at short distances from the road. They get far enough from the highway that the women can remove their veils without being seen by strangers. From their screams of laughter and the tossing of their arms, they appear the gayest of the gay. Their bearded, phlegmatic old Mormon of a husband reclines nonchalantly, smoking his *narghileh* in the center of the merry group. What a beastly thing is polygamy! These natives seem particularly to admire trees, flowers, fine horses and young children, but even the better sort appear to have no refined delights and but few pleasures, save those common to all classes.

Oh what it must have cost the Jews to part from these homes of their ancestors, when Jehovah brought upon them the king of the Chaldees, who carried away to Babylon "them that had escaped the sword." (2 Chron. xxxvi.) And again, when Titus once more destroyed the cities of their land and removed the few, whom the wars had spared, to distant colonies. To part from the homes they had created and beautified, who can tell what it cost them in tears and sighings! How powerfully Jeremiah has depictured their feelings. When only a little girl of ten years, I copied from out a lady's diary, who was here many years before, this passage; how little, at that time, I thought I should ever come here to verify its truth: "The lovely plain of Sharon is dotted with villages. Acacias are abundant there. The light wind bows the heads of the green barley fields, like a lake with clouds drifting it! When the wind lulls, the heat is oppressive."

Solomon, alluding to the matchless pastures, said: "Go thy way forth to the footsteps of the flock and feed thy flock beside the shepherds' tents. But I might note a hundred such expressions of Bible readings. None, however, affects my mind so much as the words of Jesus, referring, perhaps, to the very flower I havê just plucked at the Fountain of Abraham: "Consider the lilies how they grow! I say unto you that Solomon in all his glory was not arrayed like one of these!" How these simple, happy illustrations of Christ cling to the memory like ivy to the wall! I cannot learn why this fountain is called "Abraham's." Among the natives the name is a common one (pronounced *Ibraheem*), and it is probably one of their own Abrahams, whose name is used here. The name is very common among them, for they look upon Abraham as the father of their nation, and call him *el-Khaleel*, the Faithful. We have no account that Abraham, the patriarch, ever visited this portion of Canaan, or even came nearer than Gerar, forty miles to the South.

The Fountain of Abraham is a large, square structure of limestone and marble. A stone trough before it lies by the side of a delightful open chamber. Immense sycamore trees shade its foot. Two roads meet and the trampled appearance of the earth proves how much the place is frequented. Brother John has made an excellent sketch of it.

Not far from me there is sitting an Arab minstrel, with a strangely-shaped violin with one broad string. He rasps it and chants his mysterious Arab poetry with great energy. But I am sure he will never

"Make a swan-like end,
Fading in music;"

For to my ear the intervals in the Arabic scale are harsh and unnatural in the extreme. Now he comes up, bowing and salaaming, and when I give him a small piece of money, goes away to try some other customer. The melancholy tone of Arab music suggests Proverbs xxv: 20: "As he that taketh away a garment in cold weather, and as vinegar upon nitre, so is he that singeth songs to a heavy heart."

Here for the first time we come within the swing of the awful, monstrous "Pendulum of History" that swung from Assyria to Egypt and back, for centuries. I am reminded of it by a bronze spear head which Elliot has just picked up. Along this Plain of Sharon first swept Sesostris, going northward and deluging the fat plains of Assyria with blood and carnage. Then, many centuries afterwards the retaliation comes, first under Sennacherib, afterwards Nebuchadnezzer, Cambyses and others, each of whom brought fire and destruction from the East. Near Beyrout, I shall see the inscriptions, side by side, of five of the world's tyrants: Serostris, the Egyptian; Sennacherib, the

Assyrian; Aurelian, the Roman: then the Saracenic and the French despot, Napoleon III. Well may the Scriptures term these human monsters by such beastly names as *lion*, *bear*, *leopard* and the like, sent to destroy men. Daniel styled Alexander the Great, a *leopard with four horns*, and a *one-horned goat*, referring to his power and the rapidity of his conquests. To Elliot, who is so greatly enamored with the character of Bonaparte, I quote this instructive paragraph:

"Bonaparte, whose mandates Kings and Popes for a time obeyed, after spreading everywhere the terror of his name, after deluging Europe with blood, and clothing its nations in sackcloth, closed his days in banishment on a lonely island, almost literally exiled from the world."

NEAR RAMLEH, 5 P. M.

We have stopped in the suburbs for an hour while John goes into the village. But my first nine miles of horseback, pleasant as it is, has tired me, and I will rest in the pleasant shade. Ramleh was formerly Arimathæa, the home of good Joseph. It is where the old-caravan road between Egypt and Damascus crossed our road to Jerusalem. Probably it is also the same road as Ramathaaim Zophim, where Samuel was born. (1 Samuel i.) In view of that, I have read that affecting incident of the birth and surrender of the son of prayer (1 Chron. vi;), by the good Hannah.

Tradition makes Joseph of Arimathæa, the owner of "the large upper room" in which the Last Supper was held. It was his tomb that received the Divine body,—scourged with rods, lacerated with thorns, pierced with nails, opened with the spear,—of our Redeemer. After the Lord's Supper was over, and the party had gone to Gethsemane, Joseph, it is said, went into the room and took the cup in which Jesus had consecrated the wine of the new covenant. This Joseph used the next day in collecting the blood that flowed from our Saviour's wounds. The Roman Catholic pictures mostly represent Joseph of Arimathæa, with this cup in his hand, called "The Holy Grail" (*Sainte Greale*, or the "Blessed Cup.") It is made of glass, olive green, fifteen inches high, four wide. Mother, who is a great admirer of Tennyson, and is waiting eagerly for his new poem, "The Holy Grail," told me to note these facts in my diary when I should visit Ramleh. "The Quest of the Holy Grail" forms part of the old romance of King Arthur, written by Thomas Mallory in the reign of Henry VII.

CAMP HAZEZON-TAMAR, near Lydda. 10 P. M.

We found our tents pitched and dinner ready for us when we arrived here about 6 o'clock. It is truly romantic to eat under canvass. I have now taken my campstool outside the tent and lit my wax candle to finish my diary. How thankful ought every woman to be who is born in our happy country. To-day I saw a woman plowing and, at the same time carrying a heavy child astride of her left shoulder. The bright-eyed little fellow looked at me so proudly as I rode by; but oh, the poor mother! *She* never once looked up. I read, just before leaving home, of a young lady in Wisconsin who cultivated twenty acres in corn, last year, but, then, that was a matter of independent choice with her, so different from these women.

From the rude wall of a stone hut close by our tent, I have picked a bunch of hyssop and laid it in our large floral album to dry. It recalls that strange and dreamy verse of Tennyson:

> "Flower in the crannied wall,
> I pluck you from the crannies;
> Hold you here, root and all, in my hand,
> Little flower,—but if I could understand
> What you are, root and all, and all in all,
> I should know what God is and man is."

Lydda, now called *Lydd*, is a busy and prosperous little place of one thousand inhabitants, embowered in fine orchards of olives, pomegranates, figs, sycamores and other trees. There is an air of thrift and prosperity around it which Mr. Fountain assures me is not often seen in Palestine. A very famous Jewish College was here during the time of Christ, and no doubt much of the scepticism and bigotry that opposed his blessed teachings originated here. The Mohammedans believe that Jesus will descend here sometime before the resurrection and conquer Antichrist, whom he will destroy. (Koran, chap. xliii: note.) The town is buried in palms and has a large well near the gate. Here as Peter "came down to the saints that dwell at Lydda," he cured Æneas who "had kept his bed eight years of the palsy." (Acts ix.) It was at Lydda, too, that Peter was abiding when word came of the death of Dorcas at Joppa, ten miles west. How promptly he answered the summons! How powerfully Jesus Christ wrought in him to restore that dead sister to life. Lydda is the first town we reached after turning to the left three miles back. Within four miles of it are the old villages of Ono, (1 Chron. viii: 12;) Hadid, (Neh. vii: 37;) and Neballat, (Neh. xiii: 34.) The Pagan Emperor, Hadrian, called it Diospolis, or the *City of Zeus*, but it soon regained its old name. The remains of St. George were buried here and the ruins of his church are still grand. A beautiful creek runs by the place, along which the oleanders grow "as willows by the water courses." (Isaiah xliv: 4.) Other luxuriant bushes fringe its banks, in whose branches the blackbird, lark and other songsters pour out their lays. But I have not yet heard the *bulbul*, or Syrian nightingale, of which Oriental poets sing so much. "This lovely songster (*Ixos xanthopygius*), whose notes, for volume and variety, surpass those of the nightingale, wanting only the final cadence, and which abounds in all the wooded districts of Palestine, and especially by the banks of the Jordan, where in the early morning it fills the air with its music." (H. B. Tristam.)

I have particularly remarked to-day the number of *blind people* in this vicinity. I think one-third the natives are either blind or one-eyed or have extremely bad eyes. I knew it was a distressing malady very prevalent in the East, but was not prepared to see so much of it. The climate is very hot for half the year, and a very fine dirt enters and frets the eye. The disease of blindness must always have been common along the coast. The perpetual glare of light; the contrast of the heat with the cold; sea air; small pox, and the uncleanliness of the people, all combine to produce eye-diseases. It is a proverb that in Lydda every man is blind or one-eyed. In Joppa there are five hundred blind persons; in Cairo, one in every five is blind. The ancient Jews were enjoined by humane laws to show all kindness to the blind. (Lev. xix: 14; Deut. xxvii: 18.) To see the sore-eyed children here is the most disgusting thing that has yet fallen under my observation. Rev. W. M. Thomson thinks that the cause of this sore calamity is owing to the locality. Situated in the course of a vast plain or valley of Sharon, it is excessively hot, and the reflection of the sun from the white sand is very painful to the eyes.

But the sight that horrifies the very soul and overwhelms it with pity and sympathy is that of the *lepers*, as I saw them coming out of Joppa. Under the beautiful and luxuriant orange trees they group together, loathsome, maimed and wretched. Some lie upon the ground. Some lean upon crutches. Many are blind, their faces black and bloated,—all that you see of them a mass of putrid sores. They recall the memory of the unhappy Lazarus. (Luke xvi.) In some, the fingers had rotted off. The voices of many hissed through tongueless throats. When I had withdrawn from these dreadful images of horror, after giving them as much *backseesh* as I could spare, I felt as never before, what a perfect emblem of spiritual corruption, or sin in the heart is leprosy in the body. As such I have no doubt Moses employed it. And I also felt that when Jesus healed the leper, (Matt. viii ;) he performed one of the most fitting acts in proof of his divinity. Dr. Thomson, in "The Land and the Book," describes these wretched objects in these words: "The scab comes on by degrees in different parts of the body; the hair falls; the nails drop off; joint after joint of the fingers fall away; the gums are absorbed; the teeth disappear; the nose, eyes, tongue and palate are consumed; finally the wretched victim sinks into the earth." How sad to think that the good Dr. Goddard, who came here on purpose to study this singular disease, died at Jerusalem, before accomplishing his work.

My dear father once told me, a little girl on his knee, an affecting story of a woman martyred here at Lydda in the last days of St. John. She was an elderly lady before she ever heard the name of Jesus as the Saviour of mankind. But she at once embraced the faith and soon won all her household, husband, children and grandchildren to the same belief. It was in the times of which Jesus had prophesied. Persecutions soon followed. The contempt of neighbors; the desertion of friends; the pointing of the finger; the sarcastic speech, these were but annoyances. Imprisonment, the forfeiture of property, the breaking up of the household were the great trials. Then comes the last trial at which poor humanity shudders, the CROSS. This punishment most cruel of all, because the first stage, that of excruciatory suffering, is so greatly prolonged, was held up before her as a terror to stimulate her to recant. The family was detained in dungeon a whole year to give them time to do so. But they had decided upon their course, and one cruel winter's morning the whole household was taken to one of the low hills that I see yonder in the east, and the scourge, the nail, the wood did their work as they had done it sixty years before upon the person of Christ. All died cheerfully. The aged mother and grandmother gave her last breath to prayer for her murderers.

I spent half an hour, after my arrival, reading what Renan says about St. Paul's journey from Jerusalem to Cesaræa. What a charming and elegant writer he is; but so unfair. Such a miserable idea of historical truth as he has. A man like Renan snubbing St. Paul is like a frog criticizing a nightingale. He has taken the strangest liberties with the Holy Land. In descriptions of

Christ he strips the Lord of Glory of all his supernatural majesty; shrivels him into a mere rabbi, entangled by the prejudices of his time, performing no real miracle, neither rising from the dead nor ascending into heaven. The history of the' Holy Church as well as the Sacred Text, contains abundant argument against him. Yet I cannot help recalling the beautiful words he addressed to his dead sister, who had traveled with him, in 1860, through this famous land and died near Beyrout.

As a pleasant contrast to our visit here. I note in my diary what Sir John Maundeville said in his, when he came here A. D. 1322, more than five hundred years ago. He says, "Those who are willing to go a long time on the sea and come nearer to Jerusalem may proceed from Cyprus and by sea to the port of Joppa, for that is the nearest point to Jerusalem, the distance being only one and one-half days. The town is called Joppa because one of the sons of Noah, named Japhet, founded it and now it is called Joppa. It is one of the oldest towns in the world, because founded before Noah's flood. There is still seen in the rock, the place where the iron chains were fastened whereby Andromeda was imprisoned. A great rib, forty feet long is still shown there."

"Omitting the history, geography and biography of the Bible and teaching only *doctrines*, is not doing justice to God's book; the *whole Bible* must be taught as far as man's heart and mind can grasp the glorious theme. The days of shallowness have fallen into disrepute, the demand for thoroughness is rising fast." I have written this passage in my diary as a reminder.

Coming into this place at the close of day, the beautiful description of a traveler in 1834 recur to me. "The whole valley of Sharon from the mountains of Jerusalem to the sea, and from the foot of Carmel to the hills of Gaza, is spread before me like a map and is extremely beautiful, especially at evening, when the last rays of the setting sun gild the mountain tops. Then the weary husbandman returns from his labor, and the bleating flocks come frisking and joyful to their fold. At such a time I saw it and lingered long in pensive meditation until the stars looked out from the sky and the cool breezes of evening began to shed soft dews on the feverish land. What a paradise was here when Solomon reigned in Jerusalem and sang of the rose of Sharon and the lily of the valley. And what a little heaven upon earth will be here again, when He that is greater than Solomon shall sit on the throne of David, his father. For in His days shall the righteous flourish and abundance of peace, so long as the moon endureth."

Midnight.

Still I cannot sleep. The solemn glory of the heaven above me overcomes my soul. I sit

"Gazing at a star,
And marvelling what it is."

This exquisite couplet recurs to my memory:

"Night threw her mantle o'er the earth,
And pinned it with a star."

Just now a noise broke from near the base of the hills east of Lydda, that I knew from the description was a pack of jackals prowling among the graves. It is a mournful howl mixed with barking and sounds like the voice of a person in distress. Oh, may I not die and be buried among this evil people. I have heard of a dear lady who expired last spring among the hills east of the Jordan, who begged in her last words that her husband would inter her remains at Jerusalem, not in an Arabic burying ground. That dreadful scream of the jackals. It was

"A cry that shivered in the tingling stars,
And as it were, one voice, an agony,
O lamentation."

Every graveyard I have yet seen in this country is a Calvary, a Golgotha, a *place of skulls.* Oh, horrible, to imagine hyenas howling over one's poor remains at midnight.

I forgot to mention why we call this camp *Hazezon-Tamar.* It is the name of a place near the Dea Sea, and means in Hebrew, "the cutting down of the palm." John named our encampment from the circumstance that we purchased a dead palm tree here, had it cut down and sent it back on a camel to Joppa, to be shipped to Beyrout, and so to New York. The tree is about ten inches in diameter, and nearly as spongy as cork.

The celestial canopy stretches above me like a curtain studded with spangles of stars. I can see the base of the hill near by, girdled with groves of fruit trees. There is a quiet, pastoral air about the landscape; a soft serenity in its forms and colors. The air is fragrant with wild thyme and camomile.

Late as the hour is, our Arab servants are sitting in a circle, smoking and disturbing sleep by their loud story telling and singing. I can catch the chorus of one of their songs, *yah gazelle, yah gazelle,* that is, oh, gazelle, of which I shall try to get the remainder. But now I am reminded that we have a hard day's work before us, to-morrow, climbing the pass of Bethhoron, and I will endeavor to secure some sleep.

MR. FOUNTAIN'S DIARY.

LYDDA, Wednesday, March 17, 1869. 8 P. M.

We began our third day and the last, at Joppa, by reading the 72d Psalm, and 19th of John, in alternate verses, singing the hymn "Work, for the Night is Coming," and prayer. Quite a number of the members of the Prussian Evangelican Mission, located at Joppa, came in and joined our devotions with seeming cordiality.

The morning was spent in the distractions of preparations for departure. But that I went through this experience last year, I should almost have been distracted. The natives have but little regard for truth in their dealings with foreigners, and none for time. Their minds are trifling and light. Never in a hurry themselves, they wilfully attribute a *nonchalence* to us, which we do not possess, and nothing will move them to punctuality. Assisted by Governor Noureddin's officers and the personal aid of Mr. Floyd, I hunted up my dragoman *here,* and my mule drivers *there,* and about noon pushed the head of our little column forward to the Fountain of Abraham, where we halted to give time for the rest to overtake us. Our settlement with the Blattners, was without dispute, and one of the brothers even offered his gratuitous services to expedite our departure for Jerusalem.

After some delay at Abraham's Fountain, we came on some to Ramleh, some to Lydda, often stopping on the way, as the young people desire to gather flowers, or make sketches, or examine objects of special interest to them. Arrived here at six o'clock, we found our tents pitched, and matters in a good condition, for I had sent the baggage, mules and servants on before us. And so we begin our camp life in the Holy Land.

Our plan is to go to-morrow (Thursday) to Gibeon; return this way on Friday, by the new turnpike road; go eastward again on Saturday to some point in sight of Jerusalem, and there lie in camp over Sunday. By this means, we acquire a perfect knowledge of all the intervening country, both plain and mountain, between Joppa and Jerusalem.

In looking through the three diaries of this day, I observe a number of passages in each of them, particularly in Elliot's, which are plainly quotations from other writers, passages committed to memory during the period these young people have been preparing for this expedition, and now involuntarily recurring to the mind, by the law of association. I have observed the same thing in all books of Oriental travel, and I hail its presence here as an evidence that my young wards are thus duly qualified for their task.

My young friends are taking pleasant liberties with the names of prominent Americans, Bible teachers and Sunday school worthies, by "planting them," as they term it, upon sacred soil. At every memorable spot, they propose to leave, as seed sown in this historic earth, the names of those who are doing the best work for Jesus Christ, in their own happy land, at home.

CHAPTER IV.*

MOUNTING THE HILLS OF DAN AND BENJAMIN.

Dog of adoption—Native horses—Wely—palm tree—Judas Macchabæus—Native religion—Jackal—Packing baggage—Steep hills—Arabic Words—Honeysuckle Glen—Sardines—Beggars, and how to refuse them—Finding a skull—Almond staff—Pet lamb—Blessings of freedom—Camel fight—Church of St. George—Insults for the boys—Plowing—Ebenezer—Exploits of the Macchabees—Pool of Gibeon—The cook—Flowers on Sharon—Baking bread—Gazelle—The Noble Helena—Butter making—Giant Pool—Rain fall—Military conscriptions—In sight of Jerusalem.

ELLIOT'S DIARY.

HONEYSUCKLE GLEN, Thursday, March 18, 1869. 11 A. M.

WHEN we left Lydda, this morning, a young dog followed us out of town, anxious to make one of our party. I fed him and tied a piece of ribbon round his neck, and named him *Sweet-Home.* The dogs here are mangy and poor, when they get to any age. They don't belong to anybody. They have to fight for a living, and are welted with scars. Their tails and ears look miserable. *Sweet-Home* is not old enough yet for a warrior. If he behaves well, I will take him to America and make a *freedman* of him. The puppies here are sleek and beautiful; but the dogs, horrid. The ancient Jews used to make dogs useful in watching houses and guarding flocks, but I don't see them at it now. Hungry and half wild, they seem to be all the time wanting to eat. No wonder the Mohammedans call them unclean. They *are* unclean if ever there was anything unclean. I noticed, yesterday, in Joppa, a big, mangy dog sleeping right across the side walk. Every native, man and woman, walked around him, so as not to let their dresses touch him. If their clothes had touched him I suppose it would have been necessary to wash them. But I made the fellow hop, with my almond cane. I don't walk around a dog, if I know myself.

You can't insult anybody in this country so much as to call him *kelb*—that is, dog. So it was in Bible times. In 1 Samuel xxiv : 14, and many other places this is seen. The Mohammedans call all us Christians, dogs, when they dare do it. Some dogs to go Mecca every year with the pilgrims, and then they call them *hadjis.* *Sweet-Home* has the ears and head of a prairie wolf. He is small, sharp-nosed, red-colored, with a short tail. I will try what civilization can do for him.

---

* RUINS OF THE CHURCH OF ST. GEORGE AT LYDDA, Nine miles East of Joppa ; Viewed from the West.

This elegant bit of Crusaders' architecture cannot be excelled by anything of that period now remaining in Palestine.

These native horses don't bear the rein at all. They don't understand horse-English either. If you want them to go ahead, you must press the knees into their ribs. If you want them to stop, hiss, and they will stop so quick you will go over their heads. If you want to turn them, pull the bridle on their neck, on the opposite side.

We saw a wely, or tomb of a sheikh, near the town of Lydda. A sheikh is the mayor of a village. Some of these sheikhs are religious, and when they die, they are worshiped as the Catholics worship saints. This wely is a stone building, eight by twelve feet. Has a cupola for a roof. Mr. Fountain says there are more dead saints among the Mohammedans, now a days, than living ones. This wely is on an eminent and commanding spot like most of the welies. Rags are tied in the windows, but I don't know what for and I didn't care enough to ask Mr. Fountain the reason. This wely is whitewashed, bright and clean. It puts me in mind of the passage "Whited sepulchres, which, indeed, appear beautiful outward." (Matt. xxiii : 27.) Mr. Fountain says all the rock of this country is limestone, and that it turns into beautiful white lime, out of which this whitewash is made.

John had a difficulty this morning with some dirty Arabs, who insulted sister Harriet. He whipped them, good. If Governor Noureddin was out here I would have the rascals bastinadoed.

When we passed the last palm tree that I shall see for some days, I got John to watch my clothes while I clumb it. 'Tis as easy to climb a palm tree as a ladder. The Arabs say there are three hundred and sixty uses for the palm tree, one for every day in the year. I can name a three hundred and sixty-first—and that is, *it is good for boys to climb.* I suppose it was such a palm tree as this that Deborah dwelt under. (Judges iv : 5.)

I name this palm tree Judas Macchabæus, for we are coming now into the district where that great warrior and patriot won his immortal fame He is one of my nine heroes, and I know his history by heart. In one of his grandest fights he gave his soldiers, for a watch-word, "the help of God." And, by God's help, they did conquer. (2 Maccabees viii : 23.) Another time, when his soldiers were almost disheartened, he said, in his speech to them—"If our time be come, let us die manfully for brethren, and let us not stain our honor." (1 Maccabees ix : 10.) Yes, I named this palm tree, at Lydda, Judas Macchabæus, and carved his initials, "J. M.," on it, with my knife.

We leave it to Harriet to dedicate the tree. She selects that noble Sunday school laborer, Rev. J. L. McKee, of Louisville, Kentucky, who, for many years, has preached a sermon every Sunday afternoon to the *children of his church.* He is nearly blind. If ever his eye sight should be restored so that he may come here and see this palm tree, he will find it a tree "good for food, and pleasant to the eyes, and a tree to be desired." (Genesis iii . 6.)

I noticed this morning that when our Arabs ate their poor, scanty rations, which were nothing but black bread made of barley, and some raw onions, they returned thanks aloud to *Allah*, as they call God. But then, they have no idea of religion, unless it makes some noise or show in the world.

I saw a jackal sneaking out of a vineyard, and thought of the verse—"take us the foxes, the little foxes that spoil the vines; for our vines have tender grapes." Hassan says that jackals are very fond of grapes, and they pull down and gnaw down the vines, reaching after them. The jackal is the dog of the hills and the battle fields.

Our baggage this morning was so badly strapped upon the pack mules, that the first sharp cliffs they rounded, it caught on the rocks. This pulled the load off on one side and pushed the mule down the cliff on the other. The poor fellow fell twenty feet. But he lit on his legs, and came scrambling up the cliff as unconcerned as possible. I thought it would kill him. Then another load slipped clear over backwards, fell to the ground and rolled down the slope till somebody stopped it. Mr. Fountain then told our servants plainly, that if this thing happened again he would discharge the whole lot of them. He is just the man to do it.

A wagon could not now pass through these hills any more than a ship could pass through the rocky reefs now to yonder port of Joppa, that I can see, some twenty miles off. But these farmers have one advantage; they can cultivate *both sides of their land.* It stands up on its edges, straight as a shingle.

I used to wonder why Bonaparte did not go to Jerusalem when he was here in the Holy Land, sixty-nine years ago. But I do not wonder now. To take an army through these hills would have been as bad a job as crossing the Alps. So when he had captured the cities of the Plain of Sharon, he wrote to the sheikhs of Jerusalem and Nablous, that "the hilly country did not lie within the base of his operations." No wonder. There he showed his good sense. I never before imagined such roads. Horses must be educated to them to understand them. The only change in these roads for a thousand years is that they get worse and worse. But these cannot get much worse.

To-day I was riding donkey Bob, and wanted him to go down a hill. He stopped, smelt of the stone slabs, one by one, made his calculations mathematically, then put his fore feet together, drew his hind feet under him, and *slid down* as neatly as any New York boy could slide down hill. As Harriet says, his intelligence and sure footedness are wonderful.

I have learned twenty more Arabic words, to-day. This makes fifty in all which I know. Besides these, I am nearly through memorizing the Lord's Prayer, in Arabic. This is my day's lesson—*kariff*, means afraid; *mogidd*, lively; *hawah*, air; *kadeem*, old; *jadeed*, new; *athkarl*, baggage; *shaheer*, barley; *zanbeel*, basket; *leeyah*, beard; *jaweel*, beautiful; *tire*, bird; *noor*, flower; *kinneenah*, bottle; *leejarm*, bridle; *jamel*, camel; *shamar*, candle; *farroj*, chicken; *walad*, child; *bard*, cold; *darfee*, warm.

I name this charming little dell, where we have stopped for luncheon, Honeysuckle Glen; it is so full of wild honeysuckles. On opening a box of sardines, which makes up a very important part of our traveling rations, I thought to confuse Mr. Fountain a little, by asking him where sardines were caught? But he knew it as well as if he had been a sardine catcher all his life. He made me write it down in my diary in this way—"sardines are young pilchards. The scientific name of a sardine is *Clupea pilchardus.* They are mostly caught off the French coast. Formerly they were chiefly caught off Sardinia, and so got their names from that island. The bait is the roe of codfish, and when they come up for it they are taken in nets woven very fine.

The heads are taken off. They are pressed closely in tin boxes. Boiling olive oil is poured over them. They are soldered up, and then they are ready for Holy Land explorers to eat." I told him that he was no sardine, any how, and he thanked me for the compliment.

I discovered this morning how to get rid of the Arab Beggars. One of them, a stout, strapping fellow, asked me for *backsheesh*, that is, money. I gave him a *parah*, ten for a cent. He looked at it scornfully, and again roared *backsheesh*. Then I said to him, *Allah delek;* which means, may God give it to you. Then he stopped; for, after you say that, they have no right to ask any more of you. He threw the money on the ground and went off, mad as you please. But pretty soon he came back and picked it up. I shall often try *Allah delek* upon them. If you give to all these beggars, it takes you all your time, and all your loose change, too. Besides that, you can never satisfy them any way.

I have just found the skull of some man who was probably murdered here. It was lying under a shelving rock, with other bones around it. It has a tremendous bruise on one side of it. The beautiful maiden's hair fern was growing all around it, and a scarlet anemone had worked its way through the lower jaw bone. I am going to dig a hole and bury it decently.

Mr. Fountain has read for us a passage from an old book, and let me copy it into my diary. "We went up from Joppa to the city of Jerusalem, A. D. 1102, a journey of two days, by a mountainous road. This was very rough and dangerous on account of the Saracens who lie in wait in the caves of the mountains to surprise Christians; to surprise those less capable of resisting by the smallness of the company, or the weary who may chance to lag behind their company. At one moment you see them on every side; at another, they are altogether invisible. Numbers of human bodies lie scattered by the way side, torn by wild beasts. There is not much earth to dig graves. A man leaving his company for that purpose would dig his own.

"Not only the poor and weak, but the rich and strong are surrounded with perils. Many are cut off by the Saracens, but more by heat and thirst. Many perish for want of drink, and more from over drinking." This is a dreadful story. Mr. Fountain says that the Knights Templar Society was instituted A. D. 1118, to protect pilgrims along this road. Who knows but what this skull belonged to one of these poor pilgrims? He says, too, that if the passion for pilgrimage, in the eleventh century, sent so many travelers here, the influence of American Sunday schools and Bible classes promises to send more, and much better ones.

I got me a staff, in Joppa, of almond tree—just like the one that Jacob crossed the Jordan with. (Gen. xxxii: 10.) I am going to carry it all through the Holy Land with me, and then, when I go home, give it to our minister, in New York.

At a little village I saw something that reminded me of 2 Samuel xii: 3. An Arab was raising a lamb "to eat of his own meat; to drink of his own cup, and lie in his bosom." Hassan says that it is a very common thing among the Arabs. He says when a lamb or kid is born, on the hill sides, the shepherd brings it home in the evening, in the folds of his shirt bosom, while the mother runs bleating by his side, wild with anxiety.

I asked a boy the names of the wild trees that I was passing. He pointed to one and called it baloot, and to another and called it baloor.

Right over yonder is where the Israelites demanded of Samuel, a king. What an unfortunate demand. Yet, they would have it, although Samuel told them exactly what sort of a tyrant their king would be. If Samuel had lived A. D. 1869, he could not have described kings and queens better than he did B. C. 1095. Of all the blessings that I was born to inherit, that of a free government is one of the greatest.

To-day, I kept an account of the number of persons to whom I gave *backsheesh.* I began early, at Lydda, with a blind man who made so much noise around the tent, that I sent him a piastre to silence him so I could sleep awhile longer. Within seventy minutes I gave money to eleven other persons, all blind, and up to this time I have helped thirty-four since I got up. More than one hundred have asked me. As a general rule, I only give a few paras to each one. Ten paras make a cent.

NEAR POOL OF GIBEON, 7 P. M.

When we first left the Plain this morning, to climb the stony pass of Beth-horon, my camel, Jenny, began to make loud cries and growls of anger and impatience. These paths are especially difficult for camels. The stones cut her feet, which are like four big sponges. At the village of Beit-ur she met another camel, and they had a fight in which they bit one another around the head till the blood streamed. I never heard such noises. The roarings were frightful. Jenny finally threw the other one down and then stamped and pounded him almost to death. They reared up and twisted round one another like four-legged boa constrictors. All day long my camel driver (camelier I call him) entertains Jenny with music, song, and fairy tales, and with the plaintive tones of his voice. She likes it; and when he stops, she looks around into his face. Her neck is so long that she can twist it like a snake's, and look backwards. When she travels, she keeps her head perfectly level. In chewing her cud she throws her lower jaw so far around the upper one, that it seems as if it would fly out of joint every time.

An American traveler describes his ride over these ridges in this way: "On, on you go; now stumbling over great rocks which have rolled down from the steep cliffs over your head; now winding round the base of some high, conical mountain, and now climbing up its rugged face; now by a zigzag path, toiling up to its airy summit, from which, with scarce time enough to cast one glance upon the wild scenery round, by a path as narrow and as rough, you slip and scramble down the other side to repeat the same process." That is pretty good and very true.

JOHN'S DIARY.

ENTRANCE OF THE HILLS, Thursday, March 18, 1869. 8 A. M.

We left Lydda at seven, first giving an hour to the old Church of St. George, which we inspected with very great interest. Harriet has made a drawing of it.* What noble arches. What a grip those Crusaders took upon the Holy

* See the engraving facing this Chapter.

Land during the eighty-eight years (1099 to 1187) that they held it. They stamped upon it their style of architecture and their indefatigable building energy, in a *stony alphabet*, that the land can never cast off. The only portion of the Church of St. George that has been preserved, is the *eastern part*. Mr. Fountain says this is the case with all ruined, Christian churches. Either the Christians, when conquered, bought over their altars from spoliation, or the conquerors voluntarily spared them through veneration and fear; or they are more solidly built than other parts. Whatever may be the cause, the eastern portions are often entire when the rest of the building has completely disappeared.

By joint consent, I marked the initials "H. C. T.," upon the corner of a stone, and dedicated this noble ruin to Rev. Henry Clay Trumbull, Missionary Secretary of the American Sunday School Union, for New England. Mr. Trumbull, is the author of the work "Children in the Temple," from which we read last Sunday several chapters. He has often visited father's house, and given us great delight in his elucidations of Scripture.

Elliot wonders where all the stone has gone to that was once used in the construction of this enormous church. But this is no problem to me. The destruction of old buildings and using their remains for building materials, have been going on in Asia for three thousand years. A stone once squared is useful, and the people turn every such scrap to account. A stone of a Persian palace, for instance, has been stuck into the enclosure of a Greek temple, then into a Roman fort, then into a Christian church, then to repair the walls of Gothic, Saracenic or Genoese builders, then used by the Turks in an aqueduct; finally, set up for a grave stone, a land terminus, or a cabin window sill. The worst fate of such a stone is to be burned into lime.

I translated, while coming from New York to Liverpool, what De Vogue says in his noble volume (*Les Eglises de la Terre Sainte*) concerning these ruins. He makes them resemble, most nearly, the ruined church at Samaria, and thinks this building was erected between 1150 and 1170, and was destroyed by order of Saladin, in 1191.

We passed over a turf, blazing with yellow daisies, crimson poppies, and hosts of floral glories. The wheat spread out around us in a sea, glistening with dew. Birds sang among the fig trees. The voice of the turtle dove murmured from the olives. A cool breeze came down from the hollows of the hills, eastward, and brought memories of Jerusalem, over which it had passed. We were on the border of Sharon, "that broad, rich tract of land that lies between the Mediterranean Sea, the northern continuation of Shefaleh." I shall always remember this Plain, for the variety, fragrance and beauty of its innumerable plants and flowers. Lovely, however, as all things around us are, I cannot note them so deliberately as I should like to do; for to-day, before we sleep, *we are to sight Jerusalem.*

"Jerusalem, my happy home,
Name ever dear to me."

So often have I sung these lines, the hymn-anthem of the good old Lowell Mason.

Just in the edge of Lydda, I became provoked beyond endurance, at the indecent gestures of two young fellows. They designed to insult Harriet as she passed by. As soon as she was out of sight, I got off my horse and flogged them handsomely with my whip.

We travel from two and a half to three miles an hour, and this I find is the usual speed in this country.

In talking with one of our Arabs, he told me that he had a sister named Lalla Rookh, (that means *tulip cheek*) others named Lelia Shrine, and Dewilde. These reminded me of names in the poem of Lalla Rookh.

The last palm tree that we shall see this side of Jerusalem, was near Lydda. Elliot went to the top of it like one of the Simia tribe. This tree suggested the verses—

"Those groups of lovely date trees, bending
Languidly their leaf-crowned heads."

But the expression, *date tree*, is only poetical, for the dates grow on *palm trees*. Mr. Fountain says that all the dates that are shaken from trees by the wind, belong to travelers and to the poor. This recalls the old Jewish law in Deut. xxiv 19 to 22, that where a sheaf of the harvest, and the gleanings of grapes and olives, have been left in the field, the owner must not go again to fetch them, but "it shall be for the stranger, the fatherless, and the widow." What a beautiful provision of divine charity.

The horses in this country do not *trot*, they only *walk* and *gallop*. They are fed at night with a little barley mixed with oat straw—that is all. Father's horses, on his New Jersey farm, are bloated gluttons compared with these poor skeletons. Their owners hardly ever let them drink. They are slow, plodding beasts, with considerable endurance, but no spirit.

In some old book, a writer has described the sheep here as being of an extra kind, with short legs, long back, large, upright horns, and all of one color. That was what I expected to see; but none of the sheep, thus far, answer to the picture, and the Arabs say the description is false.

Elliot has formed a warm attachment for his camel that he calls Jenny. I cannot, however, see much to admire in a camel. Its motion is fearfully rough; a man who can endure the camel's trot is booked for any other conveyance. Jenny has a most fretful disposition, and moans reproachfully whenever a person approaches her. The proverbial patience of the camel appears to me mere stupidity. It is obstinate and vicious, and I expect to see Elliot get shockingly bitten, yet, by the cross-grained creature that he rides so joyfully. As Elliot cannot learn to sing in the way Hassan does, he has turned the tables upon that obtuse Arab by trying, this morning, to teach him Verdi's Prison Song.

Horses, on first acquaintance, abhor the smell of the camel, and it is recorded that Cyrus gained his great battle over Crœsus by making use of this instinct; so writes old Herodotus, at least.

The donkey that was hired for Elliot is truly an original animal; a practical joker, full of tricks, but without malice.

Taking a last view of the Plain of Sharon, from the edge of the hills, I note that here Shitrai, the Sharonite, fed the flocks of King David. (1 Chronicles xxvii: 29.) Here, also, the royal herds of Solomon grazed, and so long as the monarchs of Judah or Israel held this rich plain, the meat supply of the royal household must have been largely drawn from this quarter.

Of all the hundreds of pilgrims that lined the road yesterday, from Joppa to Ramleh, almost every one has gone by the shorter way of Koloniah, and up the new turnpike to Jerusalem. One bare foot friar is behind us with his rope girdle and hempen gown, who seems disposed to try the old Crusader's road by way of Beth-horon and Mount Joy.

As we pass into the hills, I regret that we must leave the old city of Antipatris, some fifteen miles to the left, on the road to Cæsarea. That place, now called Kefr Saba, is where they brought Paul, by night, on his way from Jerusalem to Cæsarea. From here the four hundred infantry that served as a guard against the Jewish assassins, returned to Jerusalem, only the seventy horsemen going on to Cæsarea. Formerly it was thought that this night march was by way of Lydda, but the best writers now agree that the soldiers turned off at Gophna, near Bethel, fourteen miles north of Jerusalem.

And now I particularly notice the style of plowing practiced here. The native plow is the simplest and crudest of instruments. It has hard work to move this stiff, stony soil. In the United States more than a thousand patents have been issued for improvements in plows. Father used to say, "show me a farmer's plow and I can describe the man." It is so here; the absurd plow is the emblem of the miserable farmer. The beam and the handle (it has but one handle) are only two sticks crossed and fastened together at the crossing point. One stick goes to the yoke, one to the hand. As it takes but one hand to guide this plow, the plowman can hold his big, heavy goad, in the other. The point of the plow is sometimes shod with iron, but such a plow as this only makes a scratch, not a furrow.

The Romans plowed only with cattle, never with horses. Usually a single pair was used. A plowman, not skillful enough to cut a straight furrow, was termed by them *delirare;* under this head I should class most of the plowmen of Sharon.

HONEYSUCKLE GLEN, 11 A. M.

Near this place was Beth-car, where the Israelites "went out and pursued the Philistines and smote them." (1 Samuel vii : 11.) Here Samuel set up a stone which he named Ebenezer, or, "the stone of help," and to this the beautiful hymn alludes—

"Here I raise my Ebenezer."

Resting here for an hour our party sung the whole piece through to Rousseau's music, "Days of Absence." Then we selected a long, square stone that lay by the roadside, and chiseled on it, "Ebenezer, 1869." This stone we told our Arabs to lift up and set against the cliff. There were five of them. The stone didn't weigh five hundred pounds but they were unable to move it.

They began upon it with the demonstrative imbecility of judgment, clatter of tongues and swinging of limbs which always accompany their movements, but they had to acknowledge their inability at last. Then Mr. Fountain, Elliot and myself took it up and raised it with ease, at which they expressed unbounded astonishment. As father's name is Ebenezer we dedicated this memorial stone to him with many a loving and grateful tear.

Somewhere in this narrow pass Judas Maccabæus defeated and slew Nicanor, B. C. 161. Here, too, Cestius, who came up at the head of the Roman army to destroy Jerusalem, was disgracefully beaten by the Jews, A. D. 67. And here the Crusaders suffered a defeat on their way to Jerusalem. No doubt many another sore fight not recorded has occurred along this world's highway. Yonder ravine may often have been heaped high with the victims of war.

We are getting pretty well towards the tops of the mountains. The hill-tops around us seem all crowded with villages, many of which are in ruins. By the route we have come, the ancient Phœnicians brought the heavy cedars and other materials that they furnished towards the erection of that magnificent and incomparable work, the Temple of Solomon. But the route must then have been in a much better condition than now. Occasionally we see traces of the old Roman road that came up this pass, connecting Joppa with Jerusalem. What road-makers those wonderful people were. And all their roads began and terminated at Rome. The broken edges of the rocks continue to rise like terraces to the tops of the hills. By some strange geological arrangement, they appear as if formed by the art of man. Perhaps the Creator arranged them in this manner to suggest to the Hebrew farmers, for whom he had designed this "chosen land," the way to build terraces and vineyards and so to cultivate these hillsides most profitably. As every foot of these mountain slopes was afterwards prepared artificially for cultivation, it is reasonable to believe that the idea was borrowed from the Divine mind.

To the north, when I get a good view, the mountains appear gray, desolate and awful. We have passed the region of grain fields, and, in fact, for several miles the land shows but little cultivation of any sort.

At the village of Jimzu the road forks; we took the left hand. The map shows that they come together again ten miles further on. A fine well is near a place called *Um Roosh.* Three trees stand together there, a fig, a carob and an oak. We dedicated them to our three Presidents, Abraham Lincoln, Andrew Johnson and U. S. Grant.

From the roof of the sheikh's house, at Upper Beth-horon (called here *Beit-oor el-foka*) we had a fine view of the country passed over since yesterday morning. Joppa, Ramleh and Lydda were in plain sight. The road to the east continues to ascend among rocky and desolate hills.

IN SIGHT OF JERUSALEM, 3 P. M.

And yonder is the city to which more eyes and more steps are now directed than ever before. Where is the scholar in all the five thousand Sunday Schools of our country who does not long to stand where I am now standing and take this view of the Holy City. Hereafter I can say as in Rev. xxi: 2: "I, John, saw the Holy City." Near this place is *Mount Joy*, said by the old chroniclers to be a very fair and delicious place where Samuel, the prophet, lies in a fair tomb. It was called *Mount Joy* because it gives joy to religious hearts, as from here *men first get view of Jerusalem.* As I was standing silently gazing towards the city, a very old man came up and kissed Elliot on the cheek, weeping bitterly. He said in French that the lad reminded him of his own dear brother sixty years ago dead. He refused *backsheesh*, and therefore I think he was in earnest. I shall never think of Jerusalem again without calling that old and venerable man to remembrance. His solemn voice, flowing robes and long grey beard reminded me of the image I have of the prophet Samuel as he appeared to Saul the night before his death on Gilboa. (1 Samuel xxviii.) He presented Elliot with a little pearl cross made at Bethlehem of the large sea shell found in the Red Sea.

We noticed at *Mount Joy* great numbers of little mounds or piles of small round stones, made by putting together three, five, seven, nine and other odd numbers of stones into diminutive pyramids. This is done by certain classes of travelers upon first coming in sight of Jerusalem; it has a superstitious charm connected with it, I do not know what. Our missionaries in Ceylon observe the same thing there by the sides of the roads leading to principal places and they charge it upon the horrid superstition of devil-worship.

The long line of battlemented wall around Jerusalum reminds me that Arculf when here, A. D. 700, counted eighty-four towers and six gates to Jerusalem. The city must then have extended much farther in this direction than it does now.

Coming up from the lower to the Upper Beth-horon, called *Beit-ur el-foka* and *Beit-ur el-tahta* we had a broken ascent that recalled most forcibly the story of the dreadful day of Gibeon "like which was no day before it or after it." Down this same steep *wady*, the five kings and their routed hosts then plunged, stumbling, falling, throwing away their armor, praying only for the darkness of night. The spear of Joshua behind them, "great stones from heaven" before them, a sun that refused to sink beneath yonder sea until their destruction was accomplished. I let my imagination run upon these facts until my blood tingled within my veins. What an awful day! The distance from our present camping place at Gibeon to Upper Beth-horon is about four miles. I observed as I passed that place that this chalky limestone presents a great number of caves and fissures, many of which have been artificially enlarged for shelter and defense. Mr. Fountain says that the dead are buried in caves in this part of Palestine for want of a sufficient depth of earth for graves. They recalled in my Bible readings many passages such as these: "Enter into the rock." (Isaiah ii: 10.) "Go into the clefts of the rocks and into the tops of the ragged rocks." (Isaiah ii: 21.)

POOL OF GIBEON, 7 P. M.

Father wants a particular description of Gibeon. The natives call it *E-lJib*. They always turn the Hebrew G into J. It stands on the northernmost of two small round hills, where the road from Jerusalem to Joppa parts into two branches, one going by the lower level of wady Suleiman; the other being the one we followed. The distance from Jerusalem is five miles in a straight line, or six and a half by the main road.

Many great events in history have occurred near this pool. Such were the celebrated duel between twelve of David's men and twelve of Ishbosheth's, in which the whole twenty-four fell down dead, (2 Samuel ii); the murder of Amasa, by Joab, at this place, (2 Samuel xx,) and Joab's own death punishment near this place. (1 Kings ii: 28.) Long after that (about B. C. 685) this place was connected with Ishmael's traitorous murder. (Jeremiah xli: 12.)

At my request Mr. Fountain has named our resting place to-night, *Camp Judas Maccabæus*, for here we may

> " Sing his heroic deeds and hapless fall
> By doom of battle."

There is no hero of romance I admire so much as this Judas whose very name, a *Hammer* exemplifies the man. In this vicinity his greatest exploits were done. His father died B. C. 166 and was buried at Modin, near Latron, where we shall pitch our tent to-morrow night. He named Judas, although only his third son, to be his successor. This indomitable warrior defeated Appollonius and Seron at Beth-horon, four miles west of this, and then Lysias at Emmans, (now called Ammas), ten miles south of Lydda. B. C. 161 he defeated and slew the great Nicanor at Beth-horon, and was himself shortly afterwards slain at Adassa, thirty stadia from this place. It was here he said to his troops, " It is better for us to die in battle than to behold the calamities of our people and our sanctuary." (1 Maccabees iii: 59.)

HARRIET'S DIARY.

ENTRANCE OF THE HILLS, Thursday, March 18, 1869. 8 A. M.

We took quite a survey of the ancient ruined church at Lydda before we started. These ruined buildings, however, are sad places for ladies' dresses and shoes.

We struck our tents and rode out of Lydda this morning in good season. Passed through a Mohammedan graveyard. Very many little mounds were there, deep enough to cast a shadow in which mourning mothers will walk all the days of their pilgrimage below. What dreary, comfortless places are these Mohammedan graveyards. No wonder all the allusions to them in the native language are gloomy. I can myself almost imagine, arising from them

> " A voice deep and dread
> As that of Monker waking up the dead
> From their first sleep ; "

According to the Mohammedan legend.

I noticed last evening, with admiration, the ingenuity of our native cook, who gets up wonderful soups, fries, fricassees, roasts, breads and puddings with a scarcity of kitchen furniture that would drive one of our New York biddies distracted. He requires no stove, no range; no fire-place. He has nothing but a long, shallow box about a feet wide and four feet long, made of sheet iron and supported by six legs that fold up under it when packed with the baggage. It has a perforated grate at the bottom. His fuel is charcoal, which we purchase at the villages from day to day as needed. Mr. Fountain says there is scarcely wood enough growing between Joppa and Jerusalem to heat his coffee pot. In this really primitive arrangement all our culinary work is done rapidly and with excellent results. Through the day our cook rides calmly along picking his fowls and preparing his viands with perfect *sang froid*.

I cannot name the tithe of the wild flowers that met my eye as I came delightedly along. The myrtle was there. The broom, lavender, hyssop, sage, wild thyme and rue are abundant. Lieut. W. F. Lynch, when here in May, 1848, described the violet-purple of the plumbago, but I do not recognize that. Perhaps it is too early in the season. He also described the hop-trefoil, a small clover with yellow flowers and hop-like heads.

The winding valley rolled in waves of wheat and barley, while the hillsides were mantled with groves of olives. It was a vast mosaic of green and brown, *jasper* and *verd-antique*. In the crystal of the morning air the very hills laughed with plenty. The whole landscape gleamed with signs of gladness upon its countenance. How beautiful must have been this plain of Sharon in the days when God was worshiped here by his own people. As near Joppa, we have passed through delightful gardens of figs, citrons, olives, pomegranates and palms.

As we approached the hills, the soil became light brown from the decomposition of the limestone. The sea shells, which we have found scattered through the soil all the way from the sea, now disappeared. We were approaching the mountains of the tribe of Dan.

Passing a low cabin in the outskirts of the village, I noticed a woman baking her daily supply of bread. In this country the prayer of our Lord is literally applicable, "Give us *each day* our daily bread;" for they *do* make their bread *every day*. The poor woman had collected a pile of thorn bushes, which burned with a fierce crackling sound and made, for a few moments, a great heat. A round stone was then laid in the flames and soon become hot. Her dough, already prepared in thin flat cakes, was then wrapped around the stone and soon the bread was baked. When removed from the stone another cake was laid upon it, and then another to the number of three or four before the stone cooled. The bread, scarcely thicker than paper, was made of dark-colored, gritty meal; smutted with soot, it resembled a blacksmith's apron.

I had seen bread making done by the Arabs the day before, at Joppa. The flour was of mixed wheat and barley, very chaffy. Made into dough, the round flat cakes were thrown into the ashes. This coarse unleavened bread, with *leban* or curdled milk, is the usual fare of the Arabs, improved sometimes by a handful of figs, olives or raisins. One writer describes an Arab party that traveled five hours a day on a pound and a half of such dry, black bread and water. We entered the hills about an hour's ride east of Lydda, wandering slowly through the flowery valleys. At the entrance of the hills I was delighted with the sight of a wild gazelle, engaged literally as the Song of Songs describes it, leaping upon the mountains, skipping upon the hills." (Cant. ii: 8.) At the distance of a half mile, the fleet little creature seemed to have no legs, it sprung so high into the air, but went like a bird out of my sight.

My favorite Dorcas, whom I mentioned in my diary two days ago, had for her Hebrew name *Tabitha*, which means *gazelle*. Perhaps in her maiden days she was noted for swiftness of foot and native gracefulness, like yonder pretty creature. Asahel, the brother of Joab, who was killed near the place where we shall pitch our tents to-night, is described "as light of foot as a young roe." (2 Samuel ii: 18.) And of the eleven Gadites who attached themselves to David when he was wandering among the hills, thirty miles south-east of us, it is said "they were as gazelles (roes) on the mountains." (1 Chronicles xii: 8.) Travelers describe the gazelle as very common here at the present day, and I hope to see them often. Perhaps I may secure a little one to take home with us, for I long to see the brilliancy in its eyes, of which I have read so much. The gentle nature of the gazelle is as proverbial as its grace and swiftness, and is well expressed in the large, soft liquid eye which has formed from time immemorial the stock comparison of Oriental poets when describing the eyes of beauty. Nor must I forget to insert in my diary here, one of the finest verses of English poetry:

"The wild gazelle on Judah's hills,
  Exulting yet may bound,
And drink from all the living rills
  That gush on holy ground;
Its airy step and glorious eye
May glance in tameless transport by."

How many objects we are hourly observing that illustrate Biblical passages. How marvelously the facts and the texts fit each other already. But then to visit the Holy Land without a good stock of Bible knowledge, is to go to sea without chart or needle, and we can never sufficiently thank our dear parents who encouraged us to commit to memory so many hundreds of scriptural texts. Already we begin to appreciate that the Biblical history is real, accurate, thoroughly veritable. No reflecting person can pass through the lands of the Bible and believe it to be a fiction. The history involves the localities; the localities illustrate the history. Finding the one to be real we irresistibly admit the truth of the other.

Helena, the mother of Constantine, came a pilgrim to this country, A.D. 326. when she was eighty years of age, more than four times my age. Probably the queenly form of that aged mother of the Roman Emperor, often passed this very road from Jerusalem to Joppa. What a woman she was. At four score years her spirits were as youthful as a girl's. After staying here a year she returned to Constantinople died, A. D. 328, and is buried at Venice. But her influence upon the mind of her son, covered this country with churches.

HONEYSUCKLE GLEN, 11 A. M.

We have now entered the hills of Dan, by the same narrow pass down which the discomfitted Canaanites scurried after the the battle of Gibeon. I want to note the incidents of that remarkable fight when I get further up the pass. These hills are stony indeed, and begin to present specimen of ilex, myrtle and dwarf oak trees. The wild purple rose appears on all sides. Some might suppose it to be the *rose of Sharon* spoken of in *Solomon's Song*, but it is not elegant enough for that. Mr. Fountain thinks that Solomon referred in that allusion to the *pink Oleander* which he says is splendid along the brooks. A fragrant, white honeysuckle, alive with honey bees, hangs over the rocks. The path here is very rough, and two persons can hardly go abreast.

We have stopped for an hour at this little dell in the hills, which rises around us an endless succession of immense regular cones, embossing the whole country, terraced to the top by natural stratification. A small, ruined mosk is close by, its broken cistern plainly to be traced. The distant whine of the jackal may still be heard, even at this hour of the day.

Passing a village, I stopped to see a woman employed in the primitive style of butter making. Our New Jersey dairymaid would have hooted at it. Yet I should be sorry to see the old methods changed in this Bible country. The milk was put into a goatskin bag, the hairy part inwards. This bag was then hung by a string to a tripod of sticks, and shaken severely backwards and forwards by a woman seated on each side. Sometimes they would strike it sharply with their fists. It takes about two hours of this churning to make the butter. It is pleasant to think that Sarah and Rebecca and Rachel used to churn in this way. Rather too much of the hair remains in it for American tastes. To preserve this butter, as they put no salt in it, they melt and simmer it for several hours, skim out the hair and other impurities and lay it down in jars. It then has the color and consistency of lard. Like the French, these people put no salt in their butter, which makes it insipid to us. Mr. Fountain has purchased a jar of butter and a jar of honey to send home.

In the little graveyard of this poor village, I noticed several women flitting around, ghost-like, enveloped in white sheets.

I went a little ways off the road to see the remains of a great reservoir in which the copious winter rains of these hills were once collected for summer use. The amount of rain that falls annually in Palestine is very great. Dr. Barclay kept a rain guage at Jerusalem for seven years and found the average for that period sixty-one and one-half inches. The greatest quantity of rain-fall in a single year was eighty-five inches. In the single month of December, 1850, there fell nearly thirty-four inches of rain. Compared with London, England, where the whole annual rain-fall is only twenty-five inches, or Devonshire, England, where it is only sixty inches, this is a wet country. But this rain all falls from October to April, scarcely a drop from March to November. As I suppose this was always so, the ruined reservoirs that abound through these hills were once of the greatest importance. They are very large, though I have not heard of one so large as that at Calcutta, that covers seven square miles and is sixty feet deep. I suppose the people occupying the sides of two adjacent hills used to unite in closing the lower part of a ravine, cleaning out and deepening its bed, cementing its sides, and then sharing the water for irrigation and domestic and religious use in the rainless seasons. And around the margin of this now dry pool, once grew water lilies and oleanders. Here the flocks and herds gathered to the watering. Here the sounds of heavy armed men were heard calling to each other. Perhaps the water was heaped up with the bodies of men slain in battle and stained with their blood. Maidens here filled their jars morning and evening for household use and chatted gaily of home things and interchanged the village news. But now,

> "The maidens come no more
> Till the sweet heavens have filled it from the heights,
> Again with living waters in the change
> Of seasons."

And here, too, or hard by, were performed the grandest exploits of the renowned warrior, Judas Machabæus, who, in his brief career, so often discomfited the enemies of Israel. It was here he said to his exhausted followers: "They come against us in much pride and iniquity to destroy us and our wives and children and to despoil us; but we fight for our lives and our lands. (1 Maccabees iii: 20.)

These naked rocks, these mountains and precipices, were those at which the ancient pilgrims used to be discouraged. Coming from the flowery Plain of Sharon they were grieved to find so inhospitable a region where formerly such pleasantness and plenty abounded.

Some of the descriptions of these hills, copied long ago in my *Index Rerum*, are wonderfully vivid, now, that I can verify them on the spot. "Rounded, swelling masses like huge bubbles." "Each one uglier than its neighbor." "A wilderness of mountain tops, in some places tossed up like waves of mud, in others, wrinkled over with ravines, like models made of crumpled, brown paper, the nearer ones whitish, strewed with rocks and bushes." "Chaotic jumble of stony hills separated by deep chasms."

UPPER PASS OF BETH-HORON, 4 P. M.

There are two Beth-horons, as the Bible says, the Upper and the Lower. The Lower is a small village on top of a low ridge separated by a narrow valley from the upper one. It is about twelve miles northwest of Jerusalem, and directly in the corner of the tribe of Benjamin. Here Judas Maccabæus defeated Nicanor. (1 Mac. vii : 39.)

The great road for transportation of materials, and travel between Joppa and Jerusalem, used to come this way.

The Upper Beth-horon is also a small village, a little larger than the other. Here I witnessed a sad thing. A man of this place was conscripted last week into the Turkish army, a most cruel act, and his mother, a widow, is as one distracted. She declared, with fearful shrieks, that he was the staff of her age, and she should never see him again. Mr. Fountain thinks she never will.

David described her condition in Ps. xxxviii, "she is bowed down greatly, and goes mourning all day long." Poor woman, may the God of the widow give her consolation. She begged us to intercede for her, with the Pasha, at Jerusalem; but of course we could have no influence there. We gave her some money and left her, while her screams were ringing in our ears.

The great Battle of Gibeon, may all be traced from this Upper Beth-horon.

MIZPEH, 5 P. M.

By a very bad road we have come from the battle-ground of Beth-horon, to the top of this commanding point, styled by the natives the Tomb of Samuel, (Neby Samuel) six hundred feet above the general level of the surrounding country. This is the great land-mark of this portion of Palestine.

The old Crusader's Church, now desecrated as a Mohammedan mosk, stands so as to afford a noble view from its minaret. It was here that the story of King Richard originated. He came as far in the direction of Jerusalem as this, leaving his soldiers encamped at Ajalon; but, when the ramparts of the Holy City were pointed out to him, he covered his face and refused to look, saying: "Ah, my God, unless I may capture that city, let me not see it." Poor man, he never did capture it; but, after a most unfortunate campaign, was glad to get back to Europe—a fugitive.

IN SIGHT OF JERUSALEM.

Oh, sacred hour! Oh, moment, never to be forgotten! Oh, blessed memorial day, this 18th of March. We all stood silent, wistfully gazing on the wondrous scene where the Redeemer died. If we interchanged our feelings at all, it was by single words. Aunt Liddy, who rarely speaks, uttered the expression, "Heavenly." Our eyes overflowed. One rushing wave of thought swept over our souls. The associations of the place were absolutely overpowering.

"Of earth's dark circlet, 'tis the precious gem
Of living light,—oh, fallen Jerusalem."

How many gems of reading that glorious sight recalls. This, from Milton, is among the most sparkling:

"The Holy City lifted high her towers;
And higher yet the glorious temple reared.
The pile, far off, appearing like a mount
Of alabaster, topped with golden spires."

Blest land of Judea, thrice hallowed of song,
Where the holiest of memories pilgrim-like throng;
In the shade of thy palm, by the shores of thy sea,
On the hills of thy beauty my heart is with thee.

With the eye of a spirit, I look on that shore,
Where pilgrim and prophet have lingered before;
With the glide of a spirit, I traverse the sod
Made bright by the steps of the angels of God.

I tread where the Twelve, in their wayfaring, trod;
I stand where they stood with the chosen of God;
Where His blessings were heard and His lessons were taught,
Where the blind was restored and the healing was wrought.

Oh, the outward hath gone: but in glory and power,
The spirit surviveth the things of an hour;
Unchanged, undecaying, its Pentecost flame
On the heart's secret altar is burning the same.

POOL AT GIBEON. 7 P. M.

Before leaving home, father told me that he was once a member of a society called the "Strong Band," and wished me, when I came to Gibeon, particularly to describe the place. It is called by the Arabs *El-jib*, by turning the Hebrew G into J, as they usually do. The town stands on top of a hill, difficult of access. It is surrounded by orchards of pears, olives, figs, apricots and apples. Vineyards abound, for here is one of the most fertile valleys in Palestine. Being nearly two thousand five hundred feet above the plain at Joppa, oranges, lemons and citrons are not found.

El-jib is but a little town, lying upon a succession of ledges. It is about five miles north west of Jerusalem. In the time of Joshua it was a royal city—no doubt both large and strong. The houses are mostly in ruins, but look as though once they were handsome edifices; the tower or castle is still standing. We are sitting by the Pool, a little ways east of the village, into which runs the water from a fine spring, west of us. All around this pool is a dense grove of olives. The Pool is one hundred by one hundred and twenty feet and is no doubt the scene of that singular duel between the men of Joab and Abner, described in 2 Samuel 2nd chapter.

At Gibeon, Solomon had that vision which left him the wisest of men. The tabernacle was here for many years, under David and Solomon, though the ark itself, was at Jerusalem.

MR. FOUNTAIN'S DIARY.

NEAR POOL AT GIBEON, Thursday, March 18, 1869. 9 P. M.

Fairly launched forth into the open country, we began our fourth day on Holy earth, by reading from Joshua 7th to 10th chapters, and the 3rd of 1 Kings, and singing the beautiful hymn—

"I'm a pilgrim, and I'm a stranger,"

to the weird, Italian air that is so popular; this was followed by prayer. An early breakfast was eaten; a profitable hour spent among the ruins of the Church of St. George, and then we struck out eastward for Gibeon.

I did not discover, until too late, that John had turned back to chastise some unruly boys who had insulted Harriet. I found it necessary to rebuke him for his rashness, and advised him to reserve such exhibitions of heroism for occasions, if any, in which his prowess will really be needed.

We have made a number of pleasant pauses, to-day, in our journey, during all which the eager eyes and swift-gliding pencils of the youthful troupe have been busy. Every hour their observations seem to me more thoughtful. The amount of Biblical and historical matter with which the pious care of their parents has charged their memories, becomes available, now, at every turning of the way. Something to the general profit may yet grow out of this little company of "Youthful Explorers." The book they most use for reference, is the Bible. As little Elliot says, "it was made on purpose for this country."

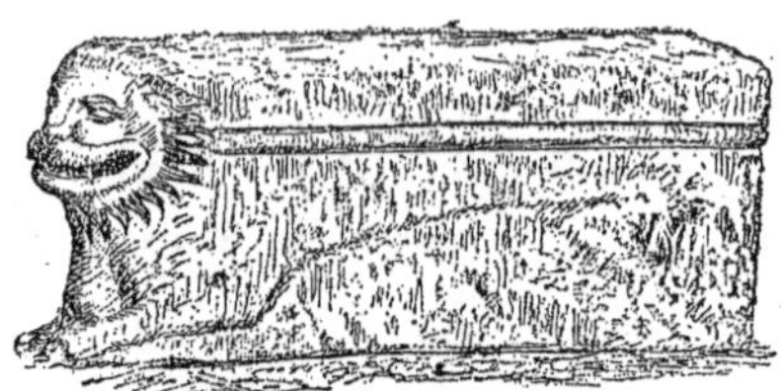

A LION'S HEAD ; A CARVING IN STONE OF THE CRUSADERS' ERA, 1099—1187.
This block is in possession of "The Scholars Holy Land Exploration."

"The Lion of the Tribe of Judah hath prevailed." Revelations v : 5.

THE POMEGRANATE.

CHAPTER V.

DOWN THE TURNPIKE, WESTWARD.

Arabic words—A talisman—The Priests and the Pope—Lost in the hills—Jackal—David's exploit—Khaus—Mosquito—Glory of the stars—Singular uses of numbers 1300 and 17—Fox—Frogs—Cucumbers—Dew—Dogs—Fig trees—Sure-footed horses—The Sheikh—Pilgrims—The Machabees—Turnpike—Joppa to Jerusalem—A Mohammedan at prayer—Bevelled stones—Temperance of the Mohammedan—Tobacco—Arabs eating—Kirjath-jearim and its history—Stone lion—The Good Thief, Dismas—Ancient tombs—Bats—Oleanders.

ELLIOT'S DIARY.

CAMP DISMAS, 6 P. M., Friday, March 19, 1869.

I HAVE not made so many notes, to-day, as usual, for I have given my time chiefly to collecting specimens of rocks, flowers, and land-shells, as we came along, and I have noticed that unless I write a thing down *the very minute it happens*, I either forget it or forget everything about it that makes it worth remembering—and then it is like drinking soda water after the effervescence goes off.

I have learned twenty more words in Arabic, to-day—*Tabbash*, means cook; *katarny*, corn; *cotn*, cotton; *fingarn*, cup; *zalarm*, darkness; *noor*, light; *nahar*, day; *lile*, night; *gadah*, dinner; *tabeeb*, doctor; *casa*, dress; *eine*, eye, or a fountain; *wajh*, face; *ab*, father; *reash*, feather; *samah*, fish; *taheen*, flour; *koot*, victuals; *jabin*, forehead; *farkeehah*, fruit; *hawargee*, gentlemen; *thabab*, gold.

When Hassan went to sleep, this morning, in the valley of Elah, I opened the little bag that hangs round his neck. It had nothing but the bones of a child's finger in it. I buried the bones and sewed up some sticks in their place, which I think will do Hassan just as much good. What a superstitious gump he is. He is the greatest coward I ever saw. I read to him the account of Judas Machabæus telling his soldiers, before the battle at Emmaus, that "every man might go home who was building a house, or had betrothed a wife, or was planting a vineyard, or was afraid of the enemy." (1 Maccabees iii : 56.) Hassan says he should have left, anyhow. I think he would.

As superstitious as Hassan is, he is not more so than most of these Catholics. In Paris they told us that the Princess Clotilde wears a belt of consecrated amulets round her waist, just as ridiculous as Hassan's dead bones.

A great many of these pilgrims are Catholics who seem to believe in the Pope more than they do in God. No matter how wicked the Pope is—and some of them have been perfect scalawags—he is the foundation-stone of their Church and the keeper of the keys of the kingdom of their heaven. He is to them the pastor of the fold of Jesus Christ. I do not believe in it. "A priest

6

in this country has neither family, name, nor legal inheritance; rights of kin, nor obligations of friendship, property nor reversion, succession nor antecedents; claims of humanity, nor benefits of legislation. To all intents and purposes of life he has passed away. His own will is surrendered. His parents are strangers to him, his brothers and sisters are aliens; his dearest friends, foes; the highest cultivations of society are but temptations. He is simply the slave of his spiritual father." So says a newspaper paragraph that I clipped out one day, and so far as I can see of the Catholic priests here, it is all true.

LOST IN THE HILLS, 10 P. M.

I have lit my wax candle—a large cord saturated with wax, that I always carry in my wallet—and have sat down to write out my day's adventures. I am *lost in the hills*, and it is a jolly thing. The night is warm. I have got my gun loaded with buck-shot. I am not a bit afraid. The katy-dids are singing merrily. I have my diary covered with oil-cloth in one pocket made on purpose for it; and my pocket Bible, bound in the same way, in another. My dog Sweet Home, has followed me. I am all right, only a little hungry, and sad to think how scared Harriet and Aunt Liddy will be about me. But I am sure of getting back to the party in the morning; so here goes to spending a whole night writing in my diary.

We left camp at Gibeon, early this morning. We came round southward, and struck the new turnpike near the Valley of Elah. I saw a jackal start near the spot where I was standing. He ran full speed half way up the hill, then stopped, looked sheepishly back to see if I was watching him, then scooted away out of sight among the rocks. I got some buck-shot after him, but failed to hit him. The jackal is as large as a middle-sized dog; color, yellow. He has the head of a wolf, the body of a dog, the tail of a fox, and the worst qualities of all three.

These Arabs cannot understand a joke. I asked one of them, to-day, where he was going? He said to El-Koods. That means Jerusalem. Then I told him that my camel always carried her *cud* with her. But he could not work it out. Such men as Artemus Ward and Josh Billings could not make a living lecturing here. I wonder if Solomon and the prophets ever joked? Some of Sampson's operations always seemed to me practical jokes, but probably the Philistines did not see it in that light.

I rode across the Valley of Elah near the place where it is said David picked up five smooth stones out of the brook, and with one of them smote the giant Goliath, in the forehead. (1 Sam. xvii.) When I was a boy I used to wonder what he did with the other four.

I visited a funny sort of tavern, as I came along, called a *khan*, which had been set up by the side of the road near the place of David's exploit. I call it *khan-carob*, because it is built under a carob tree. The sycamore is the tallest tree around here, but the carob is more plenty. The khanjee, or tavern keeper, only had to lay a few poles across from the tree to a large rock. Over them he threw some mats for shade, and so his hotel was complete. A cave under the rocks answered for his cupboard. A few dirty cushions stuffed with fleas, were sufficient to sit on. And there he sold boiled eggs, (hard as his own head,) arrack, and gritty bread, while he kept one hand at work scratching himself. A thievish looking chap. When the Knights Templar used to police these roads, seven hundred years ago, a man could leave his baggage anywhere out by the roadside, and come back again next day and find it, for nobody would touch it. But I should hate to trust that khanjee with my baggage. A *khan*, means a house built for charity. One that I stopped in yesterday, was thirty by forty yards square, as I stepped it, two feet to a step. Everybody who visits a regular khan is welcome, gratis, only he is expected to pay a small fee of a piastre or two to the khanjee. I have read a book called "The Tent and the Khan," by Mr. Stewart. The great Khan Builder of the Eastern world was the Emperor Saladin, who took possession of this country A. D. 1187. He is one of my nine heroes.

The way I got lost was this: We had stopped for the night near Latroon. While the servants were pitching the tents, I saw a large hawk chasing partridges over the side of the hill, south of the road, and started on foot in hopes to shoot him. A mile or so from the party I had a row with some Arabs. As I did not know what they wanted, and they did not know what I wanted, I just went along up the valley following my big hawk who kept ahead of me, as the bird kept ahead of the Arab hero in the story. But after all I missed the bird. Then, thinking I could strike a bee-line, and go back, I got lost in the hills. A crowd of ragamuffins followed me for an hour; but they jawed Arabic so fast tha t I could not understand them. I can talk a little of this dog's language; but when it comes to twisting a dozen words together, swallowing them, and then talking them up again from clear down your stomach, I am out. Their speaking sounds to me more like the barking of dogs than human speech. As I sit here, there is a village of Arabs just across the valley, and the gabble of the people is so like the yelping of the dogs, that I can hardly tell them apart. I am glad I am not among them at any rate, for I know that the fleas in their houses are horribly thick, to-night, and poor Sweet Home and I are doing better here.

Just now a mosquito came humming over me. He has exactly the same hum as our New York mosquitoes, and I am going to let him bite me, if only for home's sake.

I wonder what father and mother would think if they knew I was out here all alone, on this hill side, at midnight. But I forget; it is only four o'clock in the afternoon where they live, while it is nearly midnight here.

A glorious meteor has passed over me, and I turned to Rev. viii : 10 ; where there fell a great star from heaven, burning like a torch. I didn't think when I first memorized that chapter at Sunday School that I should ever read it under such circumstances as these. The Mohammedans believe that shooting stars are firebrands flung by the good angels from the gates of heaven, to keep devils off from that holy place.

Now I hear the cry of a pack of jackals; busy around some graveyard I suppose. Though people lay flat stones in the graves, the jackals are too much for them and dig them open. These sounds recall the lines I learned once:

"The jackal's cry, the distant moan
Of the hyena, fierce and lone."

I am glad the lions and bears that David encountered three thousand years ago, have been exterminated. (1 Samuel xvii: 37.)

1 A. M.

It is one o'clock in the morning. How bright and glorious the stars! I see the Pleiades in the constellation *Taurus*, so plain that I can count twenty-five stars in the group. I never saw Alcyone look half so brilliant. It really shines like a star of the first magnitude, rather than the second. No wonder it is called the *Light of the Pleiades*. How elegantly Job says, "Canst thou bind the sweet influences of the Pleiades" (Job xxxviii: 31.) And yonder, close at its side, is the brilliant star *Aldebaran* in the face of Taurus. Regular *Arab* names these stars have. Most all the stars have Arab names. But oh how magnificently Orion sparkles, to-night, a little higher up! No wonder the Leipsic College, in 1807, named those finest of gems in the sky, after my hero Napoleon. For there was nothing among the stars worthier. Only four hours ride northwest of here, was where that great man captured Joppa.

I remember here the passage "Seek him that maketh the seven stars and Orion." (Job ix: 9.) Leo, with his sickle has nearly gone down over the Mediterranean Sea. Far in the north the glorious old *Dipper* hangs just as it does in New York. How often I have looked at him there, away up the island towards Harlem!

3 A. M.

I am counting some figures in my diary. How curious it is that the number 1300 should be needed so much among the Palestine hills. It takes one 1300 feet to measure the depth of the Dead Sea. It is one 1300 feet from the surface of the Dead Sea to the surface of the Mediterranean Sea. It is *two* 1300 feet from the surface of the Mediterranean to the city of Jerusalem. It is *three* 1300 feet from the city of Jerusalem down to the surface of the Dead Sea. And it is *four* 1300 feet from Jerusalem to the bottom of the Dead Sea. It is the same way with the number 17. From Jerusalem to the Dead Sea is *one* 17 miles; from Jerusalem to Joppa is *two* 17 miles; from Jerusalem to Nazareth is *four* 17; from Nazareth to the Mediterranean Sea is *one* 17. How easy this makes it to remember these distances, and so save the trouble of looking so much at the map!

Here comes a fox stealing by me so near that I almost hit him with a stone. What a cunning, voracious, mischievous fellow the fox is! It was not more than twenty miles southwest of here that Samson caught three hundred of the rascals and took firebrands, and turned them tail-to-tail and let them go into the standing corn of the Philistines. (Judges xv.)

And now I hear distinctly from the pool between me and the village yonder, the croak of frogs, so natural that I cannot help thinking of fishhooks, pickerel and froggy's hind legs. So I have heard to-night mosquito, fox, jackal and frog.

I measured, to-day, a cucumber that an Arab was eating raw without salt or vinegar. It was twelve inches long, much greener than our cucumbers, smoother, softer and sweeter. It is more digestible, too, I should hope, or that man has had the colic awfully to-night who was eating it. The cucumber is mentioned in Numbers xi: 5.

My coat is nearly wet through with dew and I am quite chilly. Like the person in Canticles v: 2, "my head is filled with the dew and my locks with the drops of the night." I must see that the locks of my gun don't get wet, at any rate. Let me look up some of the passages where the dews of this country are mentioned. "Your goodness is as the early dew" (Hosea vi: 4); "will be as the dew unto Israel" (Hosea xiv: 5); "His body (Nebuchadnezzar's) was wet with the dews of heaven" (Daniel iv: 33); "Thou hast the dew of thy youth". (Ps. cx: 3.) How convenient my little concordance is! Here are twenty-five more allusions in the Bible to the word *dews.*

And now the dogs over yonder are barking fit to kill themselves. Mr. Fountain told me at Joppa that a child lately was torn down and killed in the streets there by the dogs. In some places the dogs even join the jackals in grubbing among the graves. Everybody hates them, Arabs as well as Jews. But there is no danger of their coming out of the village to attack me. I shall always respect the dog since the good Dr. J. T. Barclay told us how he found the entrance to the great cavern under Jerusalem by the aid of his dog. It was a dog, too, that discovered the precious and beautiful purple-dye with which the robes of King Solomon were empurpled. Come here, then, my poor *Sweet-Home* and take my last biscuit in payment for the company and comfort you have been to me to-night.

Poor Aunt Liddy, how badly she must feel now! She has all the time been warning me that I would get lost. They may name their camp to-night *Bochim.* That means *Weepings*, as the camp near Jericho was named. (Judges ii.) But I can't bear to think of that.

Let me figure up a little more. "A *cubit* is two feet; a *great cubit*, eleven feet; a *span* ten inches and seven-eighths; a palm three inches." This is what Mr. Fountain told me to memorize.

That big fig tree close by reminds me that I saw lately in the catalogue of the "London Horticultural Society," forty-two varieties of figs raised in the hot houses in England.

How sure-footed these Syrian horses are! One that I rode to-day took me up a hill so nearly perpendicular that my dog actually couldn't follow him; but had to run around the point of the ridge and overtake me at the top.

And now I will read the thirteenth chapter of 1st Corinthians, the only page of Christian literature, as my pastor once told me, that can be compared with the discourses of Jesus. Oh that I had such a gentle spirit as his!

4 A. M.

Although I didn't know that I had *gone to sleep*, yet in fact I have just woke up. It is as cold as winter. The Sheikh of the village close by, was standing by me when I woke, and his voice it was that woke me. I knew he was a Sheikh by his *arba* or cloak. He was girded around with a lot of old pistols, about as dangerous as the pop guns they sell on Broadway. He seemed disposed to be friendly but he was monstrous homely. A very tall man with a square face and cheek bones, like the portrait of Gen. Ely S. Parker. A hooked nose. Eyes deep set and piercing, like the portrait of Daniel Webster. Thick grizzly black beard. If Prof. Rawson had been here he would have sketched him in no time as a regular Arab land-pirate. The Sheikh pointed to the village and said *tefuddle*. That means welcome. I shook my head with the Arabic negative, *Lar*, *Lar*. That is No, No. Then he took me by the sleeve and made signs to me to go and eat with him. But he never offered to shake hands. People in this country never do. Still I refused to go with him; but gave him a lump of sugar and a piastre for *backsheesh*. Then he left me and I am glad he is gone. He *looks* ugly though he may be a good man.

When he first awoke me he said *Ya sidy*. That is *My lord*. Then he said *Jenaback* and *Saadatah*, that is *Your Excellency* and *Your Highness*. But big as these names sound, they are no more than one Arab beggar in the street will use to another.

It is getting day now. Around me is a sort of rocky wilderness with towering cliffs on each side, up which people can go by zigzag paths full of rolling stones. A palm tree yonder by the village is waving its starlike plumes. Close by I recognize the olive, hawthorn, ilex, dwarf oak, myrtle, laurel and laurestina, as Harriet has been showing them to me for several days. The broom plant or *planta genista* is everywhere gay.

The Sheikh has told his people about me for I see them coming this way, and it is time I was off to hunt up my party.

JOHN'S DIARY.

THREE MILES WEST OF JERUSALEM, 8 A. M.

The road from the Pool of Gibeon to this place was, unexpectedly, bad. The country, too, has changed, suddenly, into an arid, solitary and desert range of hills; strangely contrasted with the charming place of our encampment last night.

A host of pilgrims is filling the road that connects Joppa with Jerusalem, as we come into it here. One young Frenchman, dressed from head to foot in ruby colored velvet, with brilliant feathers in a Tyrolese hat, attracts every eye. The most of these pilgrims, however, are ragged and look forlorn, hungry and footsore, as they well may be. I imagine Paul went always in this way on foot, living, probably, as they do, on bread, vegetables and milk,—a *wandering pedestrian*. And yet he was not like them in anything else. I like what Renan says of his style: "It was so original, so peculiarly his own, that any addition would stand out upon the ground of the text by its very lack of color." I have just read the opening of Paul's letter to the Ephesians while waiting for this motley and noisy crowd to pass and it was this that suggested the comparison.

One of the pilgrims, a Greek, after giving me his designation, asked who we were? I told him *Chlamydates* and he went off puzzled. If he had known a very little more he would have got the definition from *Chlamys*, a traveler's cloak and understood that I simply meant *travelers*.

There is nothing to me more affecting in the associations of these hills, while the birds fill the morning air with their sweet sounds, than that among them dwelt the noble family of the Maccabees. It was here that the heroic Judas

"Fought for the land his soul adored,
For happy homes and altars free,
His only talisman *the sword*,
His only spell-word *liberty*.
Never was horde of tyrants met
With bloodier welcome; never yet
To patriot vengeance, has the sword
More terrible libations poured."

From a boy I have read that history as I read Robinson Crusoe, and Ruth and the life of Washington. Over my bed-head, at home, are the portraits of Washington, Abd-el-Kader, Garibaldi and Judas Maccabæus. How well I recall the "rising" of Mattathias, the father of the five boys, as recorded in 1 Maccabees ii; and his "Woe is me! wherefore was I born!" and how the family "rent their clothes and put on sack-cloth and mourned very sore;" and how, at his home in Modin (now *Latroon*, where we shall camp to-night) he slew the King's commissioner and pulled down the altar he had built, and how then they "fled into the mountains (B. C. 168) and left all that ever they had;" and how when "the time had drawn near that Mattathias should die" (B. C. 166), he exhorted his five sons "to be valiant and show themselves men and obtain glory." Well did the sons obey that father even to the death. *Simon*, after a life of usefulness, was assassinated as our President Lincoln, was. *Jonathan*, after a noble career, was also murdered B. C. 144. *Eleazar* was killed in battle by an elephant, in an unsuccessful attempt to slay King Antiochus Eupator. *Joannan-Caddis* was treacherously slain by "the children of Jambri." *Judas*, the greatest of the five, and the one selected by his father to be his successor, first defeated Apollonius, and slew him in battle. Then he defeated Seron. Next he gained two victories over Lysias, B. C. 166. In B. C. 163 he defeated Lysias, the *third* time. In B. C. 161 he defeated and slew Nicanor and secured the independence of his nation. Then he himself experienced the versatility of fortune, for he was killed in battle the same year at Eleasa. Of him it was said as of Judah, the son of Jacob: "in his acts he was like a lion, and like a lion's whelp roaring for his prey." (1 Maccabees iii: 4.) When he recovered Jerusalem from the hands of the heathen, he found the sanctuary desolate and the altar profaned, and the gates burnt up, and shrubs growing in the courts as in the forest, or in one of the mountains. Yea, and the priests' chambers pulled down." (1 Maccabees iv: 38.)

KULONIEH, 9 A. M.

We have journeyed for the last hour by the new turnpike built last year by orders of the Pasha of Jerusalem, to connect that city with Joppa. This is the only wagon-road in Palestine. It is about thirty-five miles in length following the windings. Lieut. Charles Warren, who is carrying on the excavations at Jerusalem, thus described the manner in which the road was built: "Each village within a certain radius, at least thirty miles, had to furnish a contingent of men for so many days. It was estimated at five days for each man, or a forfeit of thirty piastres; but some of my men have already paid fifty piastres and worked on Sundays as well, so that in one village, at least, the pressure must have been heavy. Portions of the road are told off to each village and the men are marched off there by the soldiers as if they were prisoners, and ordered to bring their own food and water. Some of them come all the way from Hebron, twenty-five miles. Seeing how energetic the Turkish Government is in the construction of this road, it would be more satisfactory did we know it is being made on sound principles. But as such is not the case, it seems hard indeed that the poor peasants should be forced to spend their time and money in a work which must certainly come to grief during the first heavy rains. There is no doubt but that the road has got on in the most astonishing manner and is fair to view on the outside. But a system of flat stones thrown about with earth patted over them with the hands, and then pressed down by rollers drawn by little children, can have little power of resisting the efforts of the winter's rain."

It was just in this way, that by forced labor and cruel compulsion, the Mahmoudich canal was built in Egypt some years ago. So all the great structures of that country were made, even the pyramids themselves.

As we came down into the valley of Elah (or *Wady Beit Haninah* as the Arabs call it), by the snake-like windings of the turnpike, I was much interested in observing the religious exercises of a Mohammedan gentleman well dressed and intelligent who had stopped for prayer near the stone bridge, under a carob tree. Although the Moslem ideas of religion seem to consist entirely in forms, and their hopes are those of a paradise altogether sensual, yet there is something, after all, impressive in their forms. This man, after washing his feet, hands and face, began his devotions by standing erect with his thumbs under his ears and his hands opened out. He repeated the words, "God is great (*Allah hu akbar*). Then he clasped his hands over his girdle; then bent forward double, hands on knees; then stood erect, hands by his sides; then knelt and laid his forehead on the ground; then leaned back on his knees and heels, at each movement repeating a series of prayers. He evidently belongs to

"The many
Who deem in outward rites and specious forms,
Religion satisfied."

Then he manipulated his rosary of one hundred beads, repeating to each bead, as he slipped it from his left hand into his right, some one of the attributes of God!

The whole took about ten minutes. It recalled to me the lines—

"Down upon the fragrant sod
Kneels with his forehead to the earth—
Lisping the eternal name of God."

Seeing that I was looking at him in respectful silence, he came up to me and saluted me, kindly. As he talked French, like all the Turkish gentlemen whom we meet, we had a pleasant chat together.

This is the people "whose God is the *Lord;* whose faith is *Islam;* whose temple is *Mecca;* whose brethren are the *Moslems;* whose prophet is *Mohammed.*" An old writer, in 1697, describes their priests as men who, by their long beards, prayers of the same standard, and a kind of Pharisaical superciliousness, which are the great virtues of the Mohammedan religion, purchase to themselves the reputation of sanctity and learning."

I am reminded, too, that this is the Mohammedan Sabbath, *Friday*. It is said that Mohammed, to show his contempt for Christ, adopted the day of the Crucifixion for the Sabbath of the Moslem. To-morrow, is the Jew's Sunday, so here are three Sundays in rotation.

From this place Mr. Fountain has sent a servant to Jerusalem with a telegraph message to Mr. Blattner, at Joppa, to meet us, to-morrow, about ten miles this side of that town. The telegraph wire runs all along, near this road, cutting across the curves, and so gaining a good deal on the road in distance. Elliot says he never knew before that the electric fluid could follow a wire just as well over a mountain as along a plain! To get good supports for the telegraph poles they have to set them up in crevices of the rocks and pile stones high around them.

In this valley I have seen the first *bevelled stones* that have come under my observation. They form part of a massive wall, a little ways west of the bridge. As I have understood that I can always recognize the old Phœnician blocks by this bevel mark, I take particular notice of it here. It is a kind of ribbon chiselled from the face of the block, next the edges, about four inches wide and two inches deep. All the great stones in the wall around Mt. Moriah are said to be figured in this way.

By agreement, we placed upon this great wall the initials of that good, Christian gentleman, Rev. Dr. Thomas R. Austin, of Indiana, and dedicated the place to him.

In this beautiful valley are fine orchards of quince and apple trees, covered with grape vines. Also, many hawthorn brushes. Some flourishing vineyards are here. The vines are simply stiff stalks, about four feet high, standing erect, without any support. I never saw any like them before. The fruit is used by the Mohammedans in the form of raisins and molasses; (*dibs*) but Mohammedans are not allowed to drink wine. In explaining this curious fact Elliot, in his funny way, says that Mohammed once got tight and killed a man; so when he became sober, his headache and remorse together, caused him to write that chapter of the Koran which forbids the use of wine. He thinks if ever a man deserved the title of "Past Most Worthy Grand Patriarch, of all the Temperance Orders in the world," Mohammed does. For the Mohammedan Church, of one hundred and fifty millions, is one great tee-total temperance society. Their total abstinence from strong drink exempts them from the application of Solomon's, "woe, sorrow, contention, babbling, words without cause, and redness of eyes." They do not "tarry at the wine, nor seek mixed wine." Yet, Mr. Fountain thinks it would injure them less, as a race, to get drunk occasionally, upon *spirits*, than to be perpetually narcotized on *tobacco*, as they are. They are never without pipe or cigarette in their mouth. To their credit I will say they do not chew tobacco or take snuff.

Although I have called this the Valley of Elah, because that is the common opinion of travelers; yet, the best writers locate the exploit of David several miles southwest of here.

This valley rises near our last night's encampment. All the wild flowers of the Plain of Sharon seem to flourish here, and the ground is like a Turkey carpet with its gay flowers. I collect the cistus, lavatera, oleander, and wild pink, whose combined fragrance is diffused in delightful profusion. The hills on each side of this great valley are high; the ravine is narrow, and if David fought here with Goliath according to one opinion, nothing is easier than to imagine the two armies in these opposing heights, challenging and insulting each other. Their voices could be distinctly heard across the valley. Close by me, under a picturesque, ruined arch, a party of Arabs is encamped, and I am confident their harsh, Shemitic gabble can be distinctly heard half a mile. In fact, I wish we could *not* hear it so plainly. They have just begun a repast upon a whole sheep, cooked in rice. They carve with their fingers, and spoon with the hollow of their hands.

So far as I see, the natives eat but little flesh—vegetable food being the prime dependance, and bread the chief article of diet. Grain of many kinds is used by them in making bread. Much use is made of onions, beans, lentils, grapes, olives, honey, olive oil, milk, butter and cheese. A very common dish is mutton, cooked to rags, and made to flavor a large pot of rice, vegetables and butter.

KIRJATH-JEARIM, 11 A. M.

It is a pleasant recollection, now, that I spent several days on the Atlantic Ocean, translating De Vogue's "Les Eglises de la Terre Sainte," (the Churches of the Holy Land.) Amongst his descriptions, I remember that of the ruined church in this village, now used for a stable, but more filthy than any stable in civilized lands. I am writing, now, upon one of the fragments of that old church. A blind man has squatted by my side, and gives his mind and voice entirely to clamoring *backsheesh*, *bachsheesh*. All the children of the place (their name is legion) are looking over my shoulder, criticising my drawing, and screaming *backsheesh*. This is seeking knowledge under difficulties. Their multitude and insolence are almost intolerable. One man in the genuine style of Oriental hospitality, has brought me a bunch of figs; he holds them out in his dirty, right hand, while he extends the left for *backsheesh*.

And yet, this is one of the neatest villages we have seen since we left Joppa. It stands on the declivity of a high hill. The houses are solidly built of stone. The village itself is embowered in groves of very large fig trees, olives, pomegranates, peaches and quinces. There is at least one palm tree, perhaps more. The present name is Kuryet El-enab, or the city of grapes, and there are many vineyards here. The hills around display those singular terraces of nature even more than those of yesterday. I set Elliot to counting the number of banks on the side of the hill, and he reckoned more than sixty. Mr. Pliny Fisk said, when he was here—"These mountains are of a peculiar formation. They seem almost as if built by the hand of man, and rise gradually step by step like pyramids. Each step, however, is so fastened into the everlasting hills, as to show you that it was placed there by the hand of Him who existed before the mountains were brought forth." The place is, outwardly, a picture of peace and happiness. The clear brook flowing down the valley gives freshness and beauty to every green thing. One tradition has made this place the Anathoth of Jeremiah, but this is doubtful; yet, it may be so. At any rate there are two circumstances connected with Kuryet that make it interesting. It was the people of Kirjath-jearim who went to

Beth-shemesh, ten miles southwest of here, across the deep valleys, and "fetched up the ark of the Lord." Here it remained twenty years, (1 Sam. vii) when David finally took it to Jerusalem. (1 Chron. xiii.) I wish I could identify "the house of Adinadab in the hill," where the sacred object so long abode ; but that is impossible. Here, too, dwelt for a long time, the celebrated robber, Abou Ghosh, the Rob Roy of these hills, who exacted a toll of fifteen piastres (sixty-three cents) from every traveler. He was an hereditary free-booter, and only did what his fathers had done before him. After he had played the big rogue for a good many years, the Turkish government seized him and sent him to Constantinople, a prisoner. I do not know what finally became of him. The American explorer, Lieut. Lynch, came leveling his line along here, May 24th, 1848. Abou Ghosh was absent at the time; but his brother was here, and peremptorily ordered the brave sailor to stop. The only answer he got was that "the government of the United States had given him his orders, and the orders should be obeyed." So the glorious "stars and stripes" went down this valley with due honor and respect.

The Ark rested here twenty years! How much there is in the fact that suggests religious thought. The Ark embodied all that was most beautiful, rare and perfect in the materials of construction; the finest linen; the most elaborate embroidery ; the rarest woods; the purest gold ; the costliest gems—nothing common or inferior was used in making it.

This old, ruined church recalls more than one poetic memory—

"There is a temple in ruin stands,
Fashioned by long-forgotten hands ;
Two or three columns and many a stone,
Marble and granite with grass o'ergrown."

In joint council of us three "Youthful Explorers," we agreed to dedicate this fine old ruin of a Crusader's Church, to Mr. Ralph Wells, of New York. How much we are benefitted in our researches here by the instructions we have had from his lectures for several years past, it is impossible to tell. His happy way of lecturing makes you feel as if you knew it all before. He is worthy to be associated with the holy memories of this place.

A native Arab brought us for sale here, a veritable *antefixa*, from some ruined temple in the plain southwest of us. Heavy as it is, and it weighs two hundred pounds. We shall pack it with our other collections and send it home. *Antefixa* is a word in architecture, meaning an ornament of a lion's head, cut on the end of a stone that was laid beneath the eaves of a building. It was perforated for the escape of water. The carving is of the Crusading style, coarse, but natural. Harriet has made a good drawing of it.*

CAMP DISMAS, 6 P. M.

It is here that tradition has established the native place of the penitant thief who, on the cross addressed Jesus, and asked to share his blessed kingdom. (Luke xxiii.) The people profess to know that his name was Dismas, and that the cross on which he was hung was preserved as late as the fourteenth century, at Cyprus. We have named our encampment, to-night, in his memory, Camp Dismas. It is about a mile south of Emmaus, where Jesus met two of

* See the engraving facing Chapter Fifth.

his disciples on the day of His resurrection; walked with them, talked with them, broke bread with them, comforted their overburdened hearts. (Luke xxiv.)

A queer incident happened this afternoon, to Elliot. He is always asking the names of places, of everybody he meets. So when he came in sight of Latroon, he enquired of a stupid Arab, who was passing along, what its name was? The Arab, without looking up, replied, *Bel maze*, that is, I do not know. So down it went in Elliot's diary. " A dirty village on the right named *Bel Maze*."

The land around Latroon is undulating, with gentle swells and broad valleys. In the winter the road along here is said to be very deep, muddy and slippery. From the opening of this valley, others can be seen, which are so many gateways for the spring brooks to issue forth from their hills to the plains, reminding me of the lines—

" Lo, where the pass expands
Its stony jaws, the abrupt mountains break."

In all books of travels, this route to Jerusalem has been delineated as extremely precipitous, craggy and fatiguing. But it is so no longer, since the turnpike was completed last year. In the French Testament the expression for smoothing the roads (as in Mark i : 3) is " aplanissez ses sentiers," that is "plane his roads;" and if ever a road way needed planing it was this one, before the Pasha of Jerusalem planed it.

A priest told me a funny story about St. Nicephorus, which illustrates the foolishness of many of their church stories. He was a good Saint, but had no whiskers, mustachios nor beard. Satan promised him as much hair as he wanted if he would do something naughty. Nicephorus refused, and immediately, as a reward for being such a good Saint, a beard burst out of his chin, clear down to his feet. The priest who told me the story, had a photograph of this bearded Saint. He was named after him Nicephorus. I told him I thought it was a very *nice* name. He did not take the joke, but I gave him *backsheesh*, and he gave me his photograph of old Nicephorus in exchange.

IN THE HILLS, 11 P. M.

A grievous calamity has befallen us. Elliot left us just as we were pitching our camp. Took his dog and gun to chase a hawk among the hills, and did not return. After waiting for an hour after dark, and firing rockets in hopes to attract his attention, Mr. Fountain and I have started out after him, leaving the servants with Aunt Liddy and Harriet. As I write this, we have stopped for a while on top of a high spur of a hill and lit some torches. A party of English gentlemen who saw our rockets, hastened to our relief, and have joined us in the search. They are military officers who have served in the East Indies, and are "driving the hills," as they call it, just as they have been accustomed to " drive the jungles " for game. They say we are sure to find him before morning. They ride through these rough crags as recklessly as the Arabs themselves.

IN THE HILLS—Midnight.

Mr. Fountain has gone back to camp to send servants to Joppa, for soldiers.

These villagers are notoriously thievish, and even murderous, and it would be directly in their line to kill the poor little boy for his gun. If the soldiers do begin on them it will be a sad day for the Arabs; for the Turkish soldiers like nothing better than to worry the villagers, who hate them, in return, with consuming hatred.

HARRIET'S DIARY.

TURNING WESTWARD. 8 A. M.

As we come around into the Joppa turnpike, three miles west of Jerusalem, the hills present the appearance of barren bleakness and ruggedness. Here we meet a great company of pilgrims of all nations, tongues and peoples, passing with their faces eastward. Among them, the swarthy, turbulent Arab, the sensual, fair-skinned Turk, the barbarous, ebony-skinned African, and the Christian of every hue and dye. Here is the down-trodden Israelite, "stranger in a strange land," and welcomed nowhere. The first caravan of Christian pilgrims consisted of Paul and the deputies of the Church of Cenchrea, who brought contributions to the faithful of the poor Christians at Jerusalem. (Acts xxi : 15.) This, indeed, was the first voyage of a band of pious, Christian converts, ever made to the cradle of Christian faith.

Although this country is literally torn to pieces by religious feuds, and its civilization delayed for centuries, by the hatreds, jealousies and acrimony of Greek and Latin Christians, Sephardim and Askenazim Jews, of Maronite and Druse, of orthodox and heretical Mohammedan; yet, as the centre of pilgrimage, Jew, Christian and Mohammedan unite in making it their *holy* land.

Among the crowd, I remarked with most interest the *monk*, with his coarse, brown cloth hood and cassock, his rope-girdle tied in curious, elegant, symbolical knots, and his well-dusted sandals, the true type of those swarms of priests who came hither in the earlier days of Christendom. One of these monks, from the south of Italy, seemed glad to converse with us when he learned that we were Americans. He thinks America will become the strongest foothold of the papal church. His idea of a pilgrimage to Palestine is to visit Ramleh, where St. George was martyred; then Jerusalem, where our Lord Jesus suffered; also, the holy places in its vicinity; then, the mountain where he fasted forty days; then, Jordan, where he was baptized; and the ruins of the church of St. John, near the baptistery; then to Bethlehem, where Christ was born, and the birthplace of John the Baptist; and finally, to the Convent of the Holy Cross, where the tree grows out of which the real cross was made. This last locality, he seemed to respect most of all.

With the crowd, although not exactly mingled in its ranks, were several very holy dervishes distinguished chiefly by their rags and filth. These were bareheaded, and went up the road prancing fantastically as they ran.

My informant, the Italian monk, dwelt with much interest upon the case of the Bishop Mastajo, of Central Africa, who had *walked* a ten months' journey, from his diocese, that in his extreme old age, he might see the spots hallowed by the steps of our divine Lord. This recalled the story of another Abyssinian ruler, who came three thousand years ago, upon an errand even more praiseworthy. (1 Kings x.)

Good arrangements are made by the different Christian communities to supply the wants of poor pilgrims. Every indigent pilgrim is allowed to stay *one day*, free of cost, at the Franciscan Convent, at Ramleh; *three days* at Bethlehem, and *thirty days* at Jerusalem. Two good meals a day are furnished them gratis. The expenses for this are of course provided for by charitable offerings from all parts of the Christian world. The same provision is made by the Jewish communities, only not quite so bountiful—as they are not so numerous or wealthy as the others. I do not know whether the Mohammedans look after the temporal wants of their pilgrims or not.

It is remarkable how many events in the Holy Scriptures are connected with caverns. And this is one strong proof of the verity of the sacred narration. Since we entered the hills above Ramleh, we have scarcely ever been out of sight of caverns, natural or artificial; and were they not thus frequently named in the Bible, their absence would be suspicious. But common as these references are on the sacred page—the legends and traditions referring to caves are far more numerous. According to local tradition, the Annunciation to Mary was made in a cave. She was born in a cave; the salutation to Elizabeth; the birth of John the Baptist; the birth of Christ; the agony in Gethsemane; the repentance of Peter; the convention to form the Apostles' Creed; the Transfiguration; these, and very many other important events in Biblical history, occurred in grottoes or caves.

VALLEY OF ELAH. 8 A. M.

The village of Kulonieh, at the entrance of this famous valley, might, by cleanliness and industry, be made a pleasant place. It is by nature a delicious vale, spacious and fertile. The ground yields good return for the little labor bestowed on it. The olive, vine and fig thrive wonderfully here, and nothing is more picturesque than the olive, when in groups, although standing by itself, I am not struck with its gracefulness, as some travelers profess to be. No doubt ancient Kulonieh was famous for the fatness of the olive and the sprightly juice of the vine. In the poor little gardens around the village, I observed great varieties of vegetables, among which I could distinguish cauliflowers, radishes, onions, beets and carrots. Beans and peas are now ripe here. How little labor would make these folks comfortable.

If there was a large town here formerly, as is most likely, such scriptural passages as these apply to it, as to so many of the older cities of Palestine: "Thou hast broken down all his hedges, thou hast brought his strongholds to ruin." (Ps. lxxxix: 40.) "Thou hast profaned his crown by casting it to the ground."

Mr. Fountain conducted us to some ancient tombs in the hillsides, near Kulonieh. But the odor of the bats that hang in them by thousands is so inconceivably noisome that I cannot remain long enough to make observations. I say nothing of the exceedingly unpleasant creatures that are parasitic to the bats, for they are too common an annoyance in this country to merit special notice. The tombs are excavated in the solid rock, no doubt taking advantage of a natural cavern, and make rooms usually about fifteen feet square.

Out of the common room, a number of small crypts were cut on every side, each one being just large enough to contain a single corpse. There were no sarcophagi or stone coffins here. Mr. Fountain thinks the Arabs steal them from the tombs for watering troughs to their flocks.

Viewing these ancient tombs, I could not help inquiring in scriptural words: "What hast thou here? and whom hast thou here that thou hast hewed thee out a sepulchre here, as he that heweth him out a sepulchre on high and that graveth an habitation for himself *in a rock*. (Isaiah xxii: 10)

They brought me a small Roman coin of bronze, found in one of these tombs. It was, no doubt placed there with the dead body as his ferry money to pass him over the river Styx, to satisfy the ferryman Charon. What absurdities those wise Romans credited! Wanting Christ they lacked everything of religious knowledge.

The bat that is so common in these tombs is named in Lev. xi: 19, as an unclean animal. It is really so. The fox-headed bat is also found here (*Xantharpya egyptiaca*), measuring twenty inches from wing to wing; this species lives on fruit.

KIRJATH JEARIM. 11 A. M.

We have enjoyed a most agreeable hour at old Kirjath-Jearim, where the ark rested twenty years. The native accessories here are charming. The beauty of the trees, the pureness of the air, the rapidity of the little mountain brook, and the luxuriousness of ferns, oleanders and other vegetation make the scene one of rare attractiveness. Butterflies of familiar forms and colors abound here. Gay and delicate flowers are numerous. The frog raises his guttural notes from the water's edge, not a whit more harsh and uncordial than the voices of the Arabs themselves. I have found but few places in my journey so agreeable as this Arab town of *Benyat El-Anab*.

This is the village that the Roman Catholic tourist Chateaubriand styles *the village of Jeremiah;* but most of travelers, *the village of Abou Ghosh*. Mr. Pliny Fisk said, when he was here in 1823, that " a little way from it was a pure stream of water flowing out of a rock, where he stopped to quench his thirst and eat some bread and fruit."

I have sketched here the branch of a pomegranate.*

The scientific name of this tree is *Punica granatam*, from the Latin *pomum granatum* or grained apple. The Romans called it *punica* because it came from Carthage. It belongs to the natural order *Myrtacœ*, but is rather a bush than a tree. The leaves are dark green, the flowers crimson. The fruit when ripe is red and juicy. It ripens here in October. Around Joppa most of the pomegranates, like the oranges, are seedless. The Hebrew name was *rimmone* and several places are named from it in Joshua xv: 32; xxi: 25; Nehemiah xi: 29. The locusts are very destructive to this tree, as in Joel i: 12; Haggai ii: 19. An orchard is named in Canticles iv: 13. The beautiful, rosy color of the fruit is compared with a lady's cheeks in Canticles iv: 3.

Carved figures of the pomegranate adorned the tops of the pillars in Solomon's temple (1 Kings vii: 18, 20, etc.), and worked representations of the

---

* See the engraving facing this chapter.

fruit ornamented the hem of the robe of the ephod in blue, purple and scarlet. It is used here chiefly in making sherbet, a sour drink like lemonade, the same, no doubt, referred to in Canticles viii: 2.

I have just been making a careful inspection of a grove of oleanders. What a mass of floral beauty. Yet Mr. Fountain says the oleander of the Jordan and the Sea of Galilee are far superior. I can scarcely conceive it possible.

A distant view of Ramleh that we passed on Wednesday, exhibits the perfectly Oriental character of the town and its scenery. Mr. Fountain says its grove of palms reminds him of a street in Naples called *Strada Nuova.* This town (Ramleh) will always be associated in my memory with the name of Joseph of Arimathæa, that "good man and just" (Luke xxiii: 50), whose privilege it was to lend to the body of Jesus a tomb. There is also a tradition that Joseph and Mary, in their flight with the infant Jesus to Egypt, tarried and spent a night here. This, however, is altogether unlikely, for this route would rather be by way of Hebron, Beersheba and Gaza. Yet upon their return from Egypt, two years afterwards, and on their way to Nazareth, such a visit is more than probable, as Ramleh stands directly upon the great highway.

As I came down again into the edge of the plain of Sharon, my horse treads odors out of its carpet of wild flowers. Passing the village of *Deir Eyub*, a place of only four or five houses, I remark that the natural arrangement of the hills form almost a complete amphitheatre, the stratification of the rocks making the seats. It is one of the strangest freaks of nature and I regret that I have not time to sketch it.

CAMP DISMAS, 9 P. M.

Near the village of Latroun just above us, stood once, in all probability, the Maccabæan city of Modin.

We had scarcely pitched our tents and gathered our comforts around us, when Mr. Fountain informed us that brother Elliot was missing. He had gone out by himself, as he is prone to do, in search of game, but did not return as promised. Mr. Fountain and John went to the foot of the hills and fired their guns in successive volleys, in hopes to hear his in return. This was the signal agreed upon in case of either one getting lost. This not succeeding, they came back and sent up a number of rockets, kept for the purpose if such a calamity should occur. The rockets summoned a party of English gentlemen camped near by, strong, sunburnt men, accustomed to adventure, and they at once offered their invaluable services in the search. Leaving the camp in charge of the servants, the entire party of six is now among the hills and we cannot doubt will find the truant. It is a night of inexpressible loveliness, but oh, a night of sorrow and sadness to us women, doomed to wait and to watch.

10 P. M.

"Refrain thy voice from weeping and thine eyes from tears; for thy work shall be rewarded, saith the Lord." How consoling these words of Jeremiah. But, oh my poor brother! Would that I too could go among the mountains and search for thee. But all that is left for Aunt Lydia and me is to pray and weep.

12 P. M.

Mr. Fountain has returned without tidings of Elliot, and sent a message to Joppa, asking for soldiers and an experienced officer to examine the villagers, who he fears have murdered our dear child for his clothing. He expects them here by daylight. Perhaps the Governor himself may accompany them. What a shocking termination to our Holy Land expedition this threatens to be. We are almost in despair. Oh, may the fatherly goodness of the Almighty protect our dear brother!

MR. FOUNTAIN'S DIARY.

CAMP DISMAS. 6 P. M.

We began our fifth day's researches in Bible lands by reading the first ten chapters of Exodus and the first three of Luke, and singing the lines "We know not what's before us." All has gone on well. The travel by the new turnpike is smoothness itself, compared with the roads we traversed yesterday. The only annoyance is the crowds of pilgrims that impede our steps.

CAMP. Midnight.

Since my brief entry above, I have been compelled to face an unexpected and a bitter trial. Our poor Elliot carelessly wandered from the party with his gun just before dark, and cannot be recovered. We are making every exertion to trace him up, and with good help from some English officers, but the character of the fellahin hereabouts is villainous, and suggests most gloomy anticipations. Leaving the rest of the company in the hills, I have hastened down here to detach a messenger to Governor Noureddin and ask for a squad of soldiers for to-morrow. After all, I have much comfort in the suggestion of his aunt "that the poor boy is only asleep somewhere under a rock and will be in by breakfast time."

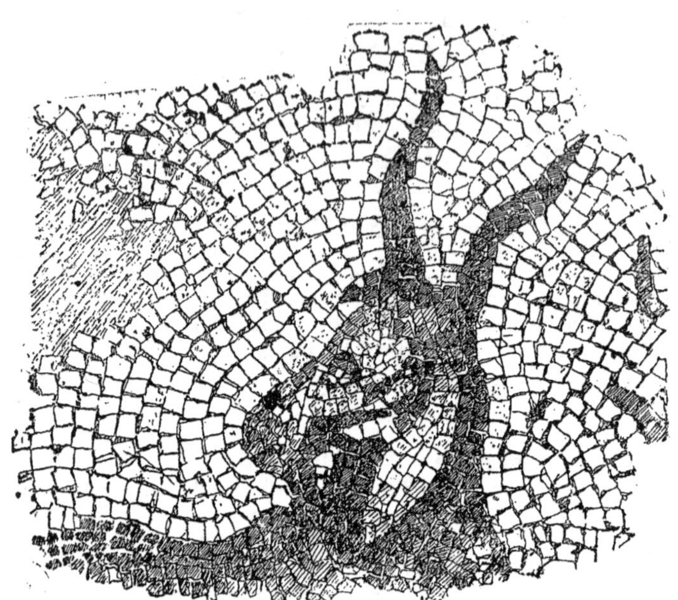

FRAGMENT OF ANCIENT MOSAIC PAVEMENT.

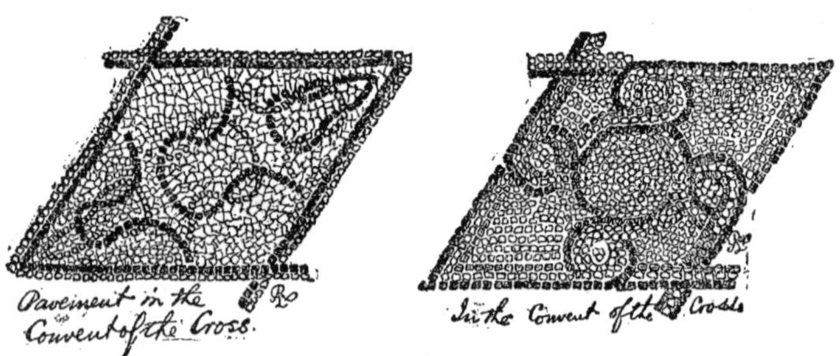

MOSAICS, FROM THE CONVENT OF THE CROSS.

(Near Jerusalem.)

CHAPTER VI.

MOUNTING THE HILLS OF JUDAH.

The recovery of Elliot—Story of a dog—Plowing and sowing—Mosaics—Arabic words—Black snake—Hospitality of Arabs—Exploit of an Arab boy—Hotel hash—Fleas—Prickly pear—Women weeping at the grave—Shepherd boy's music—Sore eyes—Tomb of Machabees—Acoustics—Insects—Scarcity of timber—Snails for food—Weights and measures—Plain of Sharon—Old coins—Counting distance by hours—Horses' shoes—Jews in Judæa—Porphyry—Agate—Dove—Onions—Performing a vow—Exploits of Lieut. Lynch—Sennacherib—Music box—Native music—Native houses—Funeral—Dragomans—Camp Sabbath.

ELLIOT'S DIARY.

CAMP DISMAS, Saturday, March 20th, 1869. 8 A. M.

MY last entry was made at 4 o'clock this morning. I like to have come to grief after all. The Sheikh left me and I started north, thinking that I must strike the turnpike, somewhere, if I kept that direction long enough. But I had not gone half a mile when a dozen scalawags of Arabs sprung from behind the rocks and pounced on me. Before I could even cock my gun at them they had me. One took my gun, one my field glass. My wallet of flowers, shells and other curiosities that I collected yesterday, they emptied. Then they began to go through me and in a minute more they wouldn't have left me a shirt to my back. But luckily, a party of English gentlemen who had been assisting Mr. Fountain in the search for me, heard *Sweet Home* barking at the robbers and galloped up in the nick of time. Gracious, how they did use those Arabs up! They not only took away from them all *my* things, but actually went through them. They tore all their clothes to rags, set them on fire and burnt the rags to ashes before their faces. Then they whipped them with ramrods on their naked backs till the blood flew. Of all the howling! Then they took me to camp on their horses. Aunt Liddy cried over me. Mr. Fountain and John came into camp about an hour afterwards.

I shall never say another word against the English so long as I live. Such kind and brave men. I showed the gentlemen my diary, and they said I was a stunning fellow to write in that way when lost in the hills.

Governor Noureddin came all the way from Joppa, post haste, to help look me up. And he seemed as glad to see me as the rest of them. I tried to get him to accept my field-glass as a present, but he wouldn't. He says, after this, when I travel alone, keep my *gun* better loaded than my *wallet*. I told him I would. He is one of the best of men. Mr. Floyd, who heard I was lost, also came out here. And so did Mr. Blattner.

I have no doubt the Governor thought I had acted very foolishly. But he only said in French to Mr. Fountain, *Les plus sages ne le sont pas toujours.* That means that the wisest of men are not always wise. I suppose he means *me!*

One of the English gentlemen, a great sunburnt man, is named Colonel Pfyffe. He told me to write it Pfyffe, and not Fife, as I was going to. As we came riding in, he told me a good dog story. When he was at Jerusalem, last week, he always left his large mastiff dog, named *Hercules*, chained to the pole of his tent, which was pitched outside of the Joppa gate. He did this to keep Hercules from fighting other dogs, a thing he was often guilty of. But day before yesterday, while Colonel Pfyffe went to the Mediterranean Hotel to see Lieut. Warren, the celebrated explorer, somebody turned Hercules loose and he followed his master clear through the city. He had to fight every dog in Jerusalem for permission to pass. Colonel Pfyffe was sitting in the hotel-parlor when the dog came in triumphant. He had won his way gallantly and got through alive. But that was all. He had lost one of his eyes and both ears. One of his legs was broken and he hadn't an inch of tail left. He died in an hour or two. Colonel Pfyffe cried when he told it.

They left Hassan here last night to watch the tents. When he saw me coming in he almost went wild with joy. He shouted. He jerked off his turban and exposed his funny shaved scalp, which is a thing the Mohammedans hardly ever do. He threw his tarboush clear up into a carob tree and then I clumb up and got it for him. He repeated to me a poem from "Antar," whatever that means, that sounded as if he was reading from a rhyming dictionary. Then he sang a war song, such as I often get him to sing, and it is wonderful what a distance you can hear that war song among these hills. I will copy that song some day and get Harriet to copy the music.

Hassan says I needn't have got lost. He says, when an Arab gets lost, if he is on horseback, he lets his horse bring him out safely. If he is on foot, he simply keeps going right along and he is sure to come out right at the place where he started. He says that a man's right foot always swings a little further than his left, and so it turns him gradually round. I don't believe that.

Mr. Fountain showed me the place where the great Ibrahim Pasha suffered a severe loss of soldiers in June, 1835. He had left Joppa with his army to go to Jerusalem, which was besieged by insurgent Arabs. Getting to this point, at the entrance of the valley, he left an officer here with one thousand men, what they call a *Bim Pasha*, while he went up the valley with the rest. When he reached the top of the mountain, he fired a cannon as a signal to the Bim Pasha to come on. But the Bim Pasha was a coward and staid below. Then the rebels rushed in upon the Bim Pasha, killed all of his thousand except two hundred, and run the balance clear back to Joppa. Ibrahim put the Bim Pasha into prison and that's the last ever heard of *him*. Ibrahim always was rough on his disgraced officers.

IN THE HILLS OF JUDAH, 4 P. M.

We started soon after breakfast. But I have been so sleepy all day that I have not paid much attention to anything. I saw a man plowing on the plain of Sharon, who had a tin funnel fixed to the handle of his plow. By this arrangement he could drop grain in one furrow while he scratched the dirt over the one before it. This was nearer civilized farming than anything I had seen in this country before, and I asked him the name of his tin funnel. He said *backsheesh*.

I found a bird's nest to-day with three speckled eggs in it. Somehow it called to memory the passage in Isaiah: "My hand hath found a nest as one gathereth eggs." As the bird ran before me and raised the dust in the path, trying to call off my attention from the nest, I remembered another passage in Nahum where it says "the clouds are the dust of God's feet." May be the prophet Nahum had this very thought in mind when he came along this way, two thousand six hundred years ago. Who knows?

As to-morrow is Sunday and we are to lie by and do no travel, I have got Mr. Fountain to let me name our camping place *Camp Sabbath*. And as soon as I get to it, I shall go directly to bed and directly to sleep.

Several times during the week I have picked up little square bits of marble, of different colors, not bigger than dice, that seem to have been made for some purpose, but never thought until to-day to ask Mr. Fountain what they are. This afternoon I discovered such a quantity of them that it excited my curiosity to know. Looking amongst them I found a piece of pavement formed of these little cubic stones and made a drawing of it. It is about two feet square.*

This head is that of the Ibex, or mountain goat. The pavement is formed by taking these cubes of marble, some white, some black, yellow and other colors, and laying them down in soft mortar. Then when the mortar hardens there is a solid pavement of pictures. Mr. Fountain says I shall find plenty of these marble pieces,—he calls them *tesseræ*,—on Mount Zion, Mount Olivet, at Shiloh, Ibneh and other places. Now that I know what they are I intend to collect them in great quantities. Mr. Fountain says there are still remaining very many vestiges of these Mosaic paintings, some as fresh and as fair as when first laid down. He tells me to write this passage in my diary concerning them: "This art was mostly confined to ornamenting floors. The work was either *large stones* of different colors cut geometrically and called *pavimenta sectilia*, or else *small cubes* cut uniformly, like those in this specimen of the ibex, and called *tesseræ*. The different colors of these cubes united to form a delineation. Mosaic, proper, consisted originally altogether of small oblong pieces of glass stones joined together with a strong cement." It was a *tesseræ* like one of these, that the Roman officers used to inscribe the *watchword* on, which they distributed among the pickets and grand-rounds of the camp.

To-day I have learned some more words in Arabic, making about eighty in all: *rah*, to go; *ainab*, grapes; *rarse*, head; *tell*, hill; *asal*, honey; *karn*, horn; *jouarn*, hungry; *gallayah*, kettle; *rokbah*, knee; *sikkeen*, knife; *bark*, lightning; *bittik*, melon; *tarjeer*, merchant.

I asked one of the village Sheikhs to-day, if he knew the name of the Sultan of Turkey? He said he didn't want to know. I told him it was *Abd-el-Asiz*, and that the name means a *leopard*. But he didn't know what a leopard was. Never heard of a leopard in this part of the country. Then he asked me the name of the Sultan of *America?* I told him *General Grant*, and I left him trying to pronounce it.

I had a jolly run to-day after a black snake. This is the first one I have

* See the engraving facing Chapter Sixth.

seen since we landed at Joppa. I run him a hundred yards at the top of my speed before I killed him. He is a black snake about six feet long. I have skinned him to take it home. Hassan says that *Eblis* lives in the hollow of a snake's tooth, and that's what made the snake turn and look so fiercely at me when I hit him. Eblis is one of their Mohammedan devils. His skin shone, in the hot sun as he scooted over the rocks, as if it had been varnished. He run as fast as the blue racers that I have chased over the Iowa prairies. The blue racer is called in Webster's Dictionary, a kind of black snake of the genus *coluber*, especially *coluber getulus*, found in the United States, and so called because it moves very quickly. Snakes are scarce here. Dr. Robinson says, in Vol. 2, page 49, that in several weeks' travel in these hills he had only seen one snake. But when Mr. R. Tod so nobly undertook to search for the martyr Assad Esh Shidiak, in his prison house on Mount Lebanon, in June, 1832, he was entreated to take care and avoid the serpents. He was told not to lie outside the buildings, lest he should be stung by serpents, and he was warned that there were serpents outside that might do him injury, perhaps take his life. I hope to find a good many when we get up in that part of the country, or else my study in *herpetology* will be wasted.

When I sat down to skin my dead snake, and Harriet began to look up Bible passages for me concerning serpents, we found that we had there, close by us, the Bible emblems of wisdom, innocence and industry. "Be ye therefore wise as serpents and harmless as doves," said our Lord, in Matthew x : 16, and here, right at my feet, is the serpent; while yonder, on a low bush, cooing most delightfully, is a pair of doves. As for industry, the ant, the emblem of that virtue, is so plenty here that you cannot walk clear of their tracks.

I was delighted, just now, to meet a real, wild Arab; a *Bedouin*. He was going across the hills on some business with the Pasha, at Jerusalem, and stopped to drink coffee with us, at our invitation. His spear was eighteen feet long, for I measured it. It was tufted at the point with ostrich feathers. He was a real, wild, savage warrior. His name was Mohammed something or other; most all these folks have Mohammed to their names. He had a gun strapped over his back, the wooden stock six feet long, with a flint lock. He says the *fellahin* are *kelben;* that means the farming Arabs are dogs. But the Bedawy, he says, are princes. He thinks no decent men will be a farmer. He says no wonder there are no old people among the farmer Arabs, for the lice and fleas eat them up before their hair turns gray. I think he is more than half right there.

Hassan told me this morning an adventure of a brave Arab boy, in these hills. He was here with two boys, younger than himself, and when night came on, they were lost as I was last night. Knowing the danger of jackals and dogs, he took his party into an old sepulchre cut in the hill side. There he built up the doorway with stones, and fought off the wild troop the whole night. The next morning the ground was trod hard and bare by the hundreds of animals that had besieged him. The people then dressed the brave fellow in man's clothes, gave him a gun and named him the "Boy Sheikh," in compliment to his gallantry. He was only about twelve years old.

CAMP SABBATH, 7 P. M.

At the dinner we have just had, I got our cook to make a dish of real, old-fashioned hash. I told him I wanted hotel hash, and showed him how to make it. He did it up wonderfully. It even had hair in it as we get it in New York, at restaurant. The next party that hires our cook may thank me for teaching him the new dish. He says he never heard of it before. He promises, after this, to have it every day or two. It is funny to hear him pronounce the name of it. He calls it *ohtelarsh*—and that is the way he will teach it to other cooks.

And now to my little iron bedstead; for to-night I have got to make up two sleeps in one.

JOHN'S DIARY.

CAMP DISMAS, 6 A. M.

All right, this morning, and every thing has passed off with a laugh. The English officers found Elliot, full six miles south of here. The dear boy had fallen among thieves, and these Englishmen proved to be his good Samaritans. They say that Elliot showed good pluck; but what can a boy of twelve do among half a dozen full grown Arabs? I only wish he had got his two barrels emptied among them, before they reached him. He says if he had not been so sleepy, watching and waiting all night, and so hungry, going without his dinner, the villains would not have surprised him as they did. I do not know about that. I have seen these Arabs peeping from behind rocks as sly as jackals, and I shall never go out by myself, after this, without keeping a hand to my gun, and my gun loaded.

The good Noureddin Effendi, with twelve soldiers, came galloping into our camp just as the Englishmen returned with the rescued boy. Their horses were white with foam. The Governor's secretary assured me that they had galloped every step of the way from Joppa, and this I can easily believe after seeing their horses. Nobody need tell me, after this, that these Turkish officers are wanting in feeling. The secretary says that the Governor would have had a hundred of the villagers in prison, at Joppa, before night, if the boy had not been found. We gave him, and the English gentlemen, and the soldiers, the best breakfast at our command. Harriet presided at the table, and when she thanked the gentlemen, in French, in her graceful and touching manner, for their kindness and humanity to the little boy, there were tears in every eye. Mr. Blattner also came to us this morning, in acknowledgment of our telegram sent him yesterday; also, Mr. Floyd.

I took an hour's stroll through the village of Latroon, after breakfast, and in spite of all my caution, came out lively with fleas. The very dust of the earth here, seems to breed them; you can stand in places and see the dust move with those insects.

The town of Latroon is strongly situated on a rocky eminence, and must once have been an important place. It abounds in prickly-pear hedges, dazzling with the most brilliant green. It is curious that this plant, the cactus, is not once alluded to in the Bible; perhaps it is a recent importation in the Holy

Land. But nothing could be better adapted to a lazy people for fencing purposes than this. I watched the process of making a fence, the other day, near Joppa, when there. First they dig a trench three feet deep, throwing up the excavated earth into an embankment. Along the top of this bank and about two feet apart, they stick the great, leathery leaves of the prickly-pear. That is all the labor required. These leaves soon send out roots, and in a few years grow up into stalks often larger than my body, and having leaves like elephant's ears. These leaves and stalks dried, make a tolerably good fuel. I saw the poorer classes of women gathering them near Joppa, for that purpose. These cacti, or prickly-pear, at Latroon, remind me of nothing so much as a gigantic hot-house.

The hill on which Latroon stands is conical in form, and crowned with the ruins of a large, strong and very ancient fortress. From the top of this I saw Joppa, Ramleh and Lydda, and beyond them the blue sea. As I entered the town of Latroon, once called Modin, the city of the great Maccabees, I encountered a group of women encircling a vacant grave, weeping and sighing. They recalled the affecting reference to Mary, the sister of Lazarus—" She goeth unto the grave to weep there." (John xi : 31.) In these Oriental customs, there is doubtless the same superstition that the Romans acknowledged, who believed that funeral solemnities conduce to the peace and happiness of the dead. I do not see the cypress used here as it is in more settled portions of the country. At Smyrna, for instance, we remarked that a cemetary resembles a *cypress swamp*, so thickly are the trees planted, one at the head of each grave. With the Romans the cypress was called the *funeral tree*, and was placed at the door of the deceased person, as an emblem of death.

I also remarked here a shepherd boy playing with all his might, upon a pipe made of two reeds. If his musical ability had been equal to his enthusiasm, I would not have hurried away from him so unceremoniously as I did. However, he stopped playing long enough to ask me for *backsheesh*, and the women stopped weeping long enough to ask me for *backsheesh*.

It was near this town that Monsieur Pierotti met with an adventure among jackals a few years ago. His horse had become fast, one cold night in the swamp, formed by this creek, and the Monsieur whiled away the slow hours of night by singing. This attracted the jackals in great numbers. They crowded round him and took evident interest in his music. Pierotti concluded that Sampson could easily have caught his three hundred foxes at Latroon, had he used " snares, cords and nets " as suggested in Psalm cxl : 5.

The houses at Latroon are all of one story, and built of uncemented stones, with flat, mud roofs. Around them are rows of small dome-roofed hovels for baking bread.

Not the slightest piece of furniture could I discover in any of the houses. There was in fact nothing in them save a few water-jars and large, earthen receptacles for grain. One of them was ornamented on the outside with a blue porcelain plate, evidently dropped by some traveler. The proprietor had framed it in a setting of dried mud, directly over his door of entrance.

The habits of these people are as filthy as their houses are empty and uncomfortable. A village in these parts is simply a *stronghold of farmers*. The villagers cultivate their little patches of ground among the hills, if they are farmers, or tend their flocks if they are shepherds; and towards sunset, return to town with all their possessions, for shelter and protection. Mr. Fountain says there is not a farmhouse in all the Holy Land, outside of a village; every shepherd and farmer lives *inside*. Consequently, there can be no such thing as domestic comfort in this country.

I was reminded of the incident of Boaz giving parched corn to Ruth (Ruth ii : 14) by noticing an Arab roasting and eating the half-ripe grains of the *doura* or millet, that grows very strong and rank in these valleys. I tasted some of it parched and found it delicious.

The worst sight I saw at Latroon was the hideous ophthalmy, or sore eyes. It is so prevalent as to render almost every child's eyes here an open sore. Their scabby faces, also, were black with those small vampires, the fleas. No happy childhood here.

In pleasing contrast with the misery of human life at Latroon, I plucked a tiny flower, the pimpernel, my favorite Sharon plant, which I found adorning the edge of a little, babbling stream—

> " One rivulet, a tiny stream
> Came lightening downward, and so spilt itself
> Among the anemones, then lost again."

By this sweet stream it was that those five noble brothers of the Machabean stock, used to play in their infancy. Such sweet, blue flowers as this, they, too, plucked, and in memory thereof, nature gives the lovely blossom to decorate their tomb.

The tomb erected here, at Modin, to the memory of the heroic Machabees, is minutely described in the apocryphal books, but there is not a trace of it left. " Simon built a monument upon the sepulchre of his father and brethren with hewn stone, behind and before. Moreover, he set up six pyramids over against another, for his father and his mother and his four brethren. And in these he made cunning devices, about the which he set great pillars, and upon the pillars he made all their armor for a perpetual memory, and by the armor, ships carved, that they might be seen of all that sail on the sea. This is the sepulchre which he made at Modin, and it standeth yet unto this day." (1 Maccabees xiii, 27 to 31.) This was written about B. C. 150. Years ago, when father first promised me this visit to the Holy Land, I made this memorandum—" As you sail on the sea, near Joppa, look for the monument of the Maccabees."

In the vicinity of Latroon I observed the acoustic properties of the atmosphere in these hills, to great advantage. Father had particularly charged us to pay attention to this subject before we should reach the mountains of Ebal and Gerizim. (Joshua viii : 30.) He gave us some special instructions in the science of acoustics for that purpose. He desired to know whether human voices can be heard at a greater distance here than in our own country. I have tested the matter several times, and this morning more particularly. A boy standing on a hill to the right of me called across to another who stood on an opposite eminence, more than half a mile off. The other one distinctly heard him and answered him. Then I could not help thinking how the blast of the Roman trumpets, as they divided the night-watches in their fortified camp here, must have echoed and re-echoed through this defile. Beyond a doubt, the garrison signals of Joppa must have been heard at Ramleh; those of Ramleh at Latroon; those of Latroon at Kolonieh; and those of Kolonieh on the ramparts of Antonio's Tower, at Jerusalem. So, when the Crusaders came into these passes, A. D. 1099, forty thousand strong, what dismay must have weakened the hearts of the infidels as they heard their clarion-notes day after day, ever drawing nearer to Jerusalem, the one grand objective-point of all their toil.

Before we left Joppa our party agreed to locate here, at Modin, five of our dead heroes, Christian warriors, who had fallen in a warfare every whit as noble as that which demanded the lives of the five Machabees—I mean the Sunday school work. Looking over our list of Sunday school workers, persons whom we have known, as visitors at father's house, or as lecturers in this branch of instruction, we find four great and good men, and make up the number by adding the name of Raikes, the founder of Sunday schools. These, then, are our "Five Machabees":—R. G. Pardee, of Pennsylvania; William Sedgewick, of Kentucky; William R. Bradbury, of New York; Stephen A. Tyng, Jr., of Pennsylvania; Robert Raikes, of England.

While Mr. Fountain assisted me to divest myself of the insects of Latroon, he gave me this suggestive sentence for my diary, which almost makes me crawl to read it: "The monstrous armor of insects, their pincers, their saws, their teeth, their nippers, their augers, their horns, and all their tools of combat, of death and of dissection with which they come armed to the battle, with which they labor, pierce, cut, rend, and fiercely divide with skill and dexterity equal to their furious blood-thirstiness, can nowhere be better studied than in the Holy Land." Mr. Fountain thinks the horrible vermin of this country is due to the filthy habits of the people; and that, in cleanly Hebrew times, the insect tribe was kept under. I like to think so. In the meantime, I shall hope never to have occasion to sleep in a village like Latroon.

HILLS OF JUDAH, 4 P. M.

In our journey this morning round the hills, from Latroon and along the Plain of Sharon, I gave careful attention to the want of forest and orchard trees in this part of the country. If heavy groves of trees were planted across this plain from the sea to the hills, say five or ten deep, the khamsin or sirocco winds that blow from the south, and cause much suffering here in warm weather, would be neutralized. The hill-floods would be far less violent if their ridges now so bare, were clothed in trees, as they were in the olden times. In parts of Belgium, trees were planted fifty feet apart, and within half a century the sandy plains were transformed into fertile lands. In Egypt this operation was marvellously successful in increasing the amount of rainfalls. A good government would offer premiums for tree planting on a large scale.

At the edge of the hills I gathered some of the large edible snails of this country, such as I have frequently seen the people roasting and eating. They call them delicious, but we have not tried them.

From a well-informed native met this morning, I gathered some information about the standard measures of the Arabs. I find that the *ruttel* is fifteen and three-fourths ounces avoirdupois weight; but in some places reckoned only at thirteen ounces. The *ukkah*, commonly called *oke*, is two and three-fourths pounds American weight; and the *kuntar* is one hundred *ruttles*.

My last view of Sharon was so grand, that although we have all said so much about it in our diaries, I can hardly help filling a page or two more. And yet, fruitful and beautiful as it appears, yet, compared with its former glory, Sharon is but a wilderness: even as Isaiah predicted two thousand six hundred years ago. No wonder the Philistines maintained war with the "Chosen Race" so many centuries, seeing that these fat corn lands, which they called *Shefalah*, were the prize for which they contended.

I have bought a good parcel of bronze coins, to-day, and shall take pains to clean them up for preservation. The mint-masters of olden time must have put considerable tin or zinc into their copper to harden it, or it would never preserve these portraits and letters so well. I have a coin of the period A. D. 333, about the time that the "Bordeaux Pilgrim" came here. He was the first visitor to Holy Land whose travels are preserved. At that date the Roman Consuls were Flavius Valerius Dalmatius, and Marcus Aurelius Xenophilus. How it brings a person face to face with history, to handle coins old as these!

In traveling here the sojourner counts his distances by hours—and not miles. Dr. Robinson adopted this plan in his books of travels. I should hope the standard measure adopted is not the hours of yonder laggard party of Arab travelers, who have been more than half an hour traveling a quarter of a mile. They stop to chat with every one they meet. They smoke. They talk with one another. They sing their monotonous chants. They do everything except go forward; although their beasts are loaded with valises and blankets—evidently the baggage of some travelers who are probably waiting for them at a watering-place further down the plain.

Climbing the sharp ridges of Judah, I recalled the expression: "My feet were almost gone, my steps had well nigh slipped." Yet, our horses are singularly sure-footed, and scarcely ever slip. This is partly owing to the manner in which they are shod. The horse-shoe made here is very light and thin. It is lengthened towards the heel, where it is thinnest. It is not turned up, but perfectly flat. To fit it to the horse's foot they hammer it cold, and nail it on with four nails. The hoof is pared with a knife. To clinch the nails they set the foot down upon a rock, and hammer upon it in the rudest manner. I think this shoe does not stay very firmly on the foot; but there is a blacksmith in every village.

We have just dined with a sheikh. A good fellow he proved to be. He sincerely believes that we people of western nations are to occupy this land some day, and drive out or Christianize his race. Alluding to this, he told Mr. Fountain, "Do not be long in coming, we expect you." His dinner was abundant, tolerably clean in the cooking, and really, under the circumstances, very good. I never saw more grace and dignity than his family displayed while waiting upon us. The only thing that made against the dinner was that he insisted upon our *seeing* the lamb that was to furnish the meal. While we were looking at it, he butchered it right before our eyes, in the doorway of the house. The dogs made it lively round that doorway all the time we were eating. The sheikh would not accept *backsheesh* for our dinner, but I gave a ten-bladed knife to one of his sons, and Elliot gave a pocket looking-glass to another.

I was greatly amused by one of the sheikh's boys who took me on top of the house to exhibit some writing, as he said, made there by "a great American Effendi." Some visitor here has played upon the credulity of these people by painting, in large, red letters, on the battlements, the inscription—"S. T.—1860—X." I found it so difficult to explain the joke to them that I did not even attempt it.

We passed a party of Jews in the hills, quietly keeping their Sabbath, which is our Saturday. They encamped here last evening, a little before sundown, and will remain till sunset, to-day. If a man endeavors to keep all the Sundays in the Holy Land he will lose three days in the week; and if he endeavors to keep the Holy Days of the Catholic and Greek Churches, he will lose the other four. This Jewish party strictly observe the injunction in Nehemiah x : 30, and elsewhere; for I saw them refuse to purchase provisions offered them by the natives, because it is their Sabbath. And they will build no fires on their Sabbath day. How this poor remnant of the eight millions, who covered these hills in the days of Christ, recalls the passage (Ezekiel xxxi: 12): "Strangers have cut him off and have left him; upon the mountains and in all the valleys his branches are fallen, and his boughs are broken."

Mr. Fountain gives me this paragraph to enter in my diary: "In England, the Jews are as 1 to 728 to the entire population; in France, 1 to 240; in Austria, 1 to 31." He does not know what they are in the United States. A member of this party of Jews has a full flowing beard, always considered by these people the noblest ornament of personal dignity and beauty. I cannot help associating it, however, with other and disgusting thoughts, when I observe many of the Arabs of this country invested with patriarchal beards, and know that they are the resort of innumerable vermin.

Among the ruins of some old edifice, I do not know what, I was surprised, to-day, to discover a fine piece of *porphyry*, which we shall take to Jerusalem to send home. How I wish it could speak its Egyptian ancestry, and tell us when, and how and by whom it was brought here. Porphyry is a compound mineral or rock, composed essentially of a base of hornstone, interspersed with crystals of feldspar. It frequently contains, also, quartz, mica and hornblende, like granite. The ancient porphyry of Egypt, of which this is a specimen, is the most esteemed. It has a ground of a fine, red color, passing into purple, having snow-white crystals of feldspar imbedded in it. The coffer of the great pyramid, which I hope to see before many months, is composed of it, and the antique, colossal statues, which we examined three weeks ago in the British Museum, and at Paris, are made of it.

We are beginning to see numbers of the beautiful Syrian dove, to-day. The dove has been regarded by mankind, from time immemorial, with peculiar sentiment, and is considered the emblem of gentleness, affection and the divine love and mercy.

One reason these natives give for the gentle disposition of the dove is that this bird has no *gall;* the gall being considered by the ancient naturalists the source and fountain of contention, the bitterness of the gall being supposed to infuse itself into the spirit. Probably, on account of this anatomical peculiarity, the dove was considered as the very best pattern for married people, and the emblem of chastity, as it lives in the strictest monogamy, never desiring another mate. Unfortunately, however, for these writers, the raven, which is always mentioned by them in strong contrast with the dove, is quite as remarkable for its attachments to its mate and young, and for the strictness of its monogamy, the same pair, when once united, residing together for the whole of their lives.

A company of Arabs sitting under a rock regaling themselves upon the onions of the plain of Sharon, attracted our attention. This onion is not the rank, harsh onion of our country, but milder and sweeter as well as considerably larger. Its skin is colored. This onion is said to be extremely wholesome, and at this season of year makes an important article of diet to the people. This is the onion mentioned in Numbers xi; for which the Israelites so greatly longed. We procured at Joppa some of the seed.

We met a man to-day who was performing a vow, almost exactly like the case in 2 Samuel xix. Some months ago, his son went out upon a peddling expedition and the father took an oath not to trim his hair nor wash his clothes till he returned. The man looked badly and smelled worse. I hope his son will soon return. He reminded me of my father's brother, Lemuel, who took a pledge in 1844 *not to shave* until Henry Clay was elected President. Of course he never did, and when Uncle Lem was killed at Bull Run in 1861, his beard was as long as a mandarin's.

I found a specimen of agate, to-day, of extraordinary beauty, semi-transparent, elegantly veined and presenting, in minature, a *bastion fort*. The agate was the second stone in the third row in the High Priest's breastplate.

Across the hills, and down by Kirjath-jearim, which we visited yesterday, our countryman, Lieut. W. F. Lynch carried his line, leveling with spirit levels every foot of the way, from the edge of the Dead Sea, through the desert of Judæa, over precipitous and mountain ridges, down and across yawning ravines, beneath a scorching sun, to the sea shore at Joppa. From a copy of his report in my lap, I make this summary of his wonderful fifty days' work: "April 10, 1848, he entered the Jordan, with his boats, from the Sea of Galilee. April 18, entered the Dead Sea. May 9, took the boats to pieces. May 10, broke up camp and left the Dead Sea. May 16, reached Jerusalem. May 24, reached Kirjath-jearim. May 29, reached the shore of the Mediterranean Sea and so finished the work." All honor to the party and its brave chief.

HARRIET'S DIARY.

CAMP DISMAS. 5 A. M.

We are made supremely happy this morning, after a sleepless night, by the return of our poor lost boy,

"While yet 't was morning, and the holy light
Of day grew bright."

I was the first to catch the sight of the party of English gentlemen coming over the hills, towards us, bringing with them dear Elliot,—

> "Straining his eyes beneath an arch of hand,"

And looking eagerly down upon those who had passed so distressed a night on his account. While he was absent he wrote down his thoughts and adventures up to daylight, sitting under a rock, by the light of his wax candle. Surely this was a brave thing for a boy of twelve to do. It would really seem as if the dear, noble fellow was inspired by the spirit of the great Mattathias, father of the five Machabees, who lie buried here, near Latroon.

It was a providential deliverance to him, that just as the Arab thieves were stripping him of his raiment, and might have consummated their brutality by murdering the lad, our English friends rode in gallantly to the rescue. It will be a lesson to Elliot in future; for he has all the time underrated the dangers of travel in this country, and is too daring. He has promised us to be more cautious.

FOOT OF THE HILLS. 11 A. M.

We are leaving the Plain of Sharon for the last time, and entering the hills of Judah to encamp, over Sunday, in sight of Jerusalem. The variety of flowers that carpet this great prairie is wonderful; chrysanthemum, camomile and the sweet smelling herbs, such as thyme, sage and lavender,—the pink broom, the purple, white and scarlet poppies, lupin, speedwell and the ubiquitous anemone,—the species of cyclamen called "cock o' the mountain" (*deck e-djebail*); around the villages the white trunks and light green foliage of the broad sycamore trees, with their old and gnarled trunks, fields of goldening wheat, giving forth a ripe, summer smell, make up a *tout ensemble* that has kept me wild with delight all the morning. The poet need not enquire,—

> "Oh, to what uses shall we put
> The wildweed flower that simply blows?"

Nothing calls out the pure, heartfelt sentiment of worship like these painted things. I have luxuriated this morning in

> "The vernal airs,
> Breathing the sweet smell of field and grove that tune
> The trembling leaves."

An English lady on the Steamer *L'Amerique*, who had traveled this whole Plain of Sharon from Carmel to Gaza, gave me this note and asked me to insert it in the diary I should keep. "The young grain, vivified by the heat, springs in prolific growth, carpeting the earth with refreshing verdure. The white and crimson aster, pale asphodel, scarlet anemone, cyclamen, blue and purple convolvulus, the butterfly-beauty of the wild poppy, the heliotrope, the pink pheasant's eye, the knotty hartwort, cover the land; while

> "The bird
> Makes his heart-voice amid the blaze of flowers."

As I stand upon a little mound and look over the plain, the grassy wastes stretch far before me, heavy with grain fields and dotted with flocks of sheep. The scarlet poppies glow like beds of live coals. The rich, crimson larkspur, golden daisy (our old home *buttercup* of girlish days), the pink convolvulus, and an army of smaller blossoms are so bright and dazzling that the earth looks richer than a pavement of precious jewels. The air is filled with a warm summer smell. How appropriately comes the thought to me here that Jehovah took the *agriculture* of his people under his own peculiar care. He discouraged *commerce* and gave them but one seaport, and that a poor and dangerous one. But He crowned the cultivator of His hills and plains with wreaths of blessings. Oh, what shoutings must have gone up from these harvest fields when the Hebrew farmers bore the last load to the garner and praised God aloud for his bounty. Upon the entrance of the hills, I hear for the first time, the *bulbul* or Oriental nightingale, singing in the briery thickets.

And from where I stand, I can see the camping-ground of the soldiers of Sennacherib, whose destruction has been made a theme of poesy by so many writers. Yonder went

"The sweep of that dark angel's wing,
Who brushed the thousands of Assyria's king
To darkness in a moment."

Then "the Lord sent an angel which cut off all the mighty men of valor, and the leaders and captains in the camp of the King of the Assyrians * * an hundred, four score and five thousand." Near Beyrout, I shall see, upon the mountain side, carved upon living rock, the boastful inscriptions which Sennacherib left there, as he came down here "conquering and to conquer." For very shame's sake, he ought, on his disgraceful return, to have had the lines *erased.*

3 P. M.

For the last three hours, *climbing* has been the watchword of our party. The moisture and slipperiness of the way, added to its steepness, has made it tedious in the extreme. It is the first really steep ascent we have been compelled to make during the week.

While resting here in this "shadow of a great rock in a weary land" (Isaiah xxxii: 2), we have amused ourselves with exhibiting our music-box to a crowd of natives. They came around clamoring and hungry for *backsheesh.* Old and young, male and female, the latter in "unwomanly rags," thrust their hands toward us, crowded us in, filled the air with their demands for *backsheesh.* One infant, not a year old, was held out by its gaunt and filthy mother, to say *batseese, batseese,* evidently the first word it had been taught. John said we should be eaten up alive. Mr. Fountain advised us to leave. Elliot was for threatening them with his gun. But I suggested *the music box.* It worked like a charm. The moment it began with Strauss' best waltz, the clamor ceased. Hands dropped. Mouths opened all agape. Smiles softened the rugged hungry faces. A low murmur of *tyeeb, tyeeb,* was the only sound heard. For a half hour I kept the changes going and all that time a sweet calm pervaded the group. Never before had I realized the force of the expression,—

"Music hath charms to soothe a savage breast."

I have succeeded to-day in taking down the notes and words of one of their marriage songs. Nobody seems to know the meaning of the words, and I think it probable it is like our "Tumty tum tidy," mere sounds without sense. I have set the harmony as well as I can.

Arab Marriage Music.

I took the opportunity, to examine with some care, one of the native houses of the better class, and I think its construction throws considerable light upon Bible passages. First, a high stone wall is built to enclose as much space as may be needed. This has but one entrance or gate. Next to the walls, on the inside, as many rooms are built as may be wanted, leaving an open court in the center, into which all the rooms as well as the gateway open. There is a well or cistern in the center of this court. The roof being flat, one can pass clear around the court on the house tops, and it is a common thing to see the dogs mounted there for convenience of barking at travelers. Small rooms are on the tops of the first story, and in these the people live, using the lower rooms for stables. A stone stairway rises from the courtyard to the house tops.

By urgent request, we partook of the hospitality of Sheikh Mustapha, the owner of this house.

Hospitality is held as a prime virtue by all genuine believers in Mohammed. If a stranger approaches at meal time, he is made to sit down like one of the family and share the food, no questions being asked as to who he is, whence he came or whither he goeth. The *Koran*, in the fourth chapter, commands, "Show kindness unto the stranger and the traveler."

Mustapha waited upon us with his wife and two sons, in accordance with the beautiful idea of hospitality derived, as they say, from El-Khalil, the name they give to Abraham, who "stood by his guests while they did eat." (Genesis xviii: 8.) It is a pleasant reflection that only a few miles south-east of here and in these very hills, that affecting incident occurred. The *lentile*, or small bean, called here *haddas*, was a portion of our repast to-day, and this, too, is connected with the story of the sale of Esau's birthright, which was made but a short distance southward.

There were no plates, knives or spoons upon the table of our kind entertainer, for, although the Turks for great feasts and for strangers, do set tables and spread out a dinner service, yet none of the Sheikhs of these Arab villages so far deviate from their ancient customs. So we all ate from the same dish and with our fingers, sitting upon the ground. The food was various and comprised, as Elliot remarked, corn, raisins, oil, milk, honey, eggs and mutton. As the bread was as thin as a wafer, we made forks and spoons of it, and so managed to eat and drink abundantly. When the repast was ended, water was brought in a skin bag and poured over our hands. Mustapha refused to receive a *backsheesh*, but I compelled him to accept a pair of scissors for his wife. The Arab women are not so particular about showing their faces to strangers as those of the Turks; but I noticed that when any of us looked steadily at our hostess, she turned her face away in confusion. The Sheikh, when I asked him through Hassan, told me that he had but one wife, but politely added that he was not at all scrupulous as to the number. I declined, however, to accept the delicate proposal so plainly implied.

Mustapha put his hand upon the cross that John wears and said: "Issa, tyeeb." That is, "Jesus, good," but whether his remark indicated any faith in Jesus, I could not understand. All these Mohammedans, however, do believe that Jesus was a *great prophet*, only second to Mohammed himself.

As Mustapha was familiar with the hospitable character of the patriarch

8

Abraham, I read to him from the book of Nehemiah, the history of that generous man. He was deeply interested. The verses I read were these: "There were at my table an hundred and fifty of the Jews and rulers, besides those that came to us from among the heathen that are round about us. Now that which was prepared for me daily was one ox and six choice sheep; also, fowls were prepared for me, and once in ten days, store of all sorts of wine; yet for all this, required I not the bread of the Governor, because the bondage was heavy upon the people. (Neh. v. 17.)

5 P. M.

We stopped for a half hour to witness a Mohammedan funeral; that of a man. The body was brought out of the village, divested of nearly all clothing, and lying upon a board covered with a sheet. At the grave, women washed it and then stuffed cotton in the eyes, ears, nose and mouth of the corpse, during which time the men were digging the grave. The body was almost hurled into the shallow pit, not the least ceremony being observed and no one seeming in the least affected by the same. After filling the grave and laying heavy stones in it as protection against jackals, dogs and hyenas, the men yelled three times, *Allah hu akbar* (God is great); and so all returned to the village, while we came away. This appeared to me the most unmannerly scene I ever witnessed.

All the English, French and American parties we meet, express surprise at the sparseness of our servants and following. They wonder particularly at our not employing one or more dragomans. Mr. Fountain tells them that we came to this country to direct, not to be directed. Freemen at home, we could little brook the tyranny to which parties are subjected who put themselves into the power of the professional dragomans. I saw one, to-day, the conventional type of his calling. Dressed in silk trowsers, with a bright *kafiah* wound, turban-like, round his head, and a dandy switch in his hand, he looked the Palestine *fop*, but he was in fact the Palestine tyrant. Taking the money of his employers in advance, he orders them about with a nonchalance that would be admirable were it not insufferable. We can call no such man master. Their affected vigilance, and frightful stories of the dangers of the way, are only parts of the system to persuade their employers of the necessity of their enormous guards. One gentleman whom we met, yesterday, had nine mules, five horses, and more than thirty servants! Poor young man. But little he will see of the Holy Land.

The only person in our party who presents any appearance of romance is our muleteer or *moukar*. He has a camel's hair sash around him actually stuffed with knives and pistols. His Syrian jacket of scarlet cloth is elaborately embroidered behind like a priest's. Yet, his face is villainous in feature, almost wolfish in repulsiveness, with a nose like a vulture's beak, a cunning, sensual mouth, small, glittering black eyes, hid under shaggy brows that almost meet over his nose, and teeth white and sharp. His three assistants are great, stupid-looking natives, dressed in flaunting red jackets and greasy turbans, but barefoot.

We have had, to-day, some most interesting conversation with a group of Israelites who are keeping their Sabbath, quietly by the roadside. Would that such intelligent men could but comprehend that the Messiah *is come*, and have already builded *that other Jerusalem*, that our foot-weary race so much need to reach!

How can we Americans look with complacency upon such systems of religious faith as papists practice here? Here, for instance, is a community of men and women who, if they simply read, circulate or defend any book named in the forbidden Index, are excluded from church-fellowship here, and from heavenly glory hereafter. I could no more summon up holy feelings while witnessing their stilted forms here, than when I saw the Shakers, at Lebanon, New York, or the Moslems, at Joppa.

MR. FOUNTAIN'S DIARY.

CAMP SABBATH, 8 P. M.

Our truant boy was brought into "Camp Dismas" by the English gentlemen shortly after daylight. We had feared our name "Dismas" would be changed into *Achor* (trouble). His return gave the glow of gratitude to our devotions. We read the 13th to 16th Chapters of Judges, and Hebrews 11th and 12th Chapters, then sung together to the "Old Hundred," the world-wide stanza "Praise God from whom all blessings flow." The deep, grand bass of our English visitors resounded through the hills around Latroon. How kind these gentlemen have been to us; and how much we owe them! In regard to Elliot, they have justly said that a boy of twelve who could light his candle amid the desolations of those hills, and cooly record his observations in his diary as he did, has the stamina of a great man. I am glad to learn from Elliot that his childish prejudice against the English, which he has expressed, sometimes offensively, is now removed. Most of our American boys imbibe this feeling to some extent from their school-books of history.

The day's journey has been with but little excitement, and we have now established our camp for the Sunday's rest.

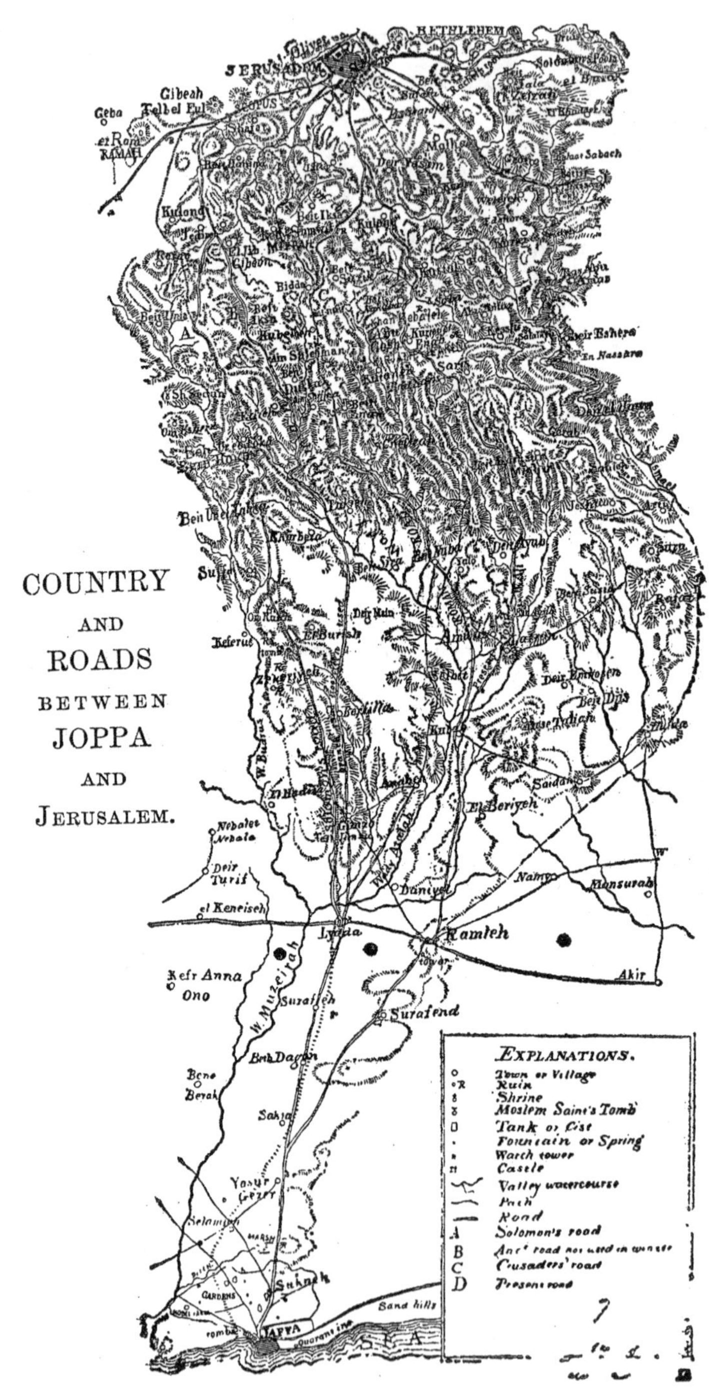

COUNTRY AND ROADS BETWEEN JOPPA AND JERUSALEM.

CHAPTER VII.

A SABBATH REST IN SIGHT OF JERUSALEM.

Arabic words—Lord's Prayer in Arabic—Native village—Dog licking sores—The wise men from the East—Twelve o'clock everywhere—Scorpion—Locust—Sugar cane—Dogs in Jerusalem—Military music—View of Jerusalem—The Koran—The Jewish party—Superstitions—The Lion of the Tribe of Judah—An altar of twelve stones—The Bible the best guide here—Sabbath musings in sight of Jerusalem.

ELLIOT'S DIARY.

SUNDAY, March 21st, 1869. 11 A. M.

TO-DAY I have finished learning one hundred Arabic words as I promised. *Kamar* means moon; *jabal*, mountain: *kinzeer*, pig; *harath*, plow; *arnab*, rabbit; *zabeeb*, raisins; *sakker*, rock; *habbul*, rope; *sarje*, saddle; *hareer*, silk; *hite*, string; *soccar*, sugar; *rard*, thunder; *tabak*, tobacco; *sharb*, young; *ams*, yesterday; *kahikah*, truth; *zoor*, lie; *tar*, fly; *kareeb*, to-morrow. Mr. Fountain says that my spelling of these words would make a grammarian titter; but that anybody can pronounce them from my spelling and that's all I want. He says that the usual method of spelling Arabic words, adopted by travelers in their books, is often funnier than mine. Even the great Dr. Robinson spelt Mohammed, *Muhammed.* He says the Arabic language is the *grandchild* of the Hebrew, in this way: Chaldee and Syriac are *children* of the Hebrew language; and Arabic is the *child* of the Chaldee and Syriac. This makes it a grandchild. Our folks at home always pronounce the words *Arab* and *Arabic* wrong. Both the words should be strongly accented on the *first* syllable, not the *second.*

Every day that I practice on this language I get it lower and lower down in my stomach. At first I spoke it as we do the English language, in the upper part of my throat and used my tongue, teeth and lips. But I soon learned that you can't talk Arabic that way. A man whose tongue was cut out by Emir Besheer, could talk just as well as ever with the stump. When one of these Arabs gets *bronchitis* it don't hurt him any as an orator; but if he has *consumption* he goes speechless. Ventriloquism is nothing in Arabic; everybody does it. They have more words for the same thing than you can imagine. For the word *snake* they have eighty-two words in Arabic; for *sword* they have one hundred and thirty words. I should like to see Webster's Unabridged in Arabic. Lucky for old Noah Webster he wasn't born out this way.

Now, too, I can say the Lord's Prayer correctly from an Arabic copy that Mr. Fountain has given me:

The Lord's Prayer In Arabic.

الصلوة الربّانيّة

ابانا الذي في السموات . ليتقدّس اسمك . ليأتِ ملكوتك .
لتكن مشيئتك كما في السماء كذلك على الارض . خبزنا كفافنا
أعطنا اليوم . واغفر لنا ذنوبنا كما نغفر نحن ايضاً للمذنبين الينا .
ولا تدخلنا في تجربةٍ . لكن نجّنا من الشرير . لان لك الملك
والقوة والمجد الى الابد .

آمين

THE WAY THE WORDS ARE PRONOUNCED.

EL SALAT EL RABBANIET.

Abana el lazi fee el samawat, layat kudus ismack. La taty malakoutack, la takoun masheyatack. Kamma fee el samawat, kazalick ala el ard. Khubzena kafafina atina el youm, wa agfour lina zinoubena kamma nuhn, ayedan, la mouznibena elayua. Wala t'dakhelna fee tajaribin, lakin naijina min ishshurrer. La in, lack el moulk, w'al kowat, w'al majd, illa el abad. Amin.

We have spent the forenoon very quietly in and near the tents. I took Hassan with me over to a village not far off and asked the people a lot of questions. First, I was introduced to the sheikh who had on a clean shirt. He kissed my hand. I asked him how he was. He answered (in Arabic) *Thanks be to God.* I asked him the same question again. He answered, *God is great.* I asked him the third time the same question. He answered, *God is bountiful.* And that's as near as he came to answering it. Then he asked me for *backsheesh* The valley outside of the village was enamelled with flowers, but oh the horrid appearance of the interior. Harriet wanted to go there, but when I came back I said *don't go.* It is too bad for human creatures to live that way. It really would seem if this profusion of flowers might teach the people some grace; but it does not.

While I was sauntering through the village, I saw a dog engaged, actually, in *licking the sores* of a poor child that lay in the sun, with nobody to keep it off. The sight made me sick but it called to memory the affecting story of Lazarus as told by our Saviour in Luke xvi; where " dogs came and licked his sores." This is one of the first stories my mother ever told me. I also saw some children munching bread at the corner of a house, one of them, a little girl, broken-nosed and ugly enough. As they stopped to look at me and ask for *backsheesh*, some dogs rushed in and snatched the bread from their hands. Then I thought of the passage in Mark vii: 27; "it is not meet to take the children's bread and to cast it unto the dogs."

From our tent door we see, a mile below us, the road that runs across the plain of Rephaim from Jerusalem to Bethlehem, and the aqueduct that used to supply the temple with water from Solomon's Pools. I imagine the wise men coming from the east across yonder plain, with their gifts, "gold, frankincense and myrrh." (Matthew ii: 11.) They passed along this very road. The Catholics pretend to know the names of those three men: Jaspar, Melchior and Balthazar, and probably they have their photographs of them, or pretend to have. But the Greek Christians also know their names and give them quite differently, Galgalatha, Malgalathe and Saraphie. I like this better. The Jews also know their names just as well, and they give them: Appelius, Amerrius and Damasus. I wish I knew their *real* names. Be they what they may, yonder is the road they traveled over on their way to Bethlehem.

Josephus tells of the young men who used to accompany King Solomon as he used to ride along this way. The young men had their hair powdered with *gold dust*. When I first read that story several years ago, I wondered to myself whether any of that gold dust could be found there now! What notions very little boys do have!

NOON.

It is curious to think as the sun comes on the meridian here, and so makes it noon, that in New York it is not yet five o'clock in the morning. At Rome, people are just going to church to *morning* service, while at Pekin, they may be going to *evening* service. As the sun moves westward, he sets the church bells ringing for Jesus, somewhere every minute in the twenty-four hours. That is grand. It is about *midnight* now at San Francisco, in California, yet I hear the church bells sounding for *noon* at Bethlehem, on my right hand, and at Jerusalem on my left. How I wish my pastor was here to enjoy the same privilege. What a sermon he could preach upon it! Why don't every preacher visit this country?

A boy brought me a locust and a scorpion preserved in arrack in a vial, and I have been reading all Bible passages where those two insects are mentioned. The locust has some curious black marks on the back of its wings which Hassan says are Hebrew words that mean, "There is only one God. He overcomes the mighty, and the locusts are part of His armies which he sends against sinners." That's what he says, but I can't see anything there but some square figures. The people here are expecting the locusts to come in great quantities next year. They were here about three years ago. They are an awful calamity. Hassan says that a full-grown locust looks like a boy soldier mounted on a pony. And in fact the book of Revelations ix: 7; has it, "the shapes of the locusts were like unto horses prepared for battle." The color of the locust is green, all but part of his head, which is yellow. It has two upper wings, green and leathery, with a white spot on each. These wings are extended, while flying, like the great sails of a ship while going before the wind. The locust has two under-wings, thin and transparent like cobwebs. When young, they say you can't tell a locust from a grasshopper. I wouldn't think, to look at this locust, that the insect could do so much mischief as it does; only, when I was in Iowa, last year, I saw what devastation the grasshoppers had made there; and they are not half so large. A locust is a sort of Goliath of a grasshopper. Some kinds of locusts, Hassan says, are so beautifully marked, that children make playthings of them. He says that women sometimes put locust eggs in their ears to cure earache. In the 8th century, the poorer classes in this country, used *to eat locusts* boiled in oil. It was only ten or fifteen miles east of here that John, the Baptist, came "preaching in the wilderness of Judæa, * * * and his meat was locusts and wild honey." (Matt. iii.) But Mr. Fountain thinks that *locusts* in this passage were not *insects* but the fruit of carob trees. Still I prefer to believe he ate *insects*. Webster's Dictionary says that the locust is a jumping orthoperous insect like the grasshopper, from which it is distinguished by the shortness of its antennæ and by having only three joints in each foot as seen from above. It has a greater power of flight than the grasshopper. The migratory locust (*locusta migratoria*) is the most injurious European species. These insects are at times so numerous in Africa and the south of Asia as to devour every green thing; and when they migrate they fly in an immense cloud.

My scorpion is nearly two inches long, and an ugly looking customer he is. He came from the rocks down by Ain Jiddy, twenty miles southeast from here, where the weather is very hot. In these hills, Hassan says, the scorpion does not *ripen* till July. That is, he does not come out of his hole sociably and appear in company, till that month. Then they are very plenty, and before you pitch your tent you must roll the stones over and pick the scorpions out and sweep them away. The Arabs call the scorpion by a word that sounds like *krab*. The old Jews called the scorpion *akrab*, and there is a place twenty miles south of here named *Akrabbim*, or the Hill of Scorpions. A delightful summer residence, a hill of scorpions must be! Something like the Iowa family I heard of, who built their house right over a snake-den, and labored all the spring months to kill them. Hassan says the scorpion's sting is not worse than a hornet's. Nobody is ever killed by them in this country. Mr. Fountain put his boot on last summer, when he was at Kedes, with three scorpions in it. That was up by Hasbeiya, in Mount Lebanon. He says he never took a boot off so quick in all his life as he did then. I do not understand what our Saviour meant in contrasting an *egg* with a *scorpion*. (Luke xi : 12.) Hassan says he once woke up and shook out more than a dozen scorpions from his *arba* or cloak. It was a cool night in the fall of the year, and the scorpions were enjoying the warm blanket as well as the Arab. But they never bit him. I have read where scorpions sting themselves when they get angry. I mean to try that, and see whether they will sting themselves, the first live ones I get hold of. The Bible passages I have just read, in which the word scorpion occurs, are these: "Their torment was as the torment of a scorpion when he striketh a man." (Rev. ix : 5.) "I will chastise you with scorpions." (1 Kings xii : 11.) "Thou dost dwell among scorpions." (Ezekiel ii : 6.) "I give unto you power to tread on serpents and scorpions." (Luke x : 19.) If I had a live one here I would build a fire around him till he should—

"Lie a beleagured scorpion, rolled
In his last deadly, venemous fold."

I wonder what that foolish son of Solomon's (Rehoboam, B. C. 975) meant when he threatened to chastise the Israelites with scorpions? (1 Kings xii : 11.)

Webster's dictionary says the scorpion is a pedipalpous arachnidan of the genus Scorpio, but this does not make it much plainer to me. I saw the constellation *Scorpio*, the eighth sign of the zodiac, last night, and a grand sight it is. The dictionary says scorpions have an elongated body, terminated by a long, slender tail, formed by six joints, the last of which terminates in an arcuated and very acute sting, which effuses a venomous liquid. This sting gives rise to excruciating pain, but is unattended either with redness or swelling, except in the axillary or inguinal glands, when an extremity is affected. It is very seldom, if ever, destructive of life. Scorpions are found pretty widely dispersed in the warm climates of both the old and new worlds.

The same boy who brought me my locust and scorpion, sold me a large bunch of sugar cane stalks, which grew just beyond Jebel-usdum. That is about forty miles southeast of here, where old Sodom once stood. He says that *sukker*, as he calls sugar, is *tyeeb*. I agree with him. That's my notion, too. The Knights Templar used to raise sugar cane down in that valley eight hundred years ago. Who knows but what all the sugar that is used in this country may some day be raised there when the Yankee farmers get hold of the Holy Land! People in this country use no sugar except loaf sugar, pure and white. Brown sugar and crushed sugar would not fetch anything in the bazaars at Joppa. The people are great on all sorts of sugar candy, and some of the best candy I ever saw is made there.

Sitting in our tent doors which are faced to the northeast, so that we can look directly towards Jerusalem, I can distinctly hear the barking of the dogs in that city, although it is three or four miles from here, so clear is the air. The city of Constantinople is said to have sixty thousand dogs, and at night the city rings with their serenadings. One traveler calls it a vast canine riot. Mr. Fountain says he never saw a native Mohammedan fondling a dog. Even the little boys and girls will not touch the pretty little puppies. I saw Hassan throw his dinner away last Friday, and go without, because Sweet-Home had merely smelt of it. He cursed the poor *kelb* in Arabic, for five minutes. Arabic curses are awful things if they *mean* as heavy as they *sound*. Sweet-Home seemed to know very well what they meant, for he fairly quailed under them. At last I had to threaten Hassan if he did not stop such slang, I would have him discharged.

While listening to the roar of dogs in yonder holy city, I recall that affecting sentence in Revelations xxii, descriptive of the New Jerusalem, that declares no *dogs* shall enter it. This is quite the opposite idea to the Indian's.

"He thinks, admitted to that equal sky,
His faithful *dog* shall bear him company."

6 P. M.

And now I hear the military music at the *Serai* or Governor's palace, which is played at sunset. Mr. Fountain says they always play at sunset. What a roar of brass instruments and drums! Surely they play no tune! Yet, it sounds well at this distance, and reminds me of the passage in Daniel iii : 15 : " The sound of the cornet, flute, harp, sackbut, psaltery and dulcimer."

JOHN'S DIARY.

CAMP SABBATH, Sunday, March 21, 1869. 4 P. M.

Mr. Fountain told us, on *L'Amerique*, two weeks ago, that Sunday would always be one of our busiest days in camp, and so we have found it, to-day, although one of the rules he laid down for us, was that we should not walk more than "a Sabbath day's journey" from camp. That means, according to the old Hebrew idea, one thousand one hundred and fifty-five yards, or eighteen yards less than two-thirds of a mile.

The "business" that Mr. Fountain referred to, however, was writing up diaries, studying Scripture applications, and contemplating the Holy Land and its objects, from the door of our tent. Thus far every step we have taken on the soil of Palestine, has offered some new witness of the truth of the sacred story. We are encamped in full view of Jerusalem, looking towards the north-east. Long lines of walls, crowned with notched parapets, and strengthened with towers, surround the city. A few domes and spires appear, as at Joppa ; also some clusters of cypress and a palm tree or two. By the aid of my field-glass, I can easily study the shape of the "Neby Daoud," or Tomb of David, and looking far over Jerusalem, and beyond Mount Olivet, can see the long, brown wall of the Mountains of Moab and Gilead, full thirty miles to the eastward.

We have spent the day chiefly in religious conversation and reading. It has been a *Dies ægyptica* to us. Much of our talk has been upon the Mohammedan religion. We took our English copy of the Koran and dipped into it, through all the one hundred and fourteen chapters, a passage or two from each. What a strange congeries of brilliant and sublime thoughts diluted with puerile absurdities and lies. The first chapter, how beautiful! "Praise be to God the Lord of all creatures; the Most Merciful; the King of the Judgment Day. We worship Thee; to Thee we make our prayers. Direct us in the right path; in the path of those with whom Thou art gracious—not of those with whom Thou art angry, or who go astray." Who can help saying AMEN to such a touching supplication as that?

Mr. Fountain thinks that the Mohammedans are in such a peculiar condition just now in regard to religious matters, that if some great reformer should rise up amongst them, such a man, for instance, as Abd-el-Kader, of Damascus, the whole following of an hundred and fifty millions might be converted to Christianity in a single generation. What a sublime thought! They believe in Moses, already; they believe, also, in Jesus; if only they would cast away their false addition, Mohammed!

A party of Jews called upon us, the same that we saw spending the Jewish Sabbath, yesterday, back among the hills. They sat for an hour. Mr. Fountain calculates that there are about fifty thousand Jews in Palestine; in Jerusalem alone about ten thousand. These are the people whom Solomon described as "a great people that cannot be numbered or counted for multitude." After the dispersion of Titus they took the name of "Mourners of Jerusalem." In 1163 their learned men were entitled Lecturers and Masters of Schools, the Flower of the Learned, the Prop of the University, etc. In 1839, a company of Presbyterian preachers came here from Scotland, to see the condition and character of God's ancient people, and I have read the "narrative" of that mission. It is full of interest.

I observe a marked difference between these Jews and those we see in America. The forehead of these is loftier, and their eyes are larger and more frank in their expression. The nose is more delicate in its prominence, and the face has a purer oval. I do not know how to account for this, yet all our party noticed it. Aunt Liddy would hardly believe these to be Jews, at all.

They talked French very well, and seemed to be pleased to converse with us. One of them read from Mr. Fountain's Hebrew Scriptures, the word of Isaiah: "I will wait upon the Lord that hideth his face from the house of Jacob, and I will look for Him." He seemed to feel deeply the force of these words in this place. He told us he had once spent several months in the United States. Unfortunate race! What are they but a by-word among the heathen, and a shaking of the head among the people? Yet, there is a simplicity in their faith, by which a Jew, transplanted thousands of miles, and after many generations, is the same genuine Jew. When I was a boy, we used to be told that the Rothschilds intended to buy up this country from the Turkish government. Mr. Fountain says the story is unfounded; that those bankers have never expressed any such intention. That great firm of money-changers has other uses for its money. If any rich Jew has a yearning in this direction, it is Mr. Moses Montefiore, of England. Our own countryman, Judah Touro, of New Orleans, did more for Palestine than any one else; but he never talked of buying it up.

The Mussulmans in Palestine are not more superstitious than the Catholics. Bayard Taylor thinks that a pious Moslem is a better man than a bigoted Catholic. The Catholic and Greek Christians have mixed so many human inventions with the simple religion of Jesus, that the Christian faith here is as badly alloyed as the Turkish coins, which are one part silver, nineteen parts alloy. Strange, what education will do. Even the historian, Rollin, (born January 13; 1661, died 1742) used to pray every day to the Virgin Mary, for mothers; to St. Joseph, for fathers; and to Jesus Christ, for children. The book does not say that he prayed to God, at all. Yet, the bible gives us no authority for using Mary, and still less Joseph, as mediators.

A native has brought me a huge jawbone taken from a cavern in the hills near by, which, upon careful examination, Mr. Fountain pronounces to be that of a *full grown lion*. This discovery has particular value to me, for we are *in the hills of Judah*, whose tribal badge was a CROWNED LION. These animals were once so numerous in Palestine, that the Hebrew language had *seven names* for lion, corresponding with the seven periods of his life. This recalls Shakespeare's division of the life of a man. First the cub; then the young lion; the full-grown lion; the lion advanced in age and strength; the lion in his utmost vigor; the aged lion, and finally, the lion in his dotage. The reasons for his disappearance from this country are the increase of population and the use of fire-arms. A few hundred miles east of this they are plenty enough. When Nebuchadnezzar destroyed the Jewish nation, B. C. 588, and the land was left desolate more than fifty years, the lions increased in great numbers. So in the State of Tennessee, during the late war, from 1861 to 1865, owing to the absence of the men in the army, rabbits, deer, turkies and other wild game increased greatly. A few more years of war and these would have become a real nuisance. Once these hills of Judah reverberated with the awful challenge of the male lion. No fox better knows hedgerows, ditches, drains and coverts around him, than the monster to which this jawbone belonged, knew the country between Jerusalem and Gaza. In the lairs of the now vanished forests, the now vanished lion once hid himself, and, as the thick roots of the oak trees are all that remain to show the former existence of great forests of oak, so the bones of the lion, exposed in the recesses of caverns, betray their existence in the days of old. Within five miles of where I write, the great Benaiah that "son of a valiant man who had done many acts," "went down and slew a lion in the midst of a pit in time of snow." (2 Sam. xxiii; 21.) Well might David honor such valor, for that poet hero himself had set an example of personal daring when he kept his father's sheep in these hills, and there came a lion and a bear and took a lamb out of the flock. Then the shepherd boy, who was a youth of sixteen years, ruddy and of a fair countenance, "went after the lion and smote him, and delivered it out of his mouth; and when he arose against the youth, he caught him by his beard and smote him and slew him." (1 Sam. xvii: 34.) The writer of the book of Ecclesiasticus (xlvii: 3;) poetizes this exploit in these words: "he played with lions as with kids and with bears as with lambs." Measuring the strong jawbone and computing the power of the muscles that must once have occupied these cavities, I can see how the king of beasts could carry in his mouth an ordinary ox. These muscles, when living, were so hard as to blunt the edge of a knife; in size and firmness they were like the wire-rope used for the rigging of ships. Observing the structure of the jaw, I see the force of the comparison used in Isaiah lxv: 25; "the lion shall eat straw like a bullock." Hezekiah's lamentation gets its force from this: "As a lion so will he break all my bones." (Isaiah xxxviii: 13.) "The righteous are as bold as a lion," said Solomon, who, doubtless, often hunted the animal among these very hills. And "the King's wrath is as a lion," he himself proved in the affair of his brother Adjoniah. (1 King's ii: 25.) "He lieth in wait secretly as a lion," said David, who had so frequently scanned these rocks, lest a crouching lion should spring from thence upon his flocks. (Ps. x: 9.) Job, amidst his despairing accusations against the chastening God could find no image so suggestive as this: "Thou huntest me as a fierce lion;" for he had often chased the royal brute among his native mountains of Gilead, away in the north-east yonder.

But all these lion images are faint when compared with the use made of the lion in describing the character of JESUS. As John stood weeping before the throne that was set in heaven, one of the four and twenty elders, clothed with white raiment and adorned with a crown of gold, said unto him: "weep not; beheld the LION OF THE TRIBE OF JUDAH, the root of David hath prevailed. This figure does not refer alone to the strength, courage and ferocity of the lion, but it is the symbol of sovereignty, and being the achievement of the princely tribe of Judah, is peculiarly applicable to JESUS CHRIST, born yonder at Bethlehem, four miles to the southward, and descended, in human line, from the tribe that once inhabited these hills. The last reference of travelers to lions in Palestine, is that of Willibald in the 8th century, who speaks of meeting one while traveling a little ways north of Jerusalem. Bones of the lion are still frequently found among the gravel on the banks of the Jordan, not far below the Sea of Galilee, seventy-five miles to the north-eastward.

8 P. M.

Elliot and I have just completed building an altar of twelve stones here, to commemorate our Sabbath encampment in sight of Jerusalem. It is four feet square and six feet high. I hope it will attract the attention of future travelers. Perhaps, long after we are dead and gone, some one will take it down. If so, he will find a scrap of parchment on which I painted, with red ochre, this verse,—

"Pilgrim, halting, staff in hand,
Even this path where thou dost stand,
Endeth in a better land,
Far away, far away,
Far, far away."

We dedicated the twelve stones of the altar to those twelve American travelers who have shed such abounding light upon the history of the Holy Land. They are Robinson, Thompson and Barclay, for the three heavy basis blocks. Next, Lynch, Durbin and Osborne compose the next tier of blocks. The third round in the pile ,we have given to Newman, Randall and Phelps, and the fourth to Taylor, Burt and Prime. We feel the right to a little national pride upon summing up the labors of these our fellow countrymen in exploring the Holy Land.

We have proved during the past week that the Holy Bible is the truest guide to a traveler in this country. The *Book* thus far has conducted us *through the land* and led us in safety to the sight of Salem's towers, even as it will lead us, infallibly, we believe, across the plains and mountains of life's pilgrimage, to the sight and to the gates and to the life of the New Jerusalem. Truly it has been "a lamp unto our feet and a light unto our path," (Ps. cxix: 105); "The word of the Lord is tried." (2 Sam. xxii: 31.) Is it not strange that in this country where it was written, the Bible is almost *a sealed book* to the Greek, Catholic, Maronite and Syrian Christians? In their breviaries or prayer books, there are less quotations from the Word of God than in Mohammed's Koran itself! And this reminds me that the prophet Amos, who lived yonder at Tekoah, about ten miles south-east of our camp, long ago threatened this very dearth of God's Word, in the well-known passage: "Behold the days come, saith the Lord God, that I will send a famine in the land, not a famine of *bread*, nor a thirst for *water*, but of *hearing the words of the Lord*." (Amos viii: 11.) This threat is already amply fulfilled. The eastern Christians neither read the Bible nor hear it read by their priests. In its place are invocations to saints, false legends, prayers not at all modelled on the Scriptural forms, and contortions of body, compared with which the seven postures of the

Mohammedans are gracefulness itself. How thankful I feel to God, who gave me Protestant parents, whose chief care has been that I should myself "search the Scriptures," thinking in them "to have eternal life."

HARRIET'S DIARY.

CAMP SABBATH, Sunday, March 21st, 1869. 4 A. M.

Our morning hour is filled with joy. *A Sabbath in Palestine;* oh, how delightful! Mr. Fountain, who is addicted to the use of coffee, rose by daylight for a cup of his needed beverage. This awoke me and I was not long in getting out to enjoy the early morning and the bright-hued flowers. But early as I was, the divine spirit of spring had preceded me, and I felt the poet's words to be true:

"I got me flowers to strew thy way,
I got me boughs off many a tree,
But THOU wast up by break of day,
And brought THY sweets along with Thee."

The poets help me at this moment with abundant aid:

"Ah, see!—the sun himself, on wings
Of glory up the east he springs!"

"King of the East although he seems, and girt,
With song and flame and fragrance slowly lifts
His golden feet on those empurpled stairs
That climbs into the windy halls of heaven!"

The murmuring bees are pursuing their voluptuous toil. The dew on the rocks brings out the singular pink streaks that we shall see upon the rocks around Stephen's Gate at Jerusalem and elsewhere. Aunt Liddy who usually indulges in a morning nap, has joined me. To give us all a delightful surprise, John has just slipped down to a low place out of sight, flute in hand, and before we knew he was out of bed at all, he salutes us with a beautiful voluntary upon the air of *Home, Sweet Home*, that fills our eyes with tears. I shall never hear that air again without associating it with the anemones, and the hills southwest of Jerusalem, and the arrowy Jordan that gleams far in the northeast yonder.

NOON.

After our customary religious exercises, which, this morning were prolonged to an hour or more, we had breakfast, and then, sitting at the entrance of our tent and looking eastward, we grouped around Mr. Fountain and questioned him upon such objects as came within our great range of vision. The longer we tarry in Palestine, the more use we make of his well-filled and experienced mind. The first two or three days we scarcely asked him any questions; now we are glad to ply him diligently with them.

Before us, in plain view is the road that leads from Jerusalem to Bethlehem. It once reflected that STAR,—

"The LIGHT, that led
The holy elders with the gift of myrrh."

This is

"Where the flying star
Led on the grayhaired wisdom of the East."

It saw Solomon, ten centuries earlier, passing daily in royal state with chariots, horsemen, and a princely following, powdered with gold dust, to his favorite "sealed fountain" and "garden of delights" at Etham, four miles to the southward. It saw, nine centuries still earlier, *Jacob* flying *northward* from the face of his brother Esau, then returning again to the south to lose in death, Rachel his best beloved, whose low, white tomb I see yonder, even now, far to the right, just upon the edge of Bethlehem. It saw *Joseph* going alone, northward, in search of his brethren—brethren only in name. It saw the ministers of Herod, hurrying to Bethlehem, to execute their Royal Master's decree. But what has not yonder pathway beheld during the forty centuries it has been used!

That plain, yonder, is Rephaim, where David won great victories over the Philistines. Well he knew every undulation of this plain, and every recess of these hills; for here, in boyhood's days, he had been himself a shepherd and fed his father's flocks. To this plain refers the beautiful song of Montgomery, which we sung this morning—

"When marshalled o'er the nightly plain."

Yonder, far to the southeast, beyond the Dead Sea, I see the Mountains of Moab, from whence the pious Ruth came, who "cared for the things of the Lord, that she might be holy, both in body and spirit." What sweet thoughts are those embraced in her immortal words: "Entreat me not to leave thee;" the model of the purest womanly devotion. I consecrate these lines to the association of ideas:

In the land of Bethlehem-judah
  Let us linger, let us wander;
Ephrath's sorrow, Rachel's pillar,
  Lieth in the valley yonder.
And the yellow barley harvest
  Floods it with a golden glory.
Let us back into the old time,
  Dreaming of her tender story,
Of her true heart's strong devotion
  From beyond the Dead Sea water,
From the heathen land of Moab,
  Mahlon's wife and Marah's daughter.

And I must not forget to include, in the events so dear to this locality, Abraham, with his son and his servants, first going northward along that road, then a *via dolorosa;* afterwards, going southward a *via triumphalis.*

Yonder, at Bethlehem and at Jerusalem, were first sung those delicious canticles of the birth and infancy of Jesus, the angel-hymns of Mary, of Zacharias, and of aged Simeon.

From where I sit, I see plainly the Mosk of Omar, on the Mount of Moriah.

"That enamelled cupola that towers
All rich with arabesque of gold and flowers
And the mosaic floor beneath."

7 P. M.

Some Arab girls, intuitively divining my love for wild flowers, have brought me a splendid bunch of them. Among these are the exquisite blossoms of the white and purple cyclamen. I have endeavored, in vain, to learn from the girls the Arab names of these floral gems. Their pronunciation of Arabic words has the defects of juvenile lisp and whisper.

One of these flowers is a lily, of which I make this drawing:

Lily of Palestine.

It was with lily-work that the Phœnician architects of Solomon's Temple decorated the capitals of the columns, and the rim of the brazen Sea was adorned in like manner. (1 Kings vii.) No country in the world abounds in so many species of lilies as the Holy Land.

One of these Syrian girls has a smooth, bronze skin, with regular features, really pretty. Another is ornamented in the most singular manner with a turquois pin fastened *into the flesh*, one on each side, and flat to the nose! She would not let me inspect, as I desired, the manner in which the pins are kept in place.

And here comes a pair of the sweet doves of Palestine, the bird which has afforded the inspired writers such acceptable types of simplicity, fidelity and innocence. (Hoz. vii : 11; Matt. x : 16.) Their cooing is a delightful sequel to our music, and no doubt was a cheering music to the three loving mothers, Rachel, Ruth, Mary, with whom this locality is associated. The dove's rapidity of flight is alluded to in Ps. lv : 6; its beauty of plumage, lxviii : 13; its dwelling in the rocks and valleys, Jerem. xlviii : 28, and Ez. vii : 16; its mournful voice, in Is. xxxviii : 14, lix : 11, and Nahum ii : 7; its amativeness, Canticles i : 15, ii : 14, etc. This emblem of the Syrian Venus abounds yet in Syria, though the legend is forgotten. This military emblem upon the standards of the Assyrians and Babylonians is referred to in Jer. xxv : 38, etc. It must long have been remembered by the Jews as their symbol of war.

To-day, begins Passion Week, which by so large a portion of the Christian world is consecrated to religious thought. The Scripture referring to it is this: "Then Jesus, six days before the Passover, came to Bethany, where Lazarus was, which had been dead, whom He raised from the dead. Then they made Him a supper; and Martha served, but Lazarus was one of them that sat at the table with Him. Then took Mary a pound of ointment of spikenard, very costly, and anointed the feet of Jesus, and wiped His feet with her hair, and the house was filled with the odor of the ointment." (John xii : 1–3.)

This affecting incident occurred in the village just beyond yonder low range of hills; I hope next Sunday to visit the spot and read the passage there.

At mother's request we had brought from home Mr. Cull's beautiful Sacred Cantata of Ruth, the words by our dear friend, Rev. Sidney Dyer. And as the sun went beyond the hills behind us, and the cool air of evening began to steal over us, we gathered in our little group, around the little book, and sang it through. Prompted by hearing some bells in Jerusalem, we began with Mr.

Lowry's "Sabbath Bells' Chime," which is inserted in the appendix to the volume. Then John played on his flute the introduction to the Cantata. Mr. Fountain sung the bass parts. Elliot, with his sweet, boyish alto, took Naomi and Orphah. My part, of course, was Ruth, while John managed the rest. The choruses rather suffered from inequality in voices; but there was no complaint from our auditory, either the five score Arabs, young and old, who sat cross-legged around us, or the companies of pilgrims, passing along the road to and from Bethlehem, who easily heard us when we took the higher parts of the music. The Arabs cried *tyeeb* in tones of most satisfactory enthusiasm, and the pilgrims waved their hands. One group of Englishmen even threw up their hats, and gave three genuine British cheers, in acknowledgment of our success.

"Oh, beautiful for situation, the joy of the whole earth is Mount Zion, on the side of the north, the city of the Great King." (Psalm xlviii : 2.)

"My soul there is a country
Afar beyond the stars,
Where stands a winged sentry
All skillful in the wars."

The number of national flags displayed at the different consulates, in Jerusalem, is quite large. We can see American, English, French, Prussian, Russian, Italian, and Austrian. The Crescent and Star of the Turkish standard flaunts, of course, above them all. But there is no *Jewish flag* seen in Jerusalem. Nowhere does the Lion of the Tribe of Judah answer to this bracing mountain breeze that so gallantly shakes the standards of other nations. Nowhere the Ravening Wolf of Benjamin, to whom these hills at first belonged. Yet, Jerusalem is the ancient possession of those tribes. I wonder do they preserve their tribal standards anywhere concealed, ready to be "full high advanced" when the promised time shall come? Oh, that the Bounding Hart of Napthali may yet float over his native mountains!

"The Land of Promise had been chosen by Supreme Wisdom, for the inheritance of a people destined to be unconquerable, while they continued pure. It was surrounded on all sides but one by mountain and desert, and that one was defended by the sea, which at the same time opened to it the intercourse with the richest countries of the west. On the north, opposed to the vast population of Asia Minor, it was protected by the double range of the Libanus and Antilibanus, a region of forests and defiles, at all seasons nearly impassable to chariots and cavalry; and, during winter, barred up with torrents and snows. The whole frontier on the east and south was a wall of mountain, rising from a desert; a durable barrier, over which no enemy, exhausted by the privations of an Asiatic March, could force their way against a brave army, waiting fresh within its own confines. But even if the Syrian wastes of sand, the fiery soil of Arabia, left the invaders strength to master the mountain defences, the whole interior was full of the finest positions for defence, that ever caught the soldier's eye. Mournful and yet beautiful to the Christian's heart must this city ever be." This sentence, from Salathiel, is full of thought to one who sits here overlooking so much of the country he describes.

9

While talking with a Jewish rabbi, to-day, I asked him if he had ever heard of the Wandering Jew? He said no. Then I read to him from Salathiel, this passage: "There has appeared from time to time, in Europe, during the last thousand years, a mysterious individual—a sojourner in all lands, yet a citizen of none; professing the profoundest secrets of opulence, yet generally living in a state of poverty; astonishing every one by the evidence of his intercourse with the eminent characters of every age, yet connected with none, without lineage, possession, or pursuit, on earth—a wanderer, and unhappy." But he had never heard of him before, and thinks there has never lived such a man.

10 P. M.

Before retiring, I make my last entries in the first portion of my diary. The various sounds of human life have mostly died out, in the village below, all but "the sound of the grinding," which is still kept up. The women are at their hard labor of preparing meal for to-morrow's bread, while their boorish husbands are asleep. This sound of the millstones gives a clear, ringing tone, mellowed as it is by distance, and suggests the idea of cheerfulness and peace. It recalls, too, that noble sentiment of the Levitical law—one of the many humane precepts that speak the very soul of God's tenderness: "No man shall take the nether or the upper millstone to pledge; for he taketh a man's life to pledge." (Deut. xxiv : 6.)

The City of Jerusalem lies yonder, as quietly is the distance, as in those glorious days when "the abomination of desolation" had been reared up in its most sacred place, and all the religion and patriotism of the people had fled to the mountains. Yet, the voices of a great people shall again be heard there—when the promised time shall come. Jerusalem shall be restored to a new and inviolate beauty. Zion, the city of solemnities, shall yet become "a great habitation," though now resounding with all the discords of religious and political factions, and a tabernacle that shall not be taken down. Not one of the stakes thereof shall be removed, neither shall any of the cords thereof be broken. (Isaiah xxxiii : 20.) Then shall the type and ante-type agree. Jerusalem below shall recall Jerusalem above—

"Where falls not hail, or rain, or any snow,
Nor ever wind blows loudly."

MR. FOUNTAIN'S DIARY.

CAMP SABBATH, 5 A. M.

The first week of our wanderings on sacred soil has ended, and I look back with satisfaction and thankfulness at the results. The young people have inaugurated such a course of private Scripture reading as will enable them during their explorations, to complete the volume while they complete the land in which it was written.

In making up our route I use the map of the British Ordnance Survey.* On that, it will be seen that—on Wednesday, we past Sukner and Yazur; took

* See a fac-simile of this map facing Chapter Seventh.

the left hand road; past Sahia, Beth-dagon and Serafieh, leaving Sarafend and Ramleh to the right, and camped at Lydda. Here comes in the cross road from Damascus to Egypt. On Thursday, we entered the hills of Dan and Benjamin; past Gimzu, Om-rush, the two Beth-horons, and other small villages, and camped at Gibeon. On Friday, we struck southward to the turnpike road (not marked on this map) and turned westward, passing Kulonieh, and Kirjath-jearim, and camped at Latroon. On Saturday, we coursed around nearly to Ramleh, turned south by the Egyptian road, passed Akir, then eastward into the hills of Judah, leaving Susia, Rafat, Suria, and many other villages on our left, and camped here in sight of Jerusalem.

CAMP SABBATH—Noon.

The morning breeze has lulled, and the heat becomes oppressive. Our religious exercises this morning were of special interest, and afforded us great enjoyment. Commencing by the alternate reading of the Book of Ruth, the 21st Chapter of Revelations, and 14th to 16th Chapters of Mark, we then sang three hymns as selected by the young people, viz: "Safely Through Another Week," "When Marshalled O'er the Nightly Plain," and "The Sweet Bye and Bye." The last of these, sung to Mr. Webster's exquisite music, with John's sweet flute accompaniment, rolled over the hills like a celestial song. A whole village of Arabs, near by, hastened across the valley to enjoy the unaccustomed treat, and complimented us with loud exclamations of *tyeeb, tyeeb*—good, good.

THE JOPPA GATE; OR, GATE ON THE WEST SIDE OF JERUSALEM.

It is called by the natives *Bab el-Khalil*, or Gate of the Faithful.

THE SIGNET OF KING SOLOMON.

Engraved over the Joppa Gate, at Jerusalem.

CHAPTER VIII.

GENERAL SURVEY OF JERUSALEM.

The first day in the city—Joppa gate—Solomon's seal—Dogs of Jerusalem—Veiled women—Cruelty of muleteers—Crowds of pilgrims—Orange merchants—Sweeping the streets—Native names—Dervish—Ornaments and cigars—The good Pasha—Heavy dews—Rephaim and its battles—Russian convent—Views from the north, east and south—Roman camp—Post-office—Banking house—Camp of the Assyrians—A ride round the walls—Promenade on the walls.

ELLIOT'S DIARY.

CAMP OF THE ASSYRIANS, NORTHWEST CORNER OF JERUSALEM,
Monday, March 22d, 1869. 6 P. M.

WE came down from the hills in the southwest, early this morning, to visit the Holy City of Jerusalem and the holy places that are round about it. We have pitched our tents here astride the walls, near the biggest and finest oak tree I have seen in all Palestine. Mr. Fountain calls it a *holm tree*; Hassan says it is a *buttum tree*, but I shall ever insist upon that it is an *oak* tree, if ever I saw an oak. Why, the ground under it is covered with acorn shells!

After the servants had set up the tents, Mr. Fountain took Harriet and John for some long and tiresome jaunts outside of the city. He has given me permission this week to work by myself, upon my pledge never to go out of sight of Hassan and a soldier he has hired for me. I am to look up the *little things* of Jerusalem, and the rest of the party the *big things*.

So I was the first of the party to enter Jerusalem. I went in by the Joppa gate, which is not far from our encampment.* This Joppa gate is distant from our house in New York, about six thousand, seven hundred miles and there is a telegraph wire runs all the way between them. As soon as I got inside I set to, to make a batch of notes for the next six days that will please my dear parents. I find that the *first* things I see in a new place are always the *best* things, and if I don't put them right down as fast as I see them, they are hardly worth putting down at all.

A week ago this morning I came out of Joppa by the *Jerusalem gate*. Now I enter Jerusalem by the *Joppa gate*. So turn about is fair play.

The moment I got inside I looked carefully over the archway at the gate for that five-pointed star that Prof. A. L. Rawson, our artist-friend, told me of.

---

* See the drawing of the Joppa gate facing Chapter Eighth.

There it is as plain as can be. I made a drawing of it.* When the soldiers saw me looking at it so closely they all came and looked at it too. They told Hassan that they had never seen it before, and thought I must have put it there! But these Turkish soldiers don't know anything.

This is the only five-pointed star I have seen, so far, in all the Holy Land. I expected to find lots of them everywhere on the old buildings. Plenty of *stars* are used in their ornaments at Joppa, but none of them *five-pointed*. Mr. Fountain says he will show me a very fine five-pointed star when we get among the ruins of Caperneum. This star is called *Solomon's seal* and *Solomon's signet*, and so this gate is what the poet called

"An archway, sealed
With the great name of Solomon."

It reminds me of that astonishing story in the Arabian Nights, of the genii who was fastened up in a casket sealed with a five-pointed star. It reminds me also of another verse:

"That like the seal of Solomon,
Has magic in in its pressure."

The fact is though, I have been writing down in my *Index Rerum* all such things as this ever since father told me I should visit the Holy Land.

My little dog *Sweet Home* followed me from camp about fifty steps into Jerusalem. Then he turned and run back to the tents. No wonder. Do you think his dog-brethren had a welcome for him? Not a very healthy welcome. A whole army of them made after him like a pack of wolves. Lucky for Sweet Home, the Jerusalem dogs don't go outside of the Joppa gate, or he never would have have lived to tell the story. Disappointed that he got away from them, the scamps then turned in to tearing and worrying each other.

None of these dogs belong to that class that Isaiah speaks of (lvi: 10): "Dumb dogs that cannot bark," for they are always barking. I wonder if old Doctor Isaac Watts didn't visit Jerusalem before he wrote the verse that I learned so long ago:

"Let dogs delight to bark and bite,
For God hath made them so!"

Dr. Barclay thinks that this Joppa gate is the same as the old *valley gate* where Nehemiah commenced his nocturnal explorations. (Nehemiah ii: 13.) The name of it here is *Bab el Khalil*. *Bab* means gate. *Khalil* means a friend or a faithful one. They call Abraham the *Friend of God*, and this gate is named after him. It is quite respectable in point of architecture. It is kept open, like all the Jerusalem gates every day from sunrise to sunset, except one hour at noon on Friday, which is the Mohammedan's Sunday.

I met lots of Turkish women here. At least Hassan says they are women. They wear their veils thinner here than they do at Joppa, and I can see the shapes of their mouths and noses through their veils. I think they are not so very handsome that they need be alarmed at anybody's seeing them.

I never noticed the cruelty of mule drivers to their animals so painfully as

* See the drawing facing Chapter Eighth.

I do here. Humanity to brutes is a virtue unknown in the Holy Land. I wish our New Yorker, Mr. Bergh, could be Pasha here for twelve months. The drivers shout at the poor, patient, willing mules. They twist their tails, overload them, kick them, curse them in that dreadful Arab slang, strike them over the head and face, and throw stones at them, oh, so cruelly!

The streets of Jerusalem to-day are full of pilgrims dressed in all sorts of costumes, and travelers who are not pilgrims, English, French, German, Americans, etc. One Yankee sea captain rolling along, full of arrack and sin, caught hold of my arm and stopped me and said, "Boy, can you tell me anything about the people of this country?" Says I, "Yes, sir, I can." "Well, then," said he, "tell it." Said I, "they never refuse *backsheesh!*" He let me go with a laugh that could be heard to the top of Mount Olivet, and said I was right. *There is* one class of people here, however, that never ask for *backsheesh*, and that is the *Jews.*

A big Arab was sitting by a pile of oranges. I don't know which was the dirtiest, the fruit or the fellow. As I knew that the oranges cost him in Joppa about ten for a cent, I priced some of them here at Jerusalem. They were five for a piastre, that is about a cent apiece. I told him that was a thousand per cent. profit. He answered *backsheesh*, and that ended the argument. His oranges, however, were not the fine large ones that I admired so at Blattner's Hotel, but a much inferior stock, not much better than we get in New York.

Ever since I can remember, mother has checked me in fault-finding by saying that "the way that Jerusalem is kept clean is, every body sweeps the pavement in front of his own house." She is mistaken. Nobody sweeps these streets. They are not swept at all. The city doesn't look as though it *ever had been* swept. A strange mistake for mother to make.

I never saw a town that has so many disgusting sights and smells as this.

I got Hassan to give me the names of such persons as he should get acquainted with to-day, so that I could write them down in my diary. They are a queer lot of words to call people by. About half the natives have *Mohammed* to their names, and the other half have *Hassan*, or *Hosseen*, or *Hosine.* As far as I can write the names he gave me, they are: Yahyah, Haroun, Yezid, Meslem, Hulakoo, Akeel, Mustarfer, Nasser, Guzzaway, Ibraheem, Awad, Karder, Abdallah, Sayid, Jussoof, Kosroo, Mosedden, Noureddeen, Solyman, Sajeeb, Soofy, Marlek, Essedeen, Haymoor, Nomarn, Nisamee, Ferhard, Majnoon, Narmer, Mnedh-dhin, Yebrood, Abdellatti, Dayood, Goorundel, Howarrer. A Russian gentleman who saw what I was doing, took my note-book and politely wrote his name in it, Kratismayoshajewsky.

When I returned to our camp for luncheon, I went by way of the Damascus gate. The soldiers there told me the name of it was Bab es-Sham. I couldn't help noticing how the ground around on that side of Jerusalem is strewed with broken glass rings and bracelets of Arab women, and the match papers, cigarette wrappers and match boxes of the men. To judge from the quantity of these that I saw here, I should think that the women did nothing else but break their glass ornaments and the men nothing else but smoke. Hassan himself is a terrible smoker. He smoked a whole package of cigarettes, that I bought for him this morning, before we got back to camp, and he has commenced on another lot, while I am copying these notes. These folks can beat General Grant himself smoking, or even Prince Albert, or the Indian chief, Hole-in-the-day.

After luncheon I returned to the city, and visited what they call the Church of the Holy Sepulchre. It is better than a Barnum's Museum for curiosities, and the curiosities are about as genuine. The priests pretend to show there, all under one roof, the place where our Saviour was scoffed by the soldiers; and where He was scourged; and where they divided His garments; and where He was shut up while they dug the hole for the cross; and where He was nailed to the wood; and where the cross was set up; and where the soldier stood that pierced His side; and where His body was anointed; and where He was buried; and where the angels appeared to the women on the resurrection morning; and where Christ appeared to Mary Magdalen; and where Adam was buried; and where the centre of the world is; and where the three crosses were found; and where Christ measured a place with His own hands as the middle of the world. (Psalms lxxiv : 12.) And a great many other things. I never saw such a museum of wonders in all the world before. But I do not believe there is a word of truth in any of them.

I saw, to-day, a fellow wearing a high sugar-loaf hat, without a rim. Hassan called him a *Dervish.* He smelt as bad as the dead cat I wrote about at Joppa. He was playing the clownish buffoon, and he played it well. He danced antic dances like the Bryant's Minstrels, only not so graceful. Then he asked me for *backsheesh.* I gave him a piastre, and advised him to have his shirt washed. He laughed, and said, *lissa fee wah;* that means there is time enough, and so he went dancing and prancing away.

JOHN'S DIARY.

CAMP ASSYRIAN, Monday, 6 P. M.

In the travels of Bertrandon de la Brocquerie, "the first esquire-carver," —whatever that means, to the Duke of Burgundy—a European gentleman, who was here A. D. 1432. I find that *his* object in preparing a diary of travels was "to animate and influence the hearts of such noble men as may be desirous of seeing the world."

The motive that animates *me* in preparing a diary is quite the opposite. To gratify my dear parents, and pastor, and friends; to bring into practice the more useful studies that I have pursued from childhood; to store my mind with practical information for manhood's days; these are the designs that influence me to draw out my pencil under the shadow of this great oak tree, at the northwest corner of Jerusalem, and record the first day's observations while yet they are fresh in phonographic characters in my note book.

How widely matters are changed around Jerusalem, within a few years, in favor of travelers! Exposed to extortions, hindrances, and every insult, without consuls to appeal to for protection or redress; with no hotels or respectable tarrying places for the sound, or hospitals for the invalid. The pilgrims of only seventy years since worshiped at the holy places at the peril of their property, their health, and their very lives. In 1697 every Christian traveler paid the sum of fourteen dollars for the privilege of entering the Holy Sepulchre.

But now, and especially since the accession of Mohammed Raschid, as Pasha General of Syria and Palestine, a great and decided advance has been made, not only here at Jerusalem, but throughout the whole of his government. By his strong hand and wise counsels he has made all the country west of the Jordan perfectly safe to travelers. He has planted a garrison at ancient Mizpah, in Mount Gilead, now called Es-Salt, and thus overawed the desert Arabs, and restrained their incursions into Palestine. He has opened new channels of trade and commerce to the people, and made Jerusalem as safe and pleasant to the pilgrim as New York.

If the central government at Constantinople would continue to choose such men for Pashas—men who profess the greatest knowledge and seek the greatest good, as they did in the case of Mohammed Raschid, the Turkish form of government would undoubtedly be the best adapted to the Oriental character of all.

When we struck our tents this morning, they were drenched with dew. They looked as if they had been exposed to a fall of rain during the night. This is the same effusion so often referred to in Scripture, that "descended upon the mountains of Zion," recalling the expressions in Psalms cxxx, and others.

The Plain of Rephaim, that lies between our camping place of yesterday and this city, was exceedingly verdant, as we passed over it, and fruitful. It is not, however, half cultivated, even in the thriftless, unhappy style of farming practiced by the native farmers. I could not help smiling to myself in supposing *The American Agriculturalist* to receive questions from these farmers, how ludicrously the answers would misfit!

Upon the Plain of Rephaim, David twice encountered the Philistines, and inflicted such destructions upon them and their idols as even to afford a *new* name to the place, that is Baal-perazim. Those robbers of the plains had come up here in great force through the deep ravines of the southwest, about the middle of May, to carry off the ripe crops for which this valley was even then proverbial. David came upon them at the head of his forces, and smote them "from Gibeon to Gaza." (1 Chron. xiv.) After reading this interesting narrative, I naturally looked for mulberry trees upon the plain, but saw none; and of course heard no "sound of going in the top" of them. (1 Chron. xiv : 15.)

Our camp, here, would be in all respects a pleasant one but for the annoyance of the huge walls and monstrous buildings of the Russian convent, close by. This tremendous pile of architecture covers nearly six acres. It is an eye-sore to all who approach Jerusalem from the west or north. The first object seen in *coming*, the last in *going*, is the Russian convent. Its religion is that of the Greek church, that still uses the old calendar which is twelve days earlier than ours. To-day, for instance, in the almanac of the Russians, is March 10. It is explained in this way: When the Catholic Pope, Gregory XII, ordained A. D. 1582, that October 5th should be considered October 15th, so as to correct the long-erring almanac, and that thenceforward the calendar should be regularly balanced by scientific rules, the Russian government refused to adopt it, and now their almanac is wrong by *twelve* days. England adopted it in 1752, nearly two hundred years after it was announced by the Pope.

It is desirable that this great mass of disfigurement, the convent, be removed. The citadel, that stood here in the days of the Maccabees, was not a greater nuisance. Simon, having captured that, leveled it to the earth, and cut away the very hill on which it stood, although it cost three years' labor to do it. (Josephus xiii : 6.)

We have named our place, *Camp of the Assyrians*, from the expression in Josephus (Wars v : 12) : "Titus began the wall from the camp of the Assyrians," because all writers are agreed that this northwest corner, outside of the city, was that Assyrian camp.

At half past eight we sallied from camp, Mr. Fountain, Harriet and myself, to ride around Jerusalem. Following the road eastward till we came opposite the Damascus Gate, we struck north for about a mile over a horrible road, but amidst fine groves of olive trees, to the top of the elevation called Mount Scopus. Along this road I noticed that the people, when cleaning out their fields and gardens, actually threw the stones into the road. How vividly this recalled the command of the herald when he went before the king : "Prepare ye the way of the people; cast up, cast up the high way; gather out the stones." (Isaiah lxii : 10.) How often these obstructed roads have thus been cleared out and smoothed to "prepare the way" for a Solomon a Nebuchadnezzar and an Alexander! Another method of disposing of the great quantity of loose stony material, is to build it up into immense stone walls, sometimes twelve feet thick and six feet high.

My first reflections upon Mount Scopus recalled that night movement of the Roman military, in which two hundred of the prison guards (the *custodia militarie*) one of whom was chained by his left hand to Paul's right hand, took that brave Apostle by night, to save him from the Jews, and with a re-inforcement of two hundred soldiers of the legion, and seventy cavalry, passed hastily over this hill by way of Antipatris to Cesaræa. (Acts xxiii.) Instead of studying the scene before me, in its relations to *existing* Jerusalem, I gave my thoughts here to the *past*. I wondered whether the affectionate Timothy was with his beloved Master in that night-march. How his youth, piety, and intelligence had won upon Paul's heart! I wondered whether these hills were blazing with the scarlet anemone then as now. It has always seemed to me that none of the other Apostles had souls so large, so open, so full of the new fire that Christ came to bring upon the earth, as Saint Paul. But, perhaps, this is because the record is so much more full in his case than theirs.

While Harriet was busy with sketch book and note book, and Mr. Fountain was looking up specimens of the calc-spar and *tesseræ*, I undertook to re-construct the Camp of Titus, that stood upon the crown of this hill.

It was a Standing Camp, (*campa stativa*) for the standards were never to be raised from their sockets, until yonder proud and doomed city should come once more under the Roman yoke. In form, it was square (*quadrata*). It was surrounded by a ditch (*fozsa*) some nine feet deep and twelve feet broad. A rampart (*vallum*) was composed of the earth which had been dug from the ditch. In this rampart sharp stakes bristled, pointing outward from every side.

The camp had four gates, one on each side. That which was so long presented to the frowning eyes that watched it morning and evening from the walls of Jerusalem, was the *porta prætoria.* The one in the rear was the *porta decumana,* those on the east and west *porta principalis dextra* and *p. p. sinistra.*

The camp was divided into two parts. The upper portion, next the enemy, contained the tents of Titus and his retinue, also the prætorium cohort. Near him were his lieutenant-generals, and the quaestor, those of the tribunes, præfects of the allies, etc., etc. Mr. H. B. Tristam, says: "There is one of the Roman camps still standing near Masada, at the southwest corner of the Dead Sea, about fifty miles southeast of here. Its lines, angles, ditch and rampart are as plainly sketched there as in the pages of a classical dictionary. And yet the head that planned it, the arms that built it, and the warlike spirits that defended it, are but the dust of 1800 years. We shall visit the place next week, and I shall enjoy a privilege, thus far denied me, of tracing out the lines of a *bona fide* Roman camp.

Here in this camp of Titus, on Mount Scopus, every evening, when the General had dismissed his chief officers and friends, after giving them his commands and distributing the watchword of the night upon *tesseræ,*—all the trumpets of the legion were sounded:

Tuba mirum spargens sonum.

This scornful challenge to the enemy was promptly taken up by the Jewish soldiers and then the hills around Jerusalem echoed with the sonorous wind-instruments used at that period. Those martial sounds, through the clear evening air, reached to an amazing distance on all sides. Flowing over the range of Olivet, they were heard by the Christian refugees at Pella, far across the Jordan in the northeast. Flowing over the range of Mizpah, the bold and thrilling peals were heard by the Jewish refugees along the Plain of Sharon. At Hebron, at Masada, at Bethel, these war-signals were recognized as tokens that the enemy was not yet in possession of Jerusalem, and great was the joy they inspired.

Next, I recalled the story of an American gentleman, which he related to me a few weeks ago, who, at the youthful age of ten, a boy at his mother's knee, conceived the purpose of visiting Jerusalem. Through a long forty years he waited, never once giving it up. Through poverty, misfortune and the vicissitudes of life, through the cares of a large family and the weakness of approaching age, he clung still to his first determination. Finally at fifty, a father and a grandfather, he achieved his desires and visited Jerusalem.

The *post-restante,* or post-office, at Jerusalem, is a queer affair, It is only open once or twice a week. It is a hard place to find and still harder to get the postmaster to understand your wishes. Mr. Fountain had quite an altercation with him before he could get his letters and papers to-day. The custom in this country is *to deliver* all postal matter, as our carriers do in New York. Therefore, if you want your letters to lie in the post-office, you must mark it "post-restante." But the best way is to have all correspondence directed to the care of the American Consulate. Letters are despatched by the French post from Jerusalem for England, on the 2d, 12th and 22d of each month; for Beyrout and Constantinople on the 8th, 18th, and 28th. Rate of postage, fifteen cents per one-quarter of an ounce. Letters arrive from England on the 10th, 20th and 30th; from Beyrout and Constantinople on the 4th, 14th and 24th. Letters from Europe and Beyrout are only prepaid as far as Joppa. Eight cents extra is charged for each letter from Joppa to Jerusalem, about 35 miles. The package containing our diaries for the past week, drawn off upon thin French paper, weighed ten ounces. The prepaid postage on it was six dollars, that is sixty cents per ounce.

I also accompanied Mr. Fountain to the counting-room of Messrs. Bergheim & Co., bankers here, who also do a general dry goods and miscellaneous business. These gentlemen are highly respected both by natives and foreigners. They have been very useful in missionary operations in Jerusalem and vicinity. The manner in which Mr. Fountain arranged his money matters for our journey, was this: father deposited with his bankers, Messrs. Brown, Brothers & Co., Wall Street, New York, the amount that he thought necessary for the journey. For this they gave him *letters of credit* in the name of Mr. Fountain, upon which he can raise money in any part of the world where there is a banking house.

I was surprised to find a first-class photographic gallery here.

HARRIET'S DIARY.

CAMP SABBATH, Daylight, Monday, March 22d, 1869.

I rise early, unable to sleep under the exciting thought, "to-day, we enter thy gates, oh, Jerusalem." To-day, "my feet shall stand within thy gates, oh, Jerusalem." I shall to-day "walk about Zion and go round about her; tell the towers thereof and mark well her bulwarks." Beyond the wilderness of Judea, and beyond the Dead Sea and over the craggy mountains of Moab, rises a bright star as if to allure me on.

"Oh, sweet STAR,
Pure in the virgin forehead of the dawn."

Oh may I be of those who "overcome" and "keep HIS works unto the end;" to whom shall be given the MORNING STAR. (Rev. ii.) Oh Thou who alone art the bright and morning star, give me the right to the tree of life, that I may enter in "through the gates into the city." (Rev. xxii.) I bless Thee for that Word that promises to many "who sleep in the dust of the earth that they shall awake to everlasting life * * to shine as the brightness of the firmament, (Daniel xii) as the stars forever and ever."

Yes, I am to see Jerusalem. I expect to find it greatly changed. Age, war, peace, friends, foes, builders, spoilers,—all have conspired to change it. The city, seventeen times beseiged and ruined, must needs have changed its garb. But the mountains are still around Jerusalem as the Lord is round about His people. (Psalms cxxv: 2.) The ancient valleys still conduct its copious winter rains to the sea. Many of the most noted localities associated in the Scriptures with Jerusalem, may yet be recognized, and it is these I seek. The glaring and clumsy miracles, the lying wonders of modern historians, have no attractions for a Protestant girl.

Camp of the Assyrians. 6. P. M.

Our tents are pitched upon the rising ground near the northwest corner of the city, where the Crusaders spread their array upon a bright and hopeful morning of June, A. D. 1099, and prepared to invest Jerusalem. More than eighteen hundred years before that time, the hosts of the Assyrians had encamped (B. C. 711) upon this same site and for a similar purpose. Ours is a more peaceful visit; and, although we cannot altogether exhibit the enthusiasm of the Crusaders, who " clothed their passions with divers gestures, some prostrate, some kneeling, some weeping, all having much ado to manage so great a gladness," yet our thanksgivings do go up to the Most High and with as sincere a gratitude as theirs. For at least we have reached Jerusalem; we have gone about its walls; viewed its bulwarks, and entered its palaces, and we hope, through an active series of explorations, to be continued through the week, to gather large and profitable fruitage for future usefulness. May God grant it. Amen.

The plan formed before we left home, six weeks ago, was to spend the whole of the first day here in acquiring *general* views of the city. Mr. Fountain thinks, from his own experience here, that we shall be the better prepared to gather in the *details* of the place if we first secure the *outline* of it, and we cheerfully defer to his judgment. Elliot, however, in his boyish impatience, begged so hard to be allowed an independent escort, and to go at once into the city, that he was was permitted to do so. He is to spend the week strolling about, asking questions and picking up "items," as he calls them, in his own juvenile manner.

We began our work by riding to the eminence entitled Scopus, from which we obtained an excellent view "from the sides of the north." As we passed over the stony paths, we were struck with the crimson anemones that spring up among the rocks on every side. They irresistibly recall the thought of "the great drops of blood falling down to the ground." (Luke xxii : 44.)

The word *Scopus*, applied to this elevation, signifies a watch tower, or a distant view. The place is about a mile from the Damascus gate, and affords from its top a fine distant view of Jerusalem.

Over it have passed the men of a hundred nations pouring down upon the city, friends and enemies, worshippers and blasphemers. The Babylonian, the Assyrian, the Persian, the Grecian, the Roman, the Christian, the Saracen, the Crusader—all, all have taken their view, as we did this morning, of the strange city at their feet. All over the hill are the little memorial heaps, such as we saw last Friday at Neby Samuel, and to them, John and myself added our own.

Mount Scopus stands out as a sort of irregular spur of Mount Olivet. The circular hillock from which I made my drawing is probably the remains of some ancient tower. From this, as I glanced southwards a little to the left hand, I could look along the valley of the Kedron nearly to Gethsemane, over which impends the noble Mount of Olives. On my right hand the view was bounded by the great Russian convent which lies northwest of the city. Directly before me was the ridge once named Moriah, on the central portion of which stands the splendid mosk of Omar, whose golden crescent was glowing in the sunlight as I gazed upon it through my glass.

From Scopus, we rode round to the left upon Mount Olivet, and selected two points at which I propose to spend a day, sketching the city. The sublime panorama, visible from the far-famed summit of Mount Olivet must be visited again and again, and somewhere upon its flowery slope we propose on Saturday to pitch our camps.

From Olivet we descended on the western side, passing through the old Hebrew burying ground; then turned to the right, crossing the little stone bridge near Gethsemane; then passed near the Pool of Siloam and Akeldama, to the Mount of Evil Counsel, south of the city. The view from this point is interesting, as giving a clear conception of the size and shape of Mount Zion, and the gloomy defile of Hinnom which skirts its base.

Leaving the Mount of Evil Counsel, we struck westward until we intercepted the roads that connects Bethlehem with Jerusalem, then took our fourth general view of the city from the western ridge, near the Hospital of the Prussian Deaconesses, over whose doorway these touching words are inscribed: *Talitha cumi* (Mark v: 41); the most affecting application of a divine text to a noble living philanthropy that I ever saw.

Having thus accomplished a circuit of Jerusalem, at distances varying from a quarter to a mile, we next circumambulated the walls immediately at their base. We had read in Mr. Prime's book in what a very few minutes he had *galloped* this distance; but we took it more soberly and occupied considerably over an hour in the undertaking.

Now we felt that we had earned the right to *enter* the city, which we did humbly and on foot at the western or Joppa gate. There the ancient Tower of Hippicus stands forward alone, gray with antiquity, among its younger companions. This is an irregular assemblage of square towers, having on the outside what we particularly noticed, *a deep ditch.* When Jerusalem surrendered to the Crusaders, in 1099, this fortress was the strongest part of the city, and the last to be surrendered. When the walls of the city were thrown down, in 1219, this fortress was spared.

From the top of this ancient tower we enjoyed a view of Jerusalem and its surroundings that can never be erased from our memories. Glimpses of the upper portion of the Dead Sea and the valley of the Jordan were a part of the splendid panorama enjoyed from this elevated spot.

Descending from the tower, we climbed up some broken steps on the northern side of the gate, and made a promenade clear around the northern side of the city to St. Stephen's gate, being all the way *on the top of the walls.* In this romantic route we were not unmindful of the ancient caution: "Remember that thou goest in the midst of snares and that thou walkest upon the battlements of the city." (Ecclesiasticus ix: 13.)

As we kept this elevated road, we saw looking inside of the city, the entire mass of houses with their square forms and flat roofs, having central elevations like domes, betraying the forms of the arches within. At some points the city wall is as much as forty feet high, and from it many views of the suburbs of Jerusalem are had of a most interesting character.

This completed our day's labors, and we have returned, wearied but delighted with our first day's researches, at Jerusalem.

10 P. M.

How silent is the humanity of Jerusalem, at this hour. Not a voice disturbs the solitude, that would betray the presence of a human being within its walls. Those dreadful barkings and yells of dogs might be the noises of savage beasts seeking their prey as they sought it through the ruins of Jerusalem, at any of those epochs when it lay long uninhabited and grew up in forest trees. The gabble and chatter and unmelodious songs that I hear in the various camps around, might be the customary sounds of Bedouin life, pitched here by the desolated city as once they did rove here at will, and as to-night, they are pitched by the fallen columns of Palmyra and the shapeless piles of Babylon.

In the religious exercises of Passion Week this is called *Monday before Easter*. The Scriptural passages commemorated are these: "On the next day much people that were come to the feast, when they heard that Jesus was coming to Jerusalem, took branches of palm trees and went forth to meet Him, and cried, Hosanna! Blessed is the King of Israel that cometh in the name of the Lord! And Jesus, when he had found a young ass, sat thereon; as it is written, Fear not, daughter of Zion; behold, thy King cometh, sitting upon an ass's colt." (John xii: 12–15.)

This was the day in the Jewish ceremonials when the children of Israel were directed to look out the Paschal Lamb that they might keep it up and have abundant time to detect any blemishes in it. So Christ, the PASCHAL LAMB, was coming into Jerusalem, to be offered up, once for all, for the sins of the world. Oh, how affecting this thought, considered *upon the very place* where the offering was made!

THE DAMASCUS GATE OF JERUSALEM; OR GATE ON THE NORTH.

It is called by the natives *Bab es-Sham*, or Gate of Damascus.

SARACENIC ORNAMENTS AT THE DAMASCUS GATE OF JERUSALEM.

CHAPTER IX.

THE POOLS AND WALLS OF JERUSALEM.

The Turkish soldier, Kosroo—Profanity—Narrow streets—Sugar cane—Tumult in the streets—Hay on the horn—Despised dogs—Houses are numbered—Taxing the farmers—The Damascus gate—Saracenic ornaments—Criticisms on priests—Kitchen fires—Statistics of Jerusalem—Birket Manilla—Birket Es-Sultan—Pool of Hezekiah—Pool of Siloam—Well of En-Rogel—Native newspapers—Pilgrimages to the Jordan—Native doctors—Solomon's coronation—Sparrows—The little girl—Man born blind—Flowers at Siloam—Bees and bee hives—The field of blood.

ELLIOT'S DIARY.

CAMP OF THE ASSYRIANS, Tuesday, March 23, 1869, 6 P. M.

I WAS so successful, yesterday, in my rambles, and filled so many pages of notes, that I am to have my own way all the week. I promise to come back to camp at eleven every morning, and stay till three. This is on account of hot weather. Then I promise to come back again at six. Hassan and the soldier are never to let me go out of their sight. The soldier's name is Kosroo. His uniform is the French zouave. His musket has the sword bayonet. He wears a tarboush. He is a lively little fellow, and don't know a word of English. I am to supply him with twenty cigarettes a day, and four cups of coffee. This is the genuine Oriental coffee, strong, black, without milk or sugar, cups as small as half a hen-egg. And he promises never to ask me for *backsheesh* till six o'clock every day. Yesterday, he behaved first rate, but made a mistake about the number of cigarettes I gave him. Kosroo was conscripted into the Turkish army, last year, at Tibnin. All his pay is his clothes and provisions. No wonder he likes to hire out in this way. He never expects to see his old mother again. We pay him five francs a day ; but the officers get this.

I spent the day mostly in the bazaars. I can pick up any quantity of items around the bazaars.

Kosroo is dreadfully profane. When Mr. Fountain asked him to guard me faithfully, he swore, by Allah, that if his own father should lay a finger on me, he would run him through with his bayonet. But he don't look it. All the Arabs in Jerusalem swear like sailors. But in the new Jerusalem "there shall be no more curse." (Rev. xxii : 3.)

The streets of Jerusalem are in no place more than eight feet wide. Generally, they are only six. They are nothing but alleys, and you keep looking all day for a street—but you never find one. These alleys run all sorts of ways. You turn up one of them and think you are going into the principal part of the city, but the first thing you know you butt up against a stone wall.

Then, you step aside, as you think, into some dark little alley, and sit down to write up your notes—when, behold, a whole caravan of people rushing down on you! You have got into the busiest street in all Jerusalem.

I laughed to see an English sailor measuring the width of the streets by *lying down* across them. He had been to Jerusalem before, and had made a bet with another sailor that he was *as long* as the street is *wide*. So he tried it in a dozen places, and won the bet every time, for his head touched one side and his feet the other. I am afraid he was drunk; at last a donkey tipped a load of oak roots on him.

The quantity of sugar cane that is sold in the bazaars of Jerusalem surprises me. Brother Harry used to write us about the little negroes, in Louisiana, who, all day long, were chewing sugar cane. The custom is almost as common among the children here. It reminds me how surprised the Crusaders were when they found at Tripoli, sweet, honeyed reeds called zookra, which they sucked and liked so much that they could not be satisfied.

The musses made sometimes in these narrow streets, make the very Turks laugh. The Turks hardly ever laugh. I watched one of the musses this morning. A camel, loaded with vegetables, was coming down the narrow street. On each side of him great sacks full bulged out. Piles of cauliflowers that grew around here, most as large as a buskel basket, were heaped mountain high, on his hump. He loomed up like Vesuvius, as he came stalking along, his head level, his monstrous under jaw swinging round the upper one like a barn door on its hinges, his wide, spongy feet flattening out on the stone pavement, in tracks like a mammoth's. As he came along, his rider roared *ruak, ruak*, that is get out of the way. And everybody *did* get out of the way. One woman, who was carrying a bread-tray on her head, dove down below the camel's stomach, and so got out. I jumped into one of the little shops where they sell cakes. The merchant was fumbling over his rosary and praying. But he stopped praying and tried to sell me some eggs—a piastre a dozen. The rest of the crowd jumped into the stores right and left as I had done.

But just as the camel had passed me, he met a procession of six donkeys, all loaded down with oak roots, the drivers on top. Here was a muss. The camel screamed. The camel driver yelled *ruak, ruak*. The donkeys raised their tails and brayed. The donkey drivers swore. I wondered how the thing would be settled, for the donkeys could not turn round for their lives, as their roots just filled up the width of the streets. The camel could not turn round without pulling down the buildings on both sides of him. Never was such an uproar. Kosroo poked the camel's legs with his bayonet to make him bite. I stopped that.

At last, the men shouldered the donkeys, roots and all, and carried them backwards into the side streets, and so let the camel pass. Such scenes must be common, here, in the business parts of the city, especially at this time when there are more than five thousand strangers here.

Right behind this camel walked a ferocious bull, who had each of his horns tied up with a wisp of hay. This reminded me of the Latin maxim, *foenum in cornu habet;* he has hay on his horns.

How the people of this country do detest and despise dogs! They seem afraid to touch them. They will suffer the poor, cowardly wretches, that look more like wolf than dog, to lie right across the side walk and block it up. Instead of driving a mangy cur out of the way, they will actually walk around him, lest their clothes should touch him. I used up a beautiful olive wood cane, to-day, that I had just bought, by striking it over the back of a monstrous brute that would not get out of the way when I halloed to him. The cane flew into slivers like glass.

These dogs bark at me incessantly. Hassan says they hate new fashioned dresses, and if I would wear the native dress they would not bark at me. May be that is the reason the people wear the same fashions that Abraham did; it pleases the dogs. The people here won't even *talk* about dogs. They won't answer my questions about dogs. If they say anything in reply to me it is *mar arrif*. That means I don't know. The Jews, too, hate dogs as bad as the Mohammedans. Yet, they lived in Egypt more than two hundred years, and the Egyptians loved the dog enough to make an idol of him. So they lived for many centuries under the Roman rule; and the Romans honored and respected the dog. But this made no difference with *them*. The Jews never will learn anything from other nations. What *they* don't know isn't worth knowing.

Jerusalem dogs are all of one breed. And such a breed! You never see here the bluff, surly, sturdy, intelligent mastiff; nor the slight-built grayhound; nor the sharp, shrewd terrier; nor the silent, courageous bull dog; nor the tawny, deep-voiced bloodhound; nor the noble Newfoundland. Instead of that, these are all gaunt, half-starved curs, mere scavengers of garbage, street-cleaners, who need cleaning themselves worse than the streets.

The dogs here seem to have a regular constitution and set of by-laws. Of course they are not written out or printed. While I was sitting, to-day, in the cool cavern of the Pool of Siloam, I jotted down what I suppose to be their regulations:

Rule 1. The City of Jerusalem is divided into ten dog districts.

Rule 2. No dog shall ever go outside of the district in which he is born. Penalty, death.

Rule 3. The strongest dog in his district shall be the dog-sheikh in that district until some stronger dog whips him. Then, the stronger dog shall take his place.

Rule 4. When the dog-sheikh barks, all the dogs in his district shall bark, too.

Rule 5. When the dogs in one district bark, all the dogs in all the other districts shall bark, too.

Rule 6. No dog shall move out of a man's way.

If that is not a good set of regulations I should like to see somebody make a better.

I was surprised to see all the houses of Jerusalem numbered on the doors. Hassan says they tax people here not according to the number of persons in the family, but according to the number of houses! So the Governor has had them all numbered. Of course they use the Arabic figures. Miyah thatata aasher, means 113. Thamarneen arbaah, is 84. Alf sittah, is 1006.

I watched a poor Fellah—that is what they call a farmer.—coming in through the Joppa gate with a load of oak roots from near Hebron. The ground in that direction is full of oak roots, although only a stray oak here and there, has been seen up that way for hundreds of years. These oak roots, when dried, burn first-rate; and the people of Jerusalem buy them for fuel.

Hassan told me how they will tax that poor farmer before he gets home to-night. His load of roots is worth in Jerusalem about a dollar, but not much good of that dollar will *he* get. For, first, the soldiers of Joppa gate will charge him eight cents for permission to pass the Custom House with a load of fuel. The gate duties on tobacco and silk are forty cents a pound; on all other articles eight per cent. At the bazaars, they will charge him ten cents more for market duties and permission to sell his fuel. Then when he goes back through the gate they will charge him ten cents more for duties on the tobacco and cloth he has bought. And finally, when he gets home to-night, the Sheikh of his village will make him pay at least ten cents more for *his* share of stealage. So there is fifty per cent., or one-half the value of his property that will be paid to-day to this extortionate iniquitous government.

I spent a good deal of time to-day at the Damascus gate. They call it here *Bab es-Sham.* This is the one that Dr. Barclay thinks was called in the Bible *The Old Gate.* (Nehemiah iii: 6.) Very considerable and interesting remains of the ancient structure are yet to be seen in the towers on each side of this gate. An old Jewish tower and stairway are perfectly preserved there. He thinks that this is the same kind of stairway named in 1 Kings vi: 8: "They went up with winding stairs into the middle chamber and out of the middle into the third."

I copied from this gate some ornaments of the modern style.* I see a great deal of this sort of figuring on the houses at Joppa and Jerusalem. It looks very pretty when well cut.

As I passed a convent, of which there are many here at Jerusalem, a lot of priests peeped out through the grated windows at me. One of them was a jolly red-nosed fellow. He said to me *min aine jaryee.* That means, where do you come from? I told him the United States of America and State of New York. Then he said *charteerah,* that is, Good bye. These priests looked to me exactly like a row of convicts squinting through their grated windows, such as I saw once at Sing Sing. They seemed unhappy and unhealthy. Of course they are. This cooping strong men in convents is like burying them alive. I am glad it is not done in the United States. There is one thing, though, that I like about these priests, that is *the singing.*

JOHN'S DIARY.

CAMP ASSYRIAN, Tuesday. 6 A. M.

In looking over the city of Jerusalem at this early morning hour, I see the scarcity of fuel singularly illustrated by the fact that the smoke of the *kitchen*

* See the drawings facing Chapter Ninth, of the Damascus Gate and the ornamental carvings that surmount it.

fires of all this city of twenty or twenty-five thousand inhabitants, increased at the present time by such multitudes of pilgrims, for whom food must be provided,—these united chimney-smokes do not equal in quantity that of *a moderate village* in the United States. I suppose there is more *tobacco* smoke rising from Jerusalem this hour, than from all the cooking that so many breakfasts demand!

6 P. M.

To-day we have given chiefly to inspecting the tanks, pools and other natural landmarks of Jerusalem. This, with yesterday's explorations, will fasten indelibly upon our minds correct ideas of the general form and surroundings of the far-famed city.

Jerusalem stands in *latitude* thirty-one degrees, forty-six minutes, north; *longitude*, thirty-five degrees, eighteen minutes east from Greenwich. In a straight line from the Mediterranean Sea, at Joppa, it is thirty-two miles; from the Jordan, eighteen; from Hebron, twenty; from Bethel, thirteen; Samaria, thirty-six; Jericho, thirteen; Ramleh, twenty-five. Its elevation is so remarkable that from every side, except the South, the ascent is perpetual, and so the old psalm expresses a reality: "Thither the tribes *go up*, the tribes of the Lord unto the testimony of Israel. (Psalm cxx: 3.) To all who approached it, in Bible days, it was emphatically a *mountain city*, breathing a mountain air, enthroned in a mountain fastness.

The western part of Jerusalem, in which our camps are pitched, is two thousand, six hundred and ten feet above the level of the Mediterranean Sea, and nearly four thousand feet above the level of the pool at the Dead Sea. The lowest point around Jerusalem is the well En-Rogel, now called Beer-ayub. Making that a basis-standard, the heights of all the prominent points in and near the city are:

Our camp	614	feet.
Mount Zion at David's tomb	541	"
Mount Moriah at Mosk of Omar	433	"
Bridge over Kedron near Gethsemane	285	"
Pool of Siloam, water-surface	118	"
Mt. Olives at Church of Ascension	728	"

By these figures, I see that our camp is pitched at the highest point near Jerusalem, except Mt. Olivet, which is one hundred and fourteen feet higher. No wonder, then, that I see Mt. Olivet so plainly over the tops of all the walls, mosks, houses and churches intervening. The Tomb of David is seventy-three feet lower than our camp; the Mosk of Omar is one hundred and eighty one feet lower; the bridge over Kedron, which we crossed yesterday, is three hundred and twenty-nine feet lower.

Our first visit to-day was to the Upper Pool of Gihon, situated about half a mile westwardly of the Joppa gate. A crowd of men and boys were bathing in the muddy water so that Harriet could not approach it. Yet the fact of two score naked persons swimming here, did not prevent the Mohammedan women from resorting here to fill their water jars! And the fact that this pool is a regular bathing place, the mud being stirred up till the water is thick with impurities, did not prevent their using it for cooking and drinking!

Josephus styles this the *Serpent's Pool;* the natives call it *Birket Mamilla.*

Their word for pool or pond is *birket ;* for spring or fountain, *aine ;* for well, *beer.* The bottom of this Birket is only four feet below the sill of the Joppa gate, and no doubt the water was formerly conducted into the city by a regular subterranean conduit. Even now there is a ditch through which its overflow in high water is taken into Hezekiah's Pool, inside the city. By my measurement, it is three hundred and fifteen feet by two hundred and eight, and from fifteen to twenty feet deep. A pair of steps descends to the pool at the southwest corner, and there is a dam on the lower side for regulating its contents.

The next pool we visited was the Lower Pool of Gihon, now called Birket es-Sultan. This is an immense reservoir covering a space of more than three and a half acres, and might once have been one hundred feet deep. It stands a quarter of a mile southwest of the Joppa gate. It is six hundred by two hundred and sixty feet in dimensions. For want of repairs it has run dry and the bottom of it is a barley field. With proper care and an expenditure of a few thousand dollars, this reservoir might be made to supply the entire population of Jerusalem with water.

The Pool of Hezekiah lies inside the city, not far from the Church of the Holy Sepulchre. It is two hundred and fifty-two by one hundred and twenty-six feet in dimensions and about ten feet deep. Its supply of water is from the Upper Pool of Gihon, and the rains collected from the roofs of adjacent houses.

Several of the coffee shops open upon the Pool of Hezekiah and we were greatly interested to see our little Elliot sitting in the embrasure of a window, note book on knee, Hassan and Kosroo on either side of him, armed with pipes and coffee cups, while a crowd of soldiers and natives filled up the rear of the picture. If he doesn't exhaust Jerusalem of its knowledge before he leaves here, it will not be for failure to ask questions.

To give Harriet the best view of the reservoir made by the good King Hezekiah (B. C. 726–698), we got leave of a family whose dwelling adjoins it and went upon the house top.

Our next move was to the Pool of Siloam, southeast of the city. This was done with anticipations of uncommon pleasure. As we passed through the Mograbbins Gate, as it is called, Mr. Fountain pointed out to me a low archway a few yards south, which was the outlet of a large sewer. Through this the soldiers of Ibrahim Pasha crept and so captured the city, in 1834.

From the Pool of Siloam it was but the crossing of a little hill to the Virgin's Fount, from which its supply of water is obtained.

From these twin fountains we went down the Valley of Jehoshaphat to the well En-Rogel, and then by a devious way returned to camp.

In the office of the American vice-consul, to-day, I saw a copy of the official newspaper, published at Beyrout. Its name is "Hadikat-el-Akhbar, Journal de Syrie et Liban." The outside forms are printed in *French,* the inside in *Arabic.* The price of the paper, weekly, per annum, is one hundred piastres, about four dollars and twenty cents. For notices, five piastres a line is charged, and "Se paient d'avance" (cash in advance) is the rule of its managers. But although the "Hadikat" seems to be in its twelfth year, not a single advertisement appears in it! The paper is well printed and makes a creditable appearance. Another one in the same style is issued, I am told, at Damascus.

Here, at Jerusalem, I find a handsome magazine published in the Armenian language, but I cannot find any one here to give me the name of it.

It was announced in the American papers that some one here at Jerusalem is printing the "Arabian Night's Entertainment," but I cannot learn anything definite about it. There is so much religious and national bigotry and hatred here, that it is almost useless to ask an Armenian anything about the Greek and Latin Christians; or the Greek and Latins anything about the Armenians. The Protestants are by far the most knowing and the most willing to communicate their knowledge. But then they are few in numbers, and their influence much less than that of other churches. At present the most influential foreign power here seems to be the French.

I spent a leisure hour this noon looking through the Concordance, for the various texts, in which the word Jerusalem occurs. I had no idea, until then, how great was the number. Expunge them from the Scriptures and what a *hiatus* would be left! Then strike out all the verses in which Jerusalem is indirectly referred to, and the sixty-six books of the Bible would remain a mere skeleton, unable to hold together, without sinew, nerve or flesh.

HARRIET'S DIARY.

CAMP ASSYRIAN, Tuesday, 6 P. M.

We began our day's researches by treading our way through the tents and camps of the pilgrims, who occupy all this quarter, waiting upon the religious services of the present (Passion) week. Very large numbers of these go down to the Jordan during their visit here. There they robe themselves in white cotton garments, bathe in the sacred river; and then, drying and preserving those garments, they take them back to their far-distant homes in Africa, Asia, Europe, and elsewhere, to be used as their *shrouds*. How much better is this superstition than that of the heathen.

I passed within the space of a mile through companies of Russians, Austrians, Poles, Turks, and a score of other nationalities, all travel-stained and foot-sore. The Russians wear the sheep skin jacket, with the wool turned inside, and red, rimless hats. Others are dressed in the flowing and parti-colored costumes of the Orientals.

I did not visit the Upper Pool of Gihon, as it is used for a public bathing-place; but I observed that it is embordered with Mohammedan cemeteries, presenting the picturesque and striking view of white-robed groups of women sitting around the broken turf of newly-made graves. Therefore, while John was making nearer observations at the Pool, I went to the *Talitha Cumi* Hospital of the Prussian Sisters. Here I fell in with a most accomplished physician, who has made his residence here for the purpose of paying attention to the diseases of the country. He informed me that the practice of medicine in Mohammedan countries is a mere bundle of superstitious observances. The Orientals have always connected religion with medicine, as the wild men of all nations do, and use charms and incantations instead of drugs. Our

American friend, Dr. J. T. Barclay, won a high reputation during the fifteen years he lived here. At first he contended with blindness, prejudice, and incredulity, but eventually overcame them all. A common method of native practice is for the doctors to write their prescriptions upon slips of parchment and cause the patient to *lick off and swallow the ink*, in place of medicine! The people of Jerusalem, now, have an excellent English physician, resident here, Thomas Chaplin, M. D. At Beyrout, they have two American physicians of the highest order of medical skill, Dr. Van Dyke and Dr. Post.

At the Lower Pool of Gihon, I was struck with the immense preparations of that wonderful monarch, King Solomon, for the water-supply of his royal city. Massive magnificence is the grand characteristic in all the remains of Solomon's work extant. This reservoir, now empty, and its bed green with barley, was a miniature lake in itself. Perhaps a miniature fleet may once have been moored here, a company of tiny vessels for the recreation of the young princes of David's house. Doubtless, the Wise King himself, often promenaded along its margin at the base of his own Mount Zion, while the royal minstrels made the echoes of the hills resound with their music. But now, nor minstrel's, nor shepherd's pipe, nor plowman's song, moves these echoes. Sadness, inexpressible, broods here. Stillness and sluggishness reign in joint dominion over Jerusalem.

My pleasantest association with this immense reservoir, this " broken cistern that holds no water," is with a blooming patch of *cyclamen*, presenting many large and handsome specimens. Its circle was so brilliant, its leaf so delicate and soft! Here, in this dry bed of King Solomon's croton-lake, it sparkles, shooting forth among its prickly neighbors, and here I gathered a number of its large bulbs to send home.

It was in the mighty amphitheatre, formed by this valley of Gihon, between the Upper and Lower Pools, that the coronation of Solomon was performed, B. C. 1015, and his brilliant reign of forty years began. No place more fitting could be desired. These hills, now so bald and covered, as to their shoulders, in sackcloth, were then crowded with the ten thousands of Jerusalem. The royal palaces upon Mount Zion, overlooking the scene—palaces whose tesselated pavements lie now in disjointed *tesseræ* through these heaps of rubbish—were thronged with women and children, elate with an event that promised so much for Israel. The city itself, upon its throne of rock, walled all around, enclosed in deep valleys and marked out as the site of a stronghold, was spectator of that memorable coronation.

I read the sacred story upon the very spot: "They caused Solomon to ride on King David's mule. And Zadok, the priest, took an horn of oil out of the tabernacle and anointed Solomon. And they blew the trumpet, and all the people said, God save King Solomon. And all the people piped with pipes, and rejoiced with great joy, so that the earth rent with the sound of them." (1 Kings i.) No wonder the band of conspirators, that had assembled on the other side of the hill, by the well En-Rogel, stood aghast at the danger they had incurred, for the people had unanimously accepted the choice of Solomon, and for a rejected prince there was but one escape.

At Hezekiah's Pool I was delighted to see many hundreds of the Jerusalem sparrows, drinking, bathing and twittering to each other in their happiest strains. This was a little world within a world. *Without*, the bustling city of many nations, intent upon cares of business, ceremonials of religion, sight-seeing—*within*, the merry family of birds congregated at their gathering place, all heedless of the distraction of humanity. Truly "the sparrow hath found a place," "and one of them shall not fall on the ground without your Father," said He who knew all the intensity of the Father's love. (Luke x 29.)

In view of this daily assemblage of birds here, this Pool better deserves the name of Struthion (sparrow) Pool, than the one now dry, north of the Tower of Antonio, to which Josephus attached that name.

These sparrows are the same species that were introduced a few years since, from England into New York, where they have increased so fast as to be familiar to every one who visits Union Park. Mr. Beecher thinks their pleasant chirp is destined to go with the English language around the world. If it does it will increase the world's cheerfulness, and lesson the number of the world's insects.

Nor do I think it trifling to write in my diary, that while upon the house top, adjacent to Hezekiah's Pool, I observed a little Jerusalem girl of five or six, rocking, and singing to her doll, with an intensity of interest and absorption of thought, deeply affecting to me.

From there we went through the Jews' quarter. This is composed of streets closed in by hovels abounding in disgusting sights and pestilential smells. The Jews were idly sauntering about, their long ringlets hanging down over their ears. Large hand-bills printed in Hebrew were posted up on the walls.

From there we went out by the Mograbbins Gate, to the Pool of Siloam. Seated upon one of its rude steps, in the southwest corner, the cool water flowing just under my feet, I read from John ix, the story of the man born blind, who came here to receive his sight. "Jesus said unto him, Go, wash in the Pool of Siloam. He went his way, therefore, and washed, and came seeing."

Even to the present day there is belief here that the water of Siloam will heal sore and inflamed eyes. Mr. Prime, in his "Tent-life," writes that he "laved his eyes in Siloam, whose waters go softly." Josephus often remarks that these waters are sweet and abundant. But of course all this is as nothing to the stupendous gift by which the MASTER, standing in the temple upon yonder eminence, communicated to it the miraculous energy of imparting light to one born blind. I, too, bathed my eyes here, and as I did so, the soft and gentle stream perfectly justified my conception of Siloam.

And here, too, in the olden time, came the Levite, with his golden pitcher, on the last and great day of the Feast of Tabernacles, to fill it with Siloam's water, to be poured over the sacrifice in commemoration of the miraculous water-supply at Rephidim. To this golden pitcher the Lord pointed, when He cried in the temple, "If any man thirst, let him come unto me and drink."

It is at Siloam that tradition locates the death of Zacharias, (Matthew xxiii: 35) and even so late as the fifth century after Christ, the stones here were fabled to be red with his blood. (*Rubra saxa.*) Our enthusiastic countrymen, Robinson, Smith, and Barclay, entered the channel of the Pool and followed it under the lofty hill through a crooked and narrow rock-hewn passage, sometimes walking, sometimes stooping, sometimes kneeling, sometimes creeping, about one thousand seven hundred feet to the Virgin's Fountain, at the upper entrance. Recently, Lieutenant Warren has performed the same feat.

Around the Pool of Siloam I gathered quite an album full of flowers, the beautiful maiden's hair fern that grows profusely here; also the hyssop "that springeth out of the wall," (1 Kings iv : 33) and others. The hyssop, I find, grows in green tufts in every ancient wall in this country.

From the Virgin's Fountain we went through the King's Gardens, anciently so called, to the Beer Ayub, or Well En-Rogel. The King's Gardens, or "royal paradise," as a writer terms them, were probably the ancient Valley of Shaveh or the King's Dale, in which occurred the affecting scene wherein participated Melchizadek, "King of Salem and Priest of the Most High," and Abraham, "the Father of the Faithful." From yonder rocky eminence of Zion on the west, came the venerable Shem, or Melchizadek with bread and wine. Here he saluted the victorious hero. "Blessed be Abram of the Most High God, possessor of heaven and earth." (Genesis xiv.) It is the greenest and loveliest nook around the whole city, and I could scarcely tear myself away from the contemplation of it, in association with events so pathetic; although the women and children from the neighboring village of Sylwan (Siloam) had crowded around me, filling the air alike with clamorous demands for *backsheesh*, and an aroma not at all derived from the sweet gardens covering the King's Dale.

These gardens, I must not neglect to write, are watered by "cool Siloam's shady rill." "The waters of Shiloah that go softly," as the prophet Isaiah describes them, flow here and make the valley the greenest spot in the vicinity, reclaimed from sterility into an oasis of fig trees, olives, pomegranates and vines by means of this tiny rill, which fertilizes and beautifies all the region through which it passes. Here, too, are the kitchen gardens which, with those of Etham, near Bethlehem, supply Jerusalem with its vegetables.

I am forgetting a pleasant fact connected with the Pool of Siloam; that is, the great number of *bees* we observed watering there. We had noticed on the west side of the city a collection of beehives, long, earthenware jars, piled horizontally one upon another to the depth of six or eight courses, upon the roof of a small outhouse, the same style of beehives observed all the way from Joppa, and several honey pedlars already have visited our tents, offering to supply us with the delectable food so often named in the sacred narration. It is the experience of all travelers, as well as our own, that the honey of Canaan possesses a finer flavor than any we have at home.

The Well En-Rogel, or Beer Eyub, is of special interest in an historical point of view. It lies just below the Akeldama, or Potter's Field, that gloomy investment of a traitor's ill-gotten gain. Such a traitor! Such a treason! As we sat for an hour in the shade of the buildings surrounding Beer Eyub, memory was faithful to recall the story of that dreadful "Field of Blood" that covers the slope of the rocky hill just above.

The enclosure termed by the Roman Catholics the *Garden of Gethsemane*, is a plot of ground a little more than half an acre in area, surrounded by a high stone wall, having but one entrance and that through a low gate. As the janitor justly said, "all must bow who enter here." Elliot measured the walls by stepping seventy-five of his short paces on a side, equal to one hundred and fifty feet. This hollow in the hills, a half-mile of garden ground, is termed *Jesmoniya* by the natives and somewhere in it, no doubt, the garden stood. It is quite likely that this is the very spot. It is neatly kept and stocked with olives, cypresses and flowers. The olive trees are eight in number, each boarded up and protected from the pilfering propensities of visitors. Such noble and venerable trees! Rough in their trunks, so aged that their cavities are built up with stone for strength, but fruitful as only such patriarchal trees can be. Each has three, four or five stems springing from a single root, and these roots the same, doubtless, that supported the trees under whose shade Jesus walked, turned aside, prayed, knelt and agonized his soul even unto death. The thought is overwhelming. My mind, while here, was chiefly occupied in the thought that the resurrection of Christ is the guarantee of the resurrection of all mankind. A young lady went past me as I sat and read of the agony, the tears and the sweat. She was making the circuit of Gethsemane upon her knees. Her costly garments already soiled and ragged by her morning's work,—sobs and tears shaking her whole frame,—her hands wildly thrown above her head. I had never seen such a sight before. It recalled the long trains of Irish Catholics that I have observed on snowy winter mornings, *on their knees*, outside the church near Sweeny's Hotel, each patiently waiting his turn to enter. It recalled the poet's words:

> "With knees of adoration wore the stone,
> A holy maid."

Though whether this was religion or fanaticism must be left to the Great Searcher of Hearts to say.

In the services of Passion week, this is "*Tuesday before Easter*." The Scriptural references are those in Matthew xi; 12–19; referring to His curse upon the barren fig tree; and the driving out of the money changers and pedlars who profaned the temple. Coming in from Bethany, where he had spent the night, our Saviour probably returned again to that village at the close of the day. It was during Tuesday that the Scribes and Pharisees plotted to take His life.

THE ST. STEPHEN'S GATE; OR GATE ON THE EAST SIDE OF JERUSALEM.

Called by the natives *Bab es-Sitti Miryam*, or Gate of Lady Mary.

CHAPTER X.

A DAY ON MOUNT OLIVET.

St. Stephen's Gate—Burial of the dead—Playing camel—Brood of puppies—Chicken merchant —Dog fight—Scanty breakfast—Arab and his horse—Broom—Brook Kedron—Martyr Stephen—Hebrew burying ground—Epitaphs—Tomb of Absalom—Story of the Great Stone—Garden of Gethsemane—View from Mount Olivet—Retrospect of Biblical history—Church now building.

ELLIOT'S DIARY.

CAMP OF THE ASSYRIANS, Wednesday, March 24th, 1869. 6 P. M.

IN going into the city, to-day, I passed clear round to the east side and entered by the St. Stephen's Gate. The people here call it the *Gate of Lady Mary*, because they think the mother of Jesus was buried in a tomb east of this gate, near the Garden of Gethsemane. But the Bible doesn't say so. There are some carved lions over this gate, just like the stone lion we got at Kirjath Jearim.*

As I went up to that gate, I saw the people burying a man in the graveyard close by. The body had been brought a good ways, and as there was no coffin, the corpse was very offensive, reminding me of the expression of Martha in John xi: 39. The grave had been dug east and west. They laid the head of the corpse to the west, placing him on his right side, with his right hand under his right ear as a man does when he is listening for something. Hassan says that they do this so that the dead man may hear Allah call him on the resurrection day. Then they sung a droning song that was terribly unpleasant to me. Then they took a number of sticks, and fastened them into the sides of the grave, crossways over the body, so as to leave quite a vacant place above it, this was so that when he shall rise on the last day, he may not have *to lift up a great deal of earth.* But I noticed all the older graves had sunk down some two feet, and I think this plan doesn't work. This dead man had a small tuft of hair on top of his head, which the angel of the resurrection will lift him up by. All the rest of his head was shaved smooth, the same way Hassan has his. Hassan says, in some places here they bury a dead man with a piece of stone in one hand and a small copper coin in the other. The *stone* is to be used at heaven's gate to knock for admission; the *money* is to pay the doorkeeper. How foolish! But none of these ceremonies are practised when a *woman* dies. Oh, no. They don't believe a woman has any soul, and therefore she can't go to heaven at all, or be raised up again by Allah or the angel.

---

* **See the drawing of Stephen's Gate facing Chapter Tenth.**

One of mother's instructions to me, which she wrote in my memorandum book, was "to take my stand at the corners of the streets of Jerusalem and describe all that I see, even to the smallest particulars; then to walk up and down and take items." So here goes for a third day in the streets of Jerusalem! I shall number my *items* in regular order:—

First. A little girl about six years old. Another little girl about twelve. They are playing camel and the big girl is the camel. She kneels down as the camels do. Then the little one climbs her back, clasps hands over her forehead, kicks her in the side and makes a noise as the cameliers do. The big girl screams and gets up awkwardly, as a camel does, turns her head back, grinds her teeth, spits and shrieks, then away they both go, laughing just as such a merry pair of sisters ought to. All the dress the two girls have on wouldn't cover a candle stand decently. Their clothes are made of blue cotton of the thinnest, cheapest and raggedest character. But, oh, what a merry game of camel they do play!

Second. A chicken pedlar comes by with strings of poultry swung all over him. The man is fairly covered with hens. A great rooster's head is sticking out where *his* head ought to be. An enormous pair of wings flaps over his shoulders, reminding me of a ridiculous old angel that I saw painted up in a Greek church yesterday.

Third. Three laboring men have sat down on the sidewalk near me to eat their breakfast. They are hungry. Their only victuals are *libbarn*, or curdled milk in a small wooden dish, and *bread* that looks like such black sawdust as mahogany wood makes. I told Hassan to buy them some boiled eggs. Nobody ever saw eggs boiled so hard as they boil them in Jerusalem. They must keep them on hand ready boiled. They boil them over night. And never was a lot of boiled eggs swallowed so fast before. Then the grateful fellows came up to thank me. Each one put his right hand under my right hand so as just to to touch it and raised it up to his lips and kissed it. This is the way they do here. They went off without even asking me for *backsheesh.* I guess they forgot it. The poor dog across the way is asking me for it in every flap of its withered tail.

Fourth. A female dog lies under the window opposite where I am sitting and suckles her four pups, young things whose eyes are not yet opened. The sidewalk there is only twenty inches wide. Thousands of people pass along that sidewalk every day. Yet the creature gave birth to them there and she will bring them up there; for nobody will disturb her even on that narrow sidewalk. At first she snarled at me, for she doesn't like the style of my clothes; but after I bought her a string of *kabobs* and some bread, she changed her mind. She saw that, after all, these outlandish clothes may cover a human heart. And now, while I am making a drawing of her family, she wags her tail and turns her one motherly eye up to me with a grateful expression.

Fifth. A furious dog fight surging down the street nearly carries me off my feet. Hassan, who was smoking outside a cafe watching me, came up with his *koorbash* and went in for them. He fairly cut holes in the dogs' sides till I stopped him. Anything like humanity seems foolishness to these people. They used to sew up their prisoners in asses' skins and then burn them alive. Used to cut their feet and hands off; burn out their eyes with hot irons; tear out their tongues by the roots. Hassan says he would love to treat his enemies that way, and I believe him. He told me of a family of four brothers, living on Mount Lebanon, whose feet, hands, tongues and eyes were destroyed by a cruel tyrant more than thirty years ago.

All the time this dog fight was going on, the mother lay perfectly unconcerned, suckling her little dogs. The heroes of the two factions had agreed that *she*, at least, shouldn't be meddled with; though, to look at them, you wouldn't think there was so much gallantry in them.

Sixth. A Bedouin Arab, from the desert, comes riding by. As it is against the laws of Jerusalem for him to bring his weapons inside, he has left his spear and his horse pistols, and his long, flint lock musket, outside the city. But he hasn't left his wild, animal face, or his lustful eye, or his cunning, thievish leer. Not a bit of it. His horse is a hundred times more of a gentleman than the rider. What a splendid horse! As the Bedouin comes so near me that I could lay my hand on him, I give him the salute, and say *salaam aleikam*, as much like an Arab as I can. Quick as a flash, he reins up his horse and looks at me. At first he hesitates, then answers my salute. He does it as much better than I do, as Harriet can sing better than I can. Then he reaches out his dry, sunburnt hand, and whispers, *backsheesh*. I gave him some and he rode off in high glee. But if his noble horse could speak, *he* would say, "You Christian dog, I scorn you and your backsheesh! I am a proud, independent Arab steed, from the desert."

I wonder how these chaps can mount their horses with those long, eighteen-feet spear handles in their hands. I must ask Hassan about that.

I forgot to say that I spent an hour with Harriet and John, this morning, on Mount Olivet, and had a good time throwing stones at the Tomb of Absalom; miserable wretch as he was.

JOHN'S DIARY.

CAMP OF THE ASSYRIANS, Wednesday, 6 P. M.

To-day has been given to viewing Jerusalem, from the Mount of Olives. Harriet sketched and described the scenery near the top, while I wandered round the base and examined the Garden of Gethsemane, the Hebrew Cemetery, and other objects of interest. After climbing to the top of the ruined Church of Ascension, I went down to the Brook Kedron, and followed its course for some distance. There is no flow of water in it; nor is the Kedron at all such a thing as, in our country, we would term a *brook*. Fifty feet of stones and loose earth have been washed in, and now encumber its bed, so that Elliot laughs at the idea of having two stone bridges to span a dry ravine. Our Christian poets have found great euphony in the name of *Kedron*. We associate it also with our Saviour's last and affecting visit to Gethsemane, and so the associations give it importance. As far back as A. D. 1322, Jerusalem had been so often destroyed, and its walls beaten down, and tumbled into the valley, that the bed of the Kedron was very much raised. The *wady* or valley of Jehoshaphat was conspicuous enough, but no brook ran in its channel any more than at present.

One of my best points of observation was the Jewish burying-ground. Innumerable white, flat stones overspread the valley here, each having a short, Hebrew inscription. It is here that aged Jews desire to be buried, that they may reach celestial happiness without having to make their way underground to the valley of Jehoshaphat, as they believe every one will, who is buried elsewhere! They expect to arise from these graves at the resurrection, and to be the first to see their Messiah. I was sorry to observe, the other day, that a number of their old grave stones had been used, at some former period, in building the walls in Mount Zion; the same thing was done in the twelfth century. It must be deemed the grossest of insults by these people. When they again get possession of their hereditary home, how quickly those walls will come down.

We had previously secured, by the assistance of some learned rabbis, translations of several of these Hebrew epitaphs. I copy two that are most beautiful. There is a peculiar accent of touching grace in them; a humility; a certain hope of universal kindness; a sense of the happiness of reposing with the just; purity of morals and sweetness of family life; a mild acceptation of death, considered as *repose*, which have not had the attention of travelers, they deserve. These epitaphs lack one thing—*faith in Jesus Christ*—to make them absolutely perfect. These two, are the epitaphs of a lady and her husband—

EPITAPH OF A WOMAN.

"Great in degree, and glorious; the heart of her husband trusted safely in her; praised as a woman that feareth the Lord. She was the king's daughter, all glorious within, who rose above all elevation, and was perfect in beauty, glory, and righteousness. She opened her mouth with wisdom, and in her tongue was the law of kindness; a stem of high descent and elevation. Was she not the Rabbiness (Mrs. Rabbi), the pleasant roe, and the widow of our master and teacher, the holy Rabbi, the holy, pious Chaim, the son of Ater, of blessed memory. She was daughter of the mighty and wise, the high prince, our honored teacher, Rabbi Moses, the son of Ater, of blessed memory."

EPITAPH OF A MAN.

"Here is a head of gold. Was he not beloved of the Almighty? A precious stone; to discourse of him, is easy. The Almighty meant it for good when he enlightened him from his glory, as they lighten the seven lamps; his shaft, and his branch, it kindled his people. And he called him by the name Hephzibah. He was a bringer to light of all that is kind; he was glory, he was brightness. Was he not the wonderful and honored Rabbi, the perfect theologian (cabbalist) of the Almighty, the holy, the pious, our honored teacher and Lord Rabbi, Chaim, son of Ater? He grew old, seeking in the Upper Geshibah (place of study); on the 15th day of the month Thamuz, in the year 5550, (i. e. the year A. D. 1790) gaining the splendor of the Shecinah. He is the author of the book 'The Lord the King,' (Hamnelech Hashene) and the book 'Taar,' (Form) and the book, 'Or Ha-haiiom,' (Light of the Living) and the book, 'Rishon le Zion,' (Is. xli : 27) (First to Zion.)"

The road, to cross the brook Kedron, goes out at St. Stephen's Gate, and here it is impossible for the Bible student not to recall the scene that occurred at the stoning of the proto-martyr. Even admitting the doubtfulness of the locality, and it has been shown even by the Catholic De Vogue, that in earlier times the place settled on as the place of Stephen's murder, was near the *Damascus Gate*, some ways from here; yet, the very name recalls the event. I read Chapters vi and vii of Acts, on the spot, and tried to imagine it; the coarse, shrivelled faces of that Jewish mob; their large eyes bulging out of their orbits; their gnashings of teeth; their vociferations; the people throwing dust into the air; tearing their clothes and twitching them convulsively; then the witnesses stoning the mild, unresisting deacon. And all this I contrasted with the conduct of the martyr himself, "calling upon God, and saying, Lord Jesus, receive my spirit;" and kneeling down, and crying with a loud voice, "Lord, lay not this sin to their charge; and when he had said this, falling asleep."

Next, I took my observations of the so-called Tomb of Absalom. It is greatly scarred by violence. This is but a modern structure, yet a very curious one. It has had rough handling from the custom of men and boys who pass it, to pick up handsfull of pebbles and make a target of it. Thus, they show their scorn for the undutiful son. I think I never saw Elliot so severely exercised as he was there. He undertook, as he said, "to stone the scallawag to death!" With his coat off, and his suspenders loosened, and his fine, boyish cheeks and eyes glowing with excitement, he quite filled the air with a shower of missiles, thrown with an aim as unerring as his determination.

I suggested to Mr. Fountain that if King David, when he went up by the ascent of Mount Olivet, yonder, fleeing from his miserable son, "and wept as he went up, his head covered and his feet bare," if he could have anticipated such an example of filial spirit, thirty centuries later, it might have afforded the unhappy father a crumb of comfort.

Dr. Robinson was struck with the resemblance between the Tomb of Absalom and some ancient tombs at Petra; "isolated masses of rock, fifteen or twenty feet square, cut out of the cliff and left some distance from it." Whenever I think of it hereafter, it will recall the memory of the youthful American who pelted it with stones, this morning, crying out, "*that* for your father; *that* for my father; *that* for Abishai; *that* for Joab; *that* for Ittai, the Hittite," while his missiles struck the front of the column, or entered the cavity previously made by the same rough procedure.

One enthusiastic writer was so pleased with the beauty of this tomb, that he called it "a connecting link between the pyramid and the Parthenon." An Israelite, who saw Elliot's proceedings, says that it is the ordinary practice of his people who live at Jerusalem, to lead their children out to this place that they may spit at it, and throw stones at it, and so learn filial obedience. He was pleased to hear from me that the Jews, everywhere, have notoriously most obedient children.

Poor Absalom! lying as he does in that distant and disgraceful pit, on Gilead (2 Samuel xviii : 17); it is his fate to furnish the world such another example of treachery as that of the apostate Judas, whose grave yard we can see from this Tomb of Absalom's, a little ways further down the valley. But

11

what an unfortunate family was that of King David! Ammon, Absalom, Adonijah, his three sons, the victims successively of lust, vengeance and ambition, how truthfully did the Spirit say to David, after the great sin of his life had been consummated, "the sword shall never depart from thine house." (2 Samuel xii : 10.)

While at Joppa, last week, the first hour that I spent upon holy earth, was given to writing the *story of the shell.* To-day, I broke a fragment of stone from the great wall that rises eighty feet on the east side of Mount Moriah, and have now written my

STORY OF THE STONE.

"I lay darkly and silently in the quarries under Mount Moriah, when the first builders of Jerusalem, the ancient Jebusites, gathered their materials, and erected their walls of defense upon Mount Zion. I slumbered there at the time of the pious meeting between Abraham and Melchizadek; and when the patriarch brought his son Isaac, here, forty-two years later, to an interrupted sacrifice upon the crown of the hill of Moriah; and when Jacob fled northward on his way to a divine vision, at Bethel; and when he returned, twenty years later, with his dying Rachel; and when Joseph passed here ten years later, in the search of his brethren. I heard the shock of the onset when Joshua took Jerusalem, at the point of the sword, two hundred and seventy-eight years later, and burnt it with fire; and the shock of the onset when King David, at the head of all Israel, took it by assault, four hundred and four years later, and made it the seat of his kingdom. I was taken, thirty-seven years afterwards, from the quarries, a great stone, hewed and squared and laid up here in the east wall, one hundred feet from its base, facing the rising sun. Here I have remained for two thousand eight hundred and eighty years, and have witnessed great events. I saw the dedication of the temple, seven and one-half years after its corner stone was laid. I heard the shout of the assembled millions who bowed their faces to the pavement and cried, 'For He is good; for His mercy endureth forever.' The gleam of the fire from heaven and the shadow of the miraculous smoke, alike passed over my polished face. I witnessed the coming of the great Chaldean, four hundred and sixteen years later, heard his battle cry, saw the irresistible assault of his armies, the city ruined and the temple burned. Fifty-two years afterwards, I saw the little company under Zerubbabel, return from Babylon and begin the pious task of rebuilding. Three hundred and seventy-one years later, I saw the greater Maccabæus perform the same pious undertaking. One hundred and forty-seven years later, I saw a third re-edification of the temple by the monster Herod. Fifty-one years later I beheld the triumphant procession of the Son of Man as he passed over the great bridge connecting Mount Olivet with Mount Moriah, when the people of Jerusalem shouted 'Hozanna to the Son of David.' A few days afterwards the same people, fickle and untrustworthy, shouted '*Crucify Him.*' Then I saw the heavens darkened at midday and felt a trembling of the solid earth such as Jerusalem rarely experiences. Thirty-seven years later I witnessed the armies of Titus fortifying the hill east of me, and drawing their lines around the doomed city; then heard those sounds of assault, resistance and final despair with which, by this time, I had become so familiar. These savage sights and sounds were often renewed afterwards. A. D. 1099 I was shaken in my place by the onset of the Crusaders who put 7,000 men to the sword upon the platform just above me, until the blood flowed over our wall like the drenchings of a great rain storm. Again and again I was an eye-witness of such scenes, until now, two thousand, eight hundred and eighty years from my first establishment in this wall, I give to an enquiring youth from distant lands, my strange story of the stone."

HARRIET'S DIARY.

CAMP OF THE ASSYRIANS. Wednesday, 6 P. M.

A morning and an afternoon upon Mount Olivet! Who would not covet so great a privilege! From 7 o'clock until 11 this morning, I sat under a temporary shade formed by stretching some green boughs upon a framework of sticks. This, I fancy, was much like the *booths* which the people made when the Tirshatha read the law of Moses in their hearing, and commanded them to go forth unto the Mount (of Olives) and fetch olive branches, and pine branches, and myrtle branches, and palm branches and branches of thick trees (probably the fig, which is the *thickest* of all) to make booths. So the people went forth and brought them and made themselves booths, everyone upon the roof of his house and in their courts, and in the courts of the house of God * * and sat under the booths," (Nehemiah viii.) From 3 o'clock till 5 this afternoon I sketched from a point about a quarter of a mile further north.

By 5 this morning, breakfast was over at our camp, for we desired to have ample time for our Olivet observations. We came around the north side of the city to its northeast corner,—through the Mohammedan burying ground, a dreary place and a hopeless,—as far as opposite St. Stephen's gate,—down the steep hill there into the Valley of Jehoshaphat,—crossed Kedron on the upper bridge, came up the slope of Olivet, leaving the Garden of Gethsemane on the the left,—through the venerable Hebrew burying ground, with the Tomb of Absalom close on the right and so to the top of the mountain. Before preparing myself to sketch Jerusalem from Olivet, I accompanied Mr. Fountain and the boys to the summit of the ancient Convent of the Ascension, now a Turkish mosk. After a little delay, the gate was opened to us by an Imaum with a white beard, the peaceable keeper of this holy place. The first care of the hospitable and tolerant old man is upon his modest settee to seat the visitors of every nation and religion, then to offer them the Oriental *fingan*, or cup of coffee.

Then he led us to the top of his minaret to admire the panorama, of which he is justly proud. It is impossible to imagine a view more satisfactory. The eye embraces at a glance, the whole city of Jerusalem and the mountains of Judæa, and extends beyond the Dead Sea to the land of Moab, evoking everywhere the grandest souvenirs of the religious history of the world. We enjoyed the view with insatiable pleasure. The Jordan gave back glimpses here and there of its silvery waters, like a flashing scimeter half sheathed in sand; its valley opening out to our left for a distance of twenty or thirty miles.

Nearly the whole of the precipitous road from Olivet to Jericho could be traced out. The village of Bethany lay distinctly at our feet. In the dewy morning, the flowers, with which the slopes of Olivet are covered, appear at their brightest. It then seems as if some rainbow has fallen to pieces here and strewn its glittering fragments over these hills. The view of the northern end of the Dead Sea, of which we got a glimpse from the walls of Jerusalem, is very commanding. On account of the marvellous purity of this mountain air, it always seems so near, although in fact fourteen miles absent, that I could throw my gold pencil case into it from the top of this minaret.

A large number of ravens making their nests in and about the mosk, perch and croak among the olive trees below us, and set us examining the various passages of Scripture in which the Bounteous Father is represented as having tender regard even for their discordant cries. What joy there must have been in heaven when the Son of God arose from this hillside and returned to his native throne and kingdom. (Acts i: 9.)

But my morning vocation was not alone to gaze. Yonder, my shelter has been made for me by the servants and I am to sketch Jerusalem from the spot where our Saviour stood when he wept over it.

All intelligent visitors to Jerusalem have united in praising the scenery from this point. It is mild and gentle, with soft variations of light and shade.* One elegant writer calls the view "a solace of holy reminiscences pure and native." Raised one hundred and fourteen feet above the highest point of Jerusalem, and two hundred and ninety-five feet above Mount Moriah, which is the nearest part of Jerusalem, the sketcher sees the city as a continuous hill, standing out singly from the surrounding mountains. Here David stood, while contemplating with a soldier's eye the strong fortress of Jebus on the opposite cliffs, and preparing with his two hundred and eighty thousand men, choice warriors of Israel, to storm it. (1 Chron. xii.) And so has Shishak stood here; and Nebuchadnezzar, and Titus, and all the conquerors of Jerusalem; for from this point the defenses could best be viewed, and arrangements made for the attack. From here, perhaps, Josephus pointed out the various localities to Titus, who with his Tenth Legion, made this his principal point of observation during the long months of the seige. To this place, probably, Solomon conducted his chief architect, and showed him the narrow, rocky ledge of Moriah which had been selected as the site of his proposed temple. From this commanding spot, all the imagery of the Levitical worship was best seen, and here Nebuchadnezzar studied it day by day during the eighteen months that *he* strove to capture Jerusalem. How it affected the royal mind may be seen from his singular dream or vision recorded in Daniel.

They also stood here when the man born blind was led down to Siloam yonder, and came back seeing. (John ix: 7.) Or when the impotent man took up his bed and walked from the margin of Bethesda yonder. (John ii; 2.) Or when the chief musician, or Neginoth, with stringed instruments and high sounding cymbals praised God according to His excellent greatness (Psalm cl),

* See the view of Jerusalem facing the Twelfth Chapter.

on yonder platform; or where the great Antiochus, swelling with anger, vowed proudly "that he would come to Jerusalem and make it a common burying place of the Jews" (2 Macc. ix: 4); or when the early American missionary, Pliny Fisk, entered the Damascus Gate yonder, in 1825, to "go about his Master's business" at Jerusalem; or when Saul, "breathing out threatenings and slaughter against the disciples of the Lord" (Acts ix), went out of that same gate to the persecution, and came back again several years afterwards the humblest of the followers of the meek and lowly Jesus; they who stood here when the Jews "stoned Stephen" on yonder hillside, "calling upon God and saying, Lord Jesus receive my spirit." (Acts vii: 59); they who stood here when the great procession passed westward along this very pathway by whose side I am sitting,—passed over garments spread in the way, and over branches of trees, and went across the stupendous bridge, now destroyed, and through the portals of the Golden Gate, yonder, while "they that went before and they that followed said, Hosanna, blessed is he that cometh in the name of the Lord" (Mark 11); and when Jesus "beheld the city," probably at this very spot where my booth has been set up, and "wept over it" (Luke xix: 41) just as he had wept over the sorrows of the disconsolate family at Bethany but a few days before (John xi); finally, they who stood here on that dark, that doleful afternoon when "the earth did quake and the rocks rent" and "darkness was over the whole land until the ninth hour" because Christ, on yonder ridge, scarcely a mile from this spot, had given up the ghost, first enduring the pangs of the cross,—— but my sentence can never be completed. *All those scenes* and a multitude of others, embracing incidents in the life of every Scriptural character from Abraham to Paul, passed within sight of spectators upon this memorable slope of Olivet where I sit.

The French Government has bought the spot of ground traditionally made the place where our Saviour gave the Lord's Prayer to His disciples and a splendid church is now erecting over it. How these lying wonders and superstitions love to cluster around a venerable and holy spot. Is it any wonder that it produces a painful coldness and incredulity in the minds of Protestants. The Turk in the old mosk told us this morning a fable quite as credible, that in old times there were two brazen columns there, so near each other that whoever could squeeze himself through was sure of *remission of sins*. Is not this a sort of fabulous adaptation of the brazen pillars that used to stand across the valley yonder? The Mohammedans even now exhibit such a pair of pillars in the Mosk El Aksar, only they are *marble ones*.

The newspapers when I left home had this paragraph, but it is difficult to learn here how much truth there is in it:

"Princess de la Tour d'Auvergne, who has obtained a grant from the Sultan of the piece of ground whereon Christ taught the Lord's Prayer, is personally superintending the erection of a temple on the spot, which will contain the prayer in every language. She has already spent over $50,000 in carrying out her project."

It of course refers to the same building that I have named above.

This janitor also rehearsed a story I had read long ago, that on every Ascension Day a strong wind used to come over this mountain and prostrate all who were in the church. This is doubtless a confused version of the descent of of the Holy Ghost upon the Apostles. (Acts ii: 2.)

This hillside recalls many other readings. As the admiring crowd threw palms and raiment in the way that the King of Peace might triumphantly assume his own (Mark xi: 8); so when King Baldwin, in A. D. 1109, met Sigurd, the crusader, at Jerusalem, "he let valuable clothes be brought and spread upon the road," that Sigurd might ride over them with honor. The same marks of respect were paid him at Constantinople, by the Emperor Alexius, by which, I suppose, it had become a common custom in that day.

The beautiful Adonis-flower, here suggests how often this tincture of blood upon flowers and stones has played a part in history. The blood of Adonis, upon this flower, the blood of Zacharius, upon the stones by the Pool of Siloam, yonder, the blood of Stephen, upon the hill side, at yonder gate, are all exhibitions of human fancy, running riot into symbolisms. Let me recall with a more solemn emotion that "blood mingled with sweat," which moistened the ground in the little enclosure at my feet.

The afternoon was spent on the slope of Olivet, a little further north, but as we are to remove our tents there on Saturday, I postpone my notes on that locality to that time.

Among the absurdities with which Jerusalem is affected, one is to bring trinkets, beads, gems, etc., into the Holy Sepulchre and lay them on what the priests call the Tomb of Christ. This makes them sell a great deal better! It reminds me of a newspaper notice that I read lately, in which twenty thousand persons laid jewels, rosaries, and other things, upon the dead body of the Bishop of Angers, in France, in order to communicate to them a supernatural virtue! I suppose people can be educated down to anything; but this appears to me very foolish, and even the Mohammedans laugh at it.

It seems, to read the old Catholic writings, as if the only purpose they had in view was to locate stories of their numberless saints, and to make each locality, in the Holy Land, a *point d'affair*, on which new inventions could rest. Their blunders, of the plainest Scriptures, are endless. Jacob's dream, at Bethel, they located on Mount Moriah; Abraham's sacrifice of Isaac, they located on Mount Akra.

I insert this quotation in my diary, from Richter: "Children are little Orientals. Dazzle them with the wide plains of the East, with brilliant dewdrops and bright-tinted flowers. Give them in stories the impulse which will carry them over our cold Northern rocks and capes, into the warm gardens of the South * * educate them religiously, through the senses."

The teachers of the various charity schools, here, tell me that the task of instructing the children of the lower classes is a most discouraging one. *Their* condition of misery and degradation is truly appalling. Tbe first necessity is to *humanize*, then *instruct* them.

Among our visitors, to-day, was a party of American gentlemen who saluted us politely. One of them, I was pained to see, carried that badge so suggestive of the days of darkness, of long struggles, of desolated homes, of bleeding hearts, an *empty sleeve*. I could not help reverting to the memory of dear friends who fell upon one side or the other, on those crimson plains of war; and the thought saddened my whole hour at Jerusalem.

The Roman Catholics, here, have eight convents, four for each sex, and four schools, two for each sex; also, a sort of theological college for training priests. To judge from what catches the eye, there seem to be more priests here, now, than work for them to do.

I was interested, to-day, in a sight that recalled to me some of the most affecting allusions in the discourses of our dear Saviour. It was that of a shepherd carrying two or three little kids and lambs in his bosom, while their distracted mothers ran after him, filling the air with their plaintive cries. He was only saving their untried feet from being bruised upon the rocks.

We agreed, the first Sunday after we left New York, that if we should ever reach Jerusalem, we would dedicate the eight veteran olive trees, in the Garden of Gethsemane, to eight of those sweet song-writers and composers whose words and music we sang together on that Sunday, and which, like the pure "oil of joy" these olive trees produce, have gladdened millions of hearts now reposing in the Family Above: Phillip Phillips, of New York; H. R. Palmer, of Illinois; J. D. Webster, of Wisconsin; Ossian E. Dodge, of Minnesota; C. R. Blackall, of Illinois; Alice Cary, of New York; Lowell Mason, of Massachusetts; B. F. Jacobs, of Illinois.

In the services of Passion Week, this is *Wednesday before Easter*. The Scriptural references of the day are those in Mark, from xi : 20 to xiv : 1–9. They include the feast at Bethany, in the house of Simon, the leper; the anointing of His head; His visit to Jerusalem and return to Bethany. The day's preaching included the memorable parable of the wicked husbandmen, the question of tribute to Cæsar; the question, by the Sadducees, relative to the resurrection; the incident of the poor widow, and the prediction of the destruction of Jerusalem.

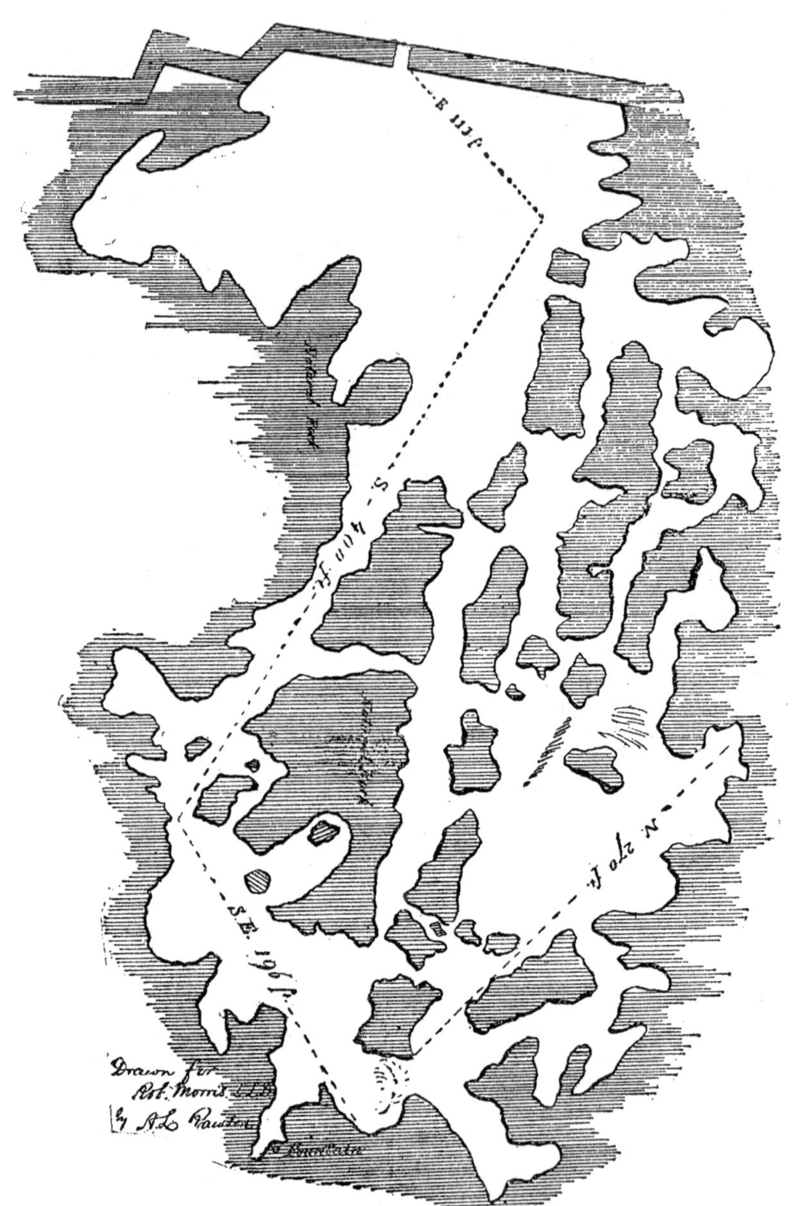

THE GREAT QUARRY UNDER JERUSALEM.

CHAPTER XI.

THE QUARRY AND THE TEMPLE.

Insulted in a coffee house—Loafing and cruel sheikhs—Street music—Queer mode of drinking—Watering the streets—A cawass—Horse shoeing—Dog districts—Mixing up things—Muldoon—Crazy man—Ancient inscription—Jews in Jerusalem—The great quarry—Mount Moriah—The accuracy of Josephus—The Mohammedan religion—Degraded state of the native women.

ELLIOT'S DIARY.

CAMP OF THE ASSYRIANS, 6 P. M., Thursday, March 25, 1869.

EVER since we arrived here, Monday morning, Mr. Fountain has permitted me to select my own field of observations, while he leads Harriet and John through their explorations. I much prefer this way of examining Jerusalem, alone. I do much better by myself. Old Dr. Peterman reads my diary and flatters my pride, that I am making *real discoveries.* Everybody stops to speak with me, because, they say, they never before saw a boy, twelve years old, going about by himself, with a cockle-shell in his hat, hunting up items. To-day, I took Hassan and my Turkish soldier, and I made their lazy legs fly over the rocky ways. But I couldn't get Sweet-Home to leave the tents.

What a lot of village sheikhs there are, hanging round Jerusalem! Hassan says they come in every day, from five or ten miles around, and loaf here. I think I have met a hundred this week. Most all of them want *backsheesh*, but they don't get it from me. If I ask them any questions, the first one is, do you know the name of the Sultan of Turkey? only about one in five can tell me. And yet his name, *Abd-el-Asiz*, is stamped on every piece of money! But it is little they can read what is stamped on money. Every village has at least one sheikh. Bethel, with only thirty houses, has two. This reminds me of the pasage, "for the transgressions of a land, many are the princes thereof." (Prov. xxviii : 2.) These sheikhs are said to be very tyrannical, in their small, mean way, and the passage in Proverbs xxviii : 3, just fits them : "The poor man that oppresseth the poor, is like a sweeping rain that leaveth no food."

I had quite an adventure in a coffee house, to-day. I had gone in to give Hassan a few cups of coffee and a smoke. The fellow had only smoked seven cigarettes since daylight, and he couldn't stand it any longer. A Turkish soldier, who was in there, told Hassan to tell me that I was a little Yankee pup. I told Hassan to tell him he was a liar. Hassan was afraid to tell him that. Then I told him myself, right to his face, that he was a dirty, worthless *kalb*—that means dog. Gracious, how mad he was. He looked as if he meant to kill me. But some French gentlemen came in just then, and when Hassan told them about it, they took the fellow and threw him out the back windows into the Pool of Hezekiah. I hadn't said a word to the soldier, and can't imagine why he acted so. It was the first time I have found a Turkish soldier uncivil. Lucky for him I had sent Kosroo off on an errand just then, or he might have killed him.

When Hassan had finished his *narghilah* and drank three cups of coffee, at my expense, we walked on again through the streets. I met a couple of musicians, one playing a sort of one-stringed fiddle, and singing like a good fellow; the other, collecting *backsheesh.* The singing was bad enough, but the one-stringed fiddle was fearful. The siring was an inch wide. If it had been wider I don't think I could have stood it at all. I asked Hassan what the song was about. He hesitated and said it was a love-song, and meant that the sun beams from a lady's eyes; the seven stars shine from her mouth; the full moon rises from her breast—and a good deal more, that he wouldn't tell me. I was quite satisfied with that specimen.

I saw a man drinking water out of a little earthen cruise. He held it six inches over his mouth and poured the water down his throat. It didn't strangle him a bit. I tried it. Poured most of the water down my bosom, and choked myself with the rest.

A man was watering the streets from large skin bags under his arms. He has the knack of it, and does'nt waste a great deal of water.

A consular dragoman or *cawass* went by with solemn mien and silver stick, a long, curved sword, long, silver-headed staff, splendid uniform, and a strut equal to the drum-major of the Forty-third New York. He reminds me of the saying here: "Buy a pipe and give a napoleon for it; let your dragoman buy it and give two." They are great cheats.

They are shoeing a horse close by. To keep him from biting, they fasten a hook-em-snivey in his upper lip, something like a clothes-pin. The blacksmith shop measures seven by nine feet; so they have to shoe the horse out in the street. The blacksmith has a hole dug in the middle of his floor so he can have the anvil on the level of his arm, and thus he need not stoop to his work.

At a corner is a place where three dog-districts meet—you can see delegates from all three of them. They will not cross the line. I tried them with a piece of bread. But they know the penalty too well, and are cautious. Such law-abiding dogs they are!

There is a donkey-stand here; a blacksmith shop; two coppersmiths, making terrific din; three baker's shops; another coppersmith, another donkey-stand, and a confectioner's, all within one hundred steps, on this side of the street.

A man with a board on his head, covered with cakes. He says they are *muldoon.* I bought some, and they are nothing but corn meal cakes, dried, without baking, and then frosted over with sugar. Muldoon is a humbug. Yet, he sold them fast, and everybody seemed to like them except me.

A man with Joppa oranges. Then a camel loaded with green grass. Then some pilgrims from Russia, wearing sheep skin dresses, with the wool inside; full of *life* were those dresses. Then a group of soldiers, all wearing *tarboushes*, and a fine looking negro for an officer. He stopped politely and talked with me; wouldn't let his soldiers ask me for *bachsheesh.* He had three medals hanging to his coat lappel. Then a stately old man with cloak trimmed with fur. In this country a common man's rank and position may be known by his dress just as much as an officer's. Then a party of men and women astride donkeys without stirrups: the saddles have an immense cushion in front to keep the rider from flying over his head when the donkey stumbles, which he is very fond of doing, and of lying down, too, right in the road. Every donkey has a boy to run behind and poke him up with a sharp stick. Then some desert Arabs with large yellow handkerchiefs on their heads in place of the *tarboush*, tied on with a black rope made of camel's hair, all of them on foot; they walked as awkwardly as sailors. Then came a flock of sheep that a man was leading through the noisy, crowded streets of Jerusalem. In all that variety of sounds, the poor things only listened for the voice of their own shepherd, and *where he led they followed.* But I might write all day and not finish this paragraph.

I took another stand about two squares off and counted a cookshop, a tinshop, a cookshop, a blacksmith shop, a cookshop and a tinshop, all in a row. Went into a number of carpenters' shops; their principal business is making, mending and ornamenting pipes, pipe-holders and pipe-handles. If there is any passage of Scripture they remind me of it is that one in which the Israelites are said to have "piped with pipes." (1 Kings i: 45.)

Going back to camp, I saw a crazy man. Among the Mohammedans crazy men are worshiped. This one was nearly naked, very crazy and very dirty. He went around among the shops taking bread and fruit, whatever he wanted to eat. Nobody interrupted him. The shopkeepers rather seemed to like it. I couldn't help thinking if he was in New York the star-police would have him locked up in ten minutes.

At the Joppa Gate of this great stone patchwork, I saw some Arabic words on the wall. Hassan says they mean that the present walls of Jerusalem were built by order of the Sultan Suleyman in 948; that is, in our way of counting, A. D. 1542. The lizards were gliding in and out of the walls there as if they cared nothing for the mortar of Suleyman.

To-day I have found mosquitoes in Jerusalem quite troublesome.

I notice that nobody I have talked to in this country, knows the real name of our country, *The United States.* As they know we came from America they call us *Americans*, and they don't know any other name for us. The British, however, call us *Yankees.* I asked an Italian gentleman how he would like to be called a *European*? He didn't understand me.

To-day I had a man to tattoo the Crusaders' "Arms of Jerasalem" on *my* arm. Many pilgrims do this as an unfading memory of their visit here. I do it as a memorial of that hero, Godfrey, the first King of Jerusalem. It is done by spreading India ink over the place and pricking it in with needles. It is not very painful and only takes a few minutes. Now I can claim some sort of connection with the great soldier of the Crusaders, who was buried near the entrance of the Holy Sepulchre. This is the figure on my arm, and it reminds me of Canticles viii: 6: "Set me as a seal upon thine arm."

Crusaders' Arms of Jerusalem.

The pattern is the Franciscan cross in the centre; the crowns of the three Wise Men of the East and the Star of Bethlehem below; and above the whole two palm branches tied together. John has copied for me the epitaph in Latin, of King Godfrey.

> Hic jacet inclytus Dux Godfridus de Bulion,
> Qui totam istam terram acquisivit cultui Christiano;
> Cujus anima regnat cum Christo. Amen.

This means, "Here lies enclosed the Duke Godfrey Boullion, who acquired all this country for the Christian faith. May his soul reign with Christ. Amen."

What a noble soul he had. When they offered to crown him King, he said: No, Jesus wore a crown of *thorns*. No golden crown for me!

JOHN'S DIARY.

CAMP OF THE ASSYRIANS. Thursday, 6 P. M.

We have to-day visited the great quarry under the City of Jerusalem. This enormous excavation, after lying for many ages sealed from the knowledge of man, was accidentally discovered by Dr. J. T. Barclay, about the year 1855. His dog was scenting in a hole under the city wall and suddenly disappeared. This led Dr. Barclay to imagine that there might be a quarry or cave worth exploring there. By enlarging the opening with a spade, he found his conjectures verified. A few years ago, quite an opening was made for the accommodation of the Prince of Wales and his party, and now it is an every day matter for visitors to enter and inspect the quarry.

In my drawing of it* the *light* portions shows where the stone was removed, the *dark* portions, where it was left in great natural columns to support the roof. But in spite of these large and frequent supports, this white limestone is so soft before it has been exposed to the air and light, that large pieces are constantly falling from the roof and accumulating in great heaps upon the floor. In entering the quarry we first went east one hundred and thirteen feet, as marked upon the map, then directly south four hundred feet, then southeast one hundred and ninety-six feet. Here is a deep circular pit in which Dr. Barclay discovered a human skeleton, some poor wretch, no doubt, who became bewildered in the windings of the great cave and fell in here unawares. With an abundant supply of candles, however, and a guide who had often traversed the quarry, we turned northward around the pit, and went two hundred and seventy feet, where the excavation seemed to end abruptly. Near the circular pit is a small basin chiselled in the rock, about five feet in diameter, and two and a half feet deep, into which the water was anciently collected for the use of the workmen. We found it full and running over; but the water is bitter and extremely disagreeable to the taste.

---

* See the drawing facing Chapter Eleventh.

That this great cavity is *a Quarry* and not a natural cave, is plain enough, both from the general appearance of it and from the marks of the chisel on every side. The floor is piled deep with clippings made by working implements. Along the sides of the quarry, deep, narrow grooves were cut lengthwise between the blocks, some of which were unusually large and these were then burst off by long levers or some other mechanical contrivance. Some magnificent halls were formed in this manner, while innumerable chambers and recesses stretch away to the right and left, showing that the rock was worked wherever it was found best in quality.

Dr. R. W. Stewart (in the "Tent and Khan") considers this quarry one of the most interesting discoveries yet made in Jerusalem. It proves that the great blocks seen in the walls of Mount Moriah, were not brought from the very great distance formerly supposed, but from a place upon the continuation of the same mountain. This quarry being higher than the top of the platform on which the Temple stood, it was easy to roll the heavy stones down the inclined plane to their places. It proves, too, from its vast capacity, how much stone was used in the various structures connected with Solomon's architecture.

Great numbers of bats were clinging to the roof of the quarry, which in places is forty feet high. Bones of various kinds, brought in here by jackals, prove the use to which the great cavern has been turned. Numerous crosses are traced upon the wall, indicating that Christians, probably Crusaders, had been here, and a few Hebrew and Arabic inscriptions, too much effaced to be readable, may be seen. In the deep and retired chamber which terminated our last traverse, we joined hands and voices to sing Mr. Robert Lowry's exquisite hymn, "Jerusalem forever bright, beautiful land of rest." This solemn place is dedicated to him as the man whose music above all others has delighted us upon our long journey, and in our Sunday School and family devotions for years past.

To-day, also, we have visited Mount Moriah; the enclosure styled by the natives the *Haram es-Shereef*, or Noble Sanctuary. It is a walled area of thirty-six acres, containing the Mosk of Omar and many other buildings. The Mohammedan religion is emphatically a thing of the *city*. It is incomplete without its mosks, its schools, ulemas and muezzins; and these are only found in the larger towns. This is one reason for this passion of pilgrimage which affects them equally with the Christian and the Jew.

My first thought on entering here recalled the fearful succession of disease, famine, suffering and slaughter by pestilence and sword, which have always accompanied the capture of Jerusalem. For this little plat of thirty-six acres is that which the conquerors of Jerusalem have chiefly coveted. This place is *haram*, equally to Jew, Christian and Mohammedan. Here the proposed sacrifice of Isaac (Genesis xxii: 10); the apparition of the destroying angel (2 Samuel xxiv: 16); the location of the Jewish Temple (2 Chron. iii: 1); and the celestial flight of Mohammed are all located, and a volume might be written to include the incidents that have occurred here.

Three places, until lately closed to the Christian traveler, are now freely opened upon the payment of *backsheesh*, viz: the Great Mosk at Damascus;

St. Sophia's at Constantinople, and this renowned mountain of our present visit. Only two places in the Holy Land yet remain closed, viz: a portion of *Neby Daoud*, or the Tomb of David on Mount Zion, and the Tomb of Abraham at Hebron. In a few years more, I have no doubt, *they* will also be opened to the influence of foreign gold.

The enclosure of the *Haram es-Shereef* lies in *length* from north to south in *breadth* from east to west. The measure of the walls, beginning at the northeast corner and going southward, is 1523½ feet; 916 feet; 1600 feet; 1038 feet. The east walls runs due north and south. The height of the walls from the ground, *as it now appears*, varies from twenty feet to eighty, the greatest height being at the *southeast* corner. But this is deceptive, because the wall is covered up from the base to the height of fifty to one hundred feet in *debris* or loose earth and stone. It is probable that if that portion of the original wall were exposed, it would stand nearly two hundred feet in height, immensely thick, and constructed of very massive stones, from six to sixty feet in length. The original Mount Moriah was a narrow ridge. On each side of it, and five hundred feet off, the workmen built those huge walls from the valleys and then filled in all that space of thirty-six acres level to the original height of the mountain. So these great walls only appear *on the outside*. Inside, they are only twelve or fifteen feet above the enclosure. The ground is nearly level, but inclines a little from north to south.

Nearly in the middle of this enclosure, is the celebrated Mosk of Omar, standing, I think, on the spot where the three successive temples of Solomon, Zerubbabel and Herod have stood. This mosk was begun A. D. 680—that is, 610 years after the destruction of Herod's temple, by Titus—and finished, like that of Solomon, in about seven years. It is a superb edifice, and I do not think Harriet's enthusiasm, at entering it, is extravagent. It is one hundred and seventy feet in diameter; an octogon in form, each side being sixty-seven feet. The height is the same as the breadth; viz.: one hundred and seventy feet, and that, too, is about the original height of the wall at the southeast corner of the enclosure. The upper part, or dome of the mosk, is circular, and a more graceful and symmetrical dome scarcely exists. The Arabic name of the Mosk of Omar is *Kubbet es-Sakhrah*, or Dome of the Rock. This refers to a remarkable stone sixty by fifty-five feet, and ten feet high, part of the original summit of Mount Moriah, that was left lying in the middle of the mosk. It is probable that here Abraham erected his altar; (Gen. xxii: 9) and here stood the Destroying Angel in the threshing floor of Aramah, the Jebusite.

I was much pleased with the beautiful Saracenic tiles, that line the great dome of this mosk. Ure, in his dictionary, says the earliest attempts to make compact stoneware with a painted glaze, was by the Arabians, in Spain, during the ninth century. This tileing is some of the oldest as well as most beautiful in the world. I sketched the design of one of the tiles, and here is my drawing. It is impossible, however, to show the elegant surface and the delicate blue glaze in which this, the arabesque pattern is drawn:

THE FIGURES UPON THE CEILING OF THE GREAT DOME IN THE MOSK OF OMAR.

Along the southern side of the enclosure is the Mosk el-Aksa, with many other buildings of but little interest to any but the historian, after seeing the Mosk of Omar. In front of one of them were buried four knights of the royal household of the English King, Henry II. They murdered the priest, Thomas a'Becket, December 29th, 1170, and fled to the Holy Wars, to escape punishment. The first quarters of the Knights Templar were located here, by King Baldwin II., in 1119, and their name was derived from their location, so near the *Temple.*

An immense cistern, now nearly dry, called the *Royal Cistern,* is also in front of El-Aksa. I descended it by a flight of forty-four steps cut in the native rock, and waded through the shallow water that covers only the bottom. It is seven hundred and thirty-six feet in circuit, and forty-two deep; therefore, its capacity is nearly two millions of gallons.

The southeastern portions of the enclosure are supported upon long streets of coverèd arches, which I was anxious to enter, but they are now closed against all visitors. We were admitted, however, to the grand, subterranean chamber under the Mosk el-Aksa and with candles surveyed it to our satisfaction.

A broad avenue opened out before us, dark, indeed, but sufficiently lighted by our candles, down which we slowly walked towards the northern end of the mosk. The passage in which we were descending, sometimes by an inclined plane, and twice, at least, by steps, was supported on both sides by heavy columns of stone, built up and connecting with each other by low, round arches. These arches were closed up with loose, dry stone walls, and on asking what was beyond, we were told that there were large cisterns of water on both sides. The middle of this passage was supported by two rows of massive monolithic round columns, every four columns supporting a dome shaped arch, of large stones, radiating exactly from the key-stone which was always a single round block, some six feet in diameter. This very peculiar style of supporting a roof is worthy of careful remark, inasmuch as I have never found it, except here and in the hewn tombs in the rock on the hill side of Aceldama.

There are three gates on the north of the enclosure and eight on the west. Of course there are none in the south and east, as the height of the pavement above the earth, would require very extensive stairways. An old gateway, called the Golden Gate (*Porta Aurea* or *Babed Dahareyeh*) in the east wall, shows where the great or "beautiful gate" (Acts iii : 2) once stood, the same, no doubt, through which Jesus entered in triumphal procession. (Mark xi : 11.) This gateway is four hundred and fifty-six feet from the northeast corner of the enclosure ; it is fifty-five feet wide.

To enter into the *Haram es-Shereef* required a special order from the Pasha of Jerusalem. But this can now be secured by any one, *except a Jew*, on the payment of small *backsheesh*. No Jew can get permission to enter upon any terms, on peril of his life. A soldier was deputed to accompany us and protect us from the African Mogrebbins or Guardians of the Haram, who are extremely fanatical.

I think I never saw such beastly and ferocious creatures as those negro guards are. They come from North Africa. Of such, the poet wrote when speaking of fanatics. He said—

"That saintly, murderous brood
To carnage and the Koran given,
Who think, through unbeliever's blood
Lies the directest path to heaven."

My drawing of the east wall of the Haram, shows the *Golden Gateway*, and the jumbled monuments, of the Mohammedan cemetery, in front. To understand the drawing properly, it must be recollected that this grave yard stands from eighty to one hundred feet *above the original level of the earth;* that is, the actual base of the wall is nearly one hundred feet below the foot of the wall, as it now appears.

East Wall of the Haram,
from the Golden Gate to the S.E. Corner

My drawing of a part of the south wall only, shows another of the gateways. This is now and long since closed up.

All American visitors to Jerusalem join in regretting that there are no missions or religious enterprises of any sort now on foot here that have an *American* basis. The American Board of Commissioners for Foreign Missions (instituted in June, 1810; incorporated June 20, 1812) made several earnest and expensive attempts to establish their work here, but all failed. The first missionaries to Palestine, Pliny Fisk and Levi Parsons, sailed from the United States in 1819. Mr. Parsons died in Egypt while preparing for this work, Feb. 10, 1822. Mr. Fisk came here, 25th of April, 1823, with Rev. Jonas King (who is still, 1869, in the missionary work at Athens, Greece), and Mr. Wolff, the converted Jew. They established their headquarters here, and it was anticipated by the American churches, that a great and good work could be done. They remained till the 27th of June, then removed to Beyrout, being convinced that better work could be accomplished there for the missionary cause. Mr. Fisk died at Beyrout soon after.

Nine years later (1834) Mr. and Mrs. W. M. Thomson, and afterwards another party of American missionaries, made attempts to establish their work here, but for various reasons, all efforts have failed. About the year 1850, an American society, "The *Christians*," founded an establishment, at the head of which was the celebrated Dr. J. T. Barclay, but this only lasted about twelve years, and all have passed away.

An agent of the German society, "The Jerusalem Friends," is here now making arrangements to bring a large number of its members next year. But we have not been able to learn what are the objects of the Society.

An American friend objects to my spelling the word Mosk, insisting upon it that *Mosque* is the correct form. I point to *Webster's Dictionary*, where the shorter and easier form is allowed. This is his definition of the word: "MOSQUE, *n.* (Fr. *mosquee*, It. *moschea*, Sp. *mezquita*, Pg. *mesquita*, Ar. *masjid*, from *sajada*, to bend, bow or adore.) A Mohammedan church or place of religious worship, (written also *mosk.*)"

HARRIET'S DIARY.

CAMP ASSYRIAN, 6 P. M.

I cannot understand why Mr. Bayard Taylor should say that Jerusalem left no impression upon his mind, save that of filth, ruin, poverty and degradation. Had he began his researches as we did, by taking *general* views of the city, his impressions would have been more ennobling. The view of Mount Moriah, for instance, from any point of observation, is inspiring. A fitter place for an august building cannot be found in the whole world, than this eminence. The Mosk of Omar, in the centre, makes a most stately figure, if only from the advantage of situation. Its dome, a vast hemisphere of arabesque tileing, is a collection of rainbows, braided into one bright tissue, and belted round at the base by a rainbow brighter than all the rest. It leaves an image upon the mind that is quite dazzling. Of all the fourteen hundred mosks built by Omar, this was the largest and fairest, and it quite redeems Jerusalem, even were there nothing else, from Mr. Taylor's aspersions. It is glorious to the eye, and not an unworthy successor of the DIVINE FANE that Solomon once reared here. It is magnificent in its marble pillars. Its dome studded with Saracenic devices on a pure gold ground, is one of those " those things of beauty " that are "a joy forever." Should I ever return to Jerusalem my first object of re-visit, will be the *Mosk of Omar*.

I found the descriptions of this memorable eminence, by Josephus, more real and vivid than I could have imagined. Writing many years after he left Jerusalem, and writing from *memory*, it is not strange that in some measurements he should have erred; especially as in the Oriental spirit, he adopted a little exaggeration; but in the main, he is very correct. I was fortunate in having read Traill's edition of Josephus. In regard to his figures, I suppose were I to attempt, to-day, from memory, to give the dimensions of the house in New York, in which I have lived for so many years, I should come no nearer literal accuracy, than Josephus did, in regard to the temple.

To Elliot, who caviled at our Saviour's expressions, in Luke xxi : 6, "There shall not be left one stone upon another that shall not be thrown down," I explained that this threat appplied to *the Temple*, not the vast, surrounding walls. It has been literally fulfilled so far as *the Temple* is concerned; not a ragment of the Temple-building, or its magnificent arcades, in which Christ walked and taught, can now be identified. Not that I think those marbles are turned to dust—rather, they were broken to pieces and thrown into the profound valleys right and left, and now help to make up the enormous accumulations of stone and earth that choke the valleys and hide the walls to the depth of one hundred feet. We spent an hour, this morning, digging with trowels in the loose earth, near the southeast corner of the wall, outside, and found pieces of Parian marble, porphyry, red granite, gray granite, verd antique and other precious materials, which, perhaps, once helped to make and adorn the Temple of Solomon.

After I had satiated myself with the view of this elegant mosk, I set my imagination loose among the events that have been crowded so thickly into this little inclosure of thirty-six acres. Here an infant boy was brought, eighteen hundred and sixty-nine years ago, from Bethlehem, the village just beyond yonder eminence on the south, "to present him to the Lord," and with him a simple offering for a sacrifice, "a pair of turtle doves or two young pigeons." (Luke ii.) I reviewed it all, and the image entered my soul. I heard the speech of Simeon, that "just and devout" man. I heard Anna, that "widow of about four score and four years." Not a word that they uttered, fell to the ground. Then I saw "the certain poor widow," who came "to cast money into the treasury." (Mark xii: 7.) But why fill my pages with a history that forms a part of every Christian's life!

Here, in the Mosk El-Aksa, on the southern line of the enclosure, they pointed out to me "a praying place for women." Is not this the only Mohammedan church in the Holy Land, where women are even admitted? I think so. And I looked with special interest and pleasure upon that isolated apartment at the eastern end of that edifice, where the guide said "only women are permitted to worship." But when *I* offered to enter, he curtly said, "only *Moslem* women!"

The only instance in which I have remarked a Mohammedan using a Koran during religious worship was to-day in the Mosk of Omar. Here was one reading aloud in a singsong tone, emphasizing with hand and voice. The sound appears to improve the sense with them. Amongst these people the man who practices the ceremonies of his creed openly is esteemed the *honest* man; the *respectable* man. It is a common reproach with them in talking to Christians, to say "we, practice our religion openly; you never do. We show the *crescent* everywhere; you are ashamed to show the *cross!*" Why then have we not before observed the Moslem devotees reading what they conceive to be their inspired Book? Simply because every devout worshiper of Mohammed *knows the Koran by heart*, and has only *to repeat*, and needs no more *to study* it!

Before leaving the great inclosure of Mount Moriah, I beheld one sight and listened to one sound, than which nothing more painful rests in my memory. The *sight* is *the Crescent* over the center of this memorable hill, the very "Abomination of Desolation" that our Saviour predicted. The *sound* was the Muezzins' call from the minaret on the northern side of the area, recalling so forcibly the downfall of Israel, as in Amos viii: 3: "songs of the temple shall be howlings in that day." Yes, that cracked and unnatural voice, hoarser in its croakings than the utterances of the ravens who cry in the olive trees upon yonder hill in the east, is all that now remains of the grand minstrelry that once shook these mountains with the praises of God. "Howlings in that day;" cried the prophet Amos, who, more than eight hundred years before the event, saw by faith, what we now see by sight, the *desolation of the sacred hill.*

I came out of the gate by which only we are allowed to visit this remarkable precinct. I mean the one at the northwest corner, with my mind full of the degradation of my sex in Oriental lands. It excites my commisseration more and more, the longer I stay here. With the exception of a few noble families, and those under great restriction, women do not visit the mosks or take any part in religious exercises. The Turkish adage, "No one can look upon my women and live" expresses the whole story, in a few words.

While I was slowly promenading the circuit of the Mosk of Omar, this morning, I remembered that it was of this place Jehovah promised, in reply to the fervent prayer of Solomon; mine eyes shall be open and mine ears attend unto the prayer that is made in this place." (2 Chron. vii: 15,) Then I breathed a silent prayer that the followers of the false prophet may soon be banished from this hill, and the descendants of Israel, perfected by suffering and inspired by faith in the *Messiah who has* come, reinstated here to serve and praise him "while the sun and moon shall endure."

In the services of Passion Week this is *Thursday before Easter*. The Scriptural references of the day are found in Mark xiv: 12–16. The place where the MASTER decided to eat the passover was selected. Then in the evening, at the head of the twelve, He came into the city from Bethany, entered the large upper room selected, and sat down to the feast. Having eaten, he then instituted the new ceremony which was to show forth his death until he should come again. Towards midnight HE left the city with eleven of the company and went to Gethsemane.

VIEW OF JERUSALEM FROM THE SPOT WHERE JESUS WEPT OVER THE CITY.

CHAPTER XII.*

THE MOHAMMEDAN SABBATH.

Spraining an ankle—The legends of Jerusalem—Gate of St. John's Hospital—Greek patriarch—Armenian patriarch—Sparrows—Ancient lamp—Native costumes—Women coloring the eyes—Akeldama—Solitary palm tree—American kerosene—Dr. Peterman—Ancient coins Story of the coin—The Jews waiting—Character of Judaism—Jews' benevolent societies—Bishop Gobat—Prussian Deaconesses—Sweet music—Via Dolorosa.

ELLIOT'S DIARY.

CAMP OF THE ASSYRIANS, Friday, March 26th, 1869, 6 P. M.

I SPRAINED my ankle, yesterday, jumping out of Jeremiah's Cave, and Mr. Fountain advised me to sit quietly, to-day, in camp, and recruit under charge of Aunt Liddy. But time is too precious, and I had Hassan and Kosroo carry me in a chair to the different places in Jerusalem where I could best take items. This was a busy day here. Good Friday to the Christians, Wailing Day to the Jews and Sunday to the Mohammedans, all three came together.

In addition to taking items, I have been looking through our books for all the legends and hard old stories I could find in them about Jerusalem. Not that I believe in them all, for I don't. I don't believe anything here unless it is in the Bible or Josephus, or some other ancient and reliable history. But there are plenty of people, Protestants as well as Catholics, who *do* believe them,—if they didn't they would hardly believe there was such a place as Jerusalem at all.

There is enough of these stories, if written out, to make a library. The Jews manufacture them; the Mohammedans manufacture them, and the Christians manufacture them. If you hire a guide to go around the city with you and tell you things, he will show you anything you want to see and tell you anything you can swallow. Ask him for the fishhook that Peter cast into the sea (Matt. xvii: 27) and he will go into some church, disappear out of sight for a half hour, and then bring you a rusty old *hook* that he is prepared to say is the very identical one. Ask him to show the cup and platter whose outside the Pharisees made clean (Matt. xxiii: 25), he will do it. Ask him to show you the place where the wicked and slothful servant digged in the earth and hid his lord's money (Matt. xxv: 18), he will lead you to the very hole. I am not sure but what, if you pay him enough for it, he will find you the *talent*

* A VIEW OF JERUSALEM FROM THE SOUTH-EAST. The dome on the right is the Mosk of Omar; the deep ravine in front is the Valley of Jehoshaphat, through which the channel of the Kedron runs.

itself. I heard a man ask a guide, yesterday, if all the righteous blood shed upon the earth from the blood of righteous Abel was to be seen still preserved anywhere in Jerusalem. The guide said he thought *it was*. At any rate he would go and see. Of course the traveler was joking, but the guide didn't see it.

In the church of St. Augustine, in Rome, are exhibited the cord with which Judas Iscariot hung himself; a wing of the Angel Gabriel; the comb of the cock that crowed when Peter denied his Lord; the beard of Noah, and the staff with which Moses divided the Red Sea.

The funniest thing about these traditions is they prove so much. Suppose you want to know where Elijah slept the night when he went on south, past Jerusalem. The guide will take you about four miles south of here and exhibit the very spot. If you ask them how they know that to be the spot, they show where Elijah *lay down on the limestone rock;* there is a *dent* made by his head, dents made by his shoulders, his hips, his knees. If you ask how came the limestone soft enough to leave such marks, they answer *backsheesh.*

Suppose you want to see the place where the Saviour ascended to heaven, instead of going across Olivet to near Bethany, as the New Testament describes it, they take you to the top of Olivet, right in sight of Jerusalem, and point to the spot. If you ask for the evidence, they show you the mark of Christ's foot in the stone. If you tell him that mark looks no more like a man's foot than like a glass bottle, they say our Saviour's foot was not shaped like any other man's foot. Then they point to a small hole in the rock close by, that they say was punched by our Saviour's cane. If you remind them that the Bible doesn't say that Jesus used *a cane*, they answer, the Bible doesn't tell us *everything* about Jesus.

Every part of the human body,—toes, feet, fingers, hands, head, shoulders,—has left its marks here *in the rock*, as if the rock was no harder than putty, wax or dough. Yet this rock is very hard indeed, and always was. The stones that lie loose on the side of Mount Olivet are black flint stones, as hard as any flint I ever saw. I set set some tinder on fire with my knife blade and a piece of that flint. The soldiers who guard travelers to the Dead Sea use that flint in their muskets for flint locks. A priest told me that our Saviour meant these flint stones when he said in Matthew xix: 40, "if these should hold their peace the stones would immediately cry out." Then I asked him how people's feet could make holes in such hard stones as that? He said I was heretic. I told him he was another; he begun it and to go there himself.

In John's cabinet at home is a lot of red sandstone that has the marks of leaves, scales, birds' tracks and drops of rain on it, made when the stone was soft. John calls it paleontology. These priests are paleontologists, too, only they don't pretend that the stone here was ever *soft*.

I paid my fee of five francs four different times over, to go into the Garden of Gethsemane. I looked at it over and over again. One time while I was reading there, Matthew xxvi, and Mark xiv, and Luke xxii, and John xviii, the guides were telling the pilgrims all manner of stories. "This is the spot where Peter's eyes were heavy." "This is the spot where James could no longer keep awake." "This is the spot where John lay down and slept."

Here the Blessed Saviour withdrew from his disciples about a stone's cast and kneeled down and prayed." "Here the drops of sweat fell like blood to the ground." "This is the spot where one of them smote the servant of the High Priest and cut off his right ear." "This is the spot where Judas betrayed the Son of Man with a kiss." "This is the spot where the young man left the linen cloth and fled from them naked." And every one of these spots they pretended to identify as exactly as one of the spots on the sun that the astronomers tell us so much about, lately.

These are the Roman Catholics. Now, if you get a guide who belongs to the Greek Church, a larger and more intelligent body here than the Catholics, only they wear different shaped caps, they will tell you plainly that the Catholic *stories* are *lies*, and that the Garden of Gethsemane is a little further up the hill. And if you will pay them for it they will take you there and show it to you.

There is, also, a large Christian society here called the Armenians, and very nice people they are. But they, too, have got their traditions, any quantity of them. They showed me the stone that was rolled back from the door of the sepulchre, the very one that the angel sat on, (Matt. xxviii : 2) and the place where the Apostle James was buried. They showed me the prison into which Jesus was placed when the guards first took Him from Gethsemane, before the high priest was ready to examine Him. One lady said, "it was a well, and that Jesus sat there with His hands tied behind Him. The sun rose and sent a ray of light upon Him, and as He raised His eyes to meet it, His face was pale as death. He was disfigured with blood, and earth, and spittle. His hair was drenched, matted and disordered. His hands were manacled and pinioned. His vesture was disfigured and disarranged." All this is beautiful, but the Bible doesn't say anything about it. And the Armenians, also, showed me the tree to which to our Lord was fastened, when He was smitten on the face, for His reply to the high priest. This makes three trees I have seen around Jerusalem, with stories to them. The first was an old mulberry tree near the Pool of Siloam, that shows the place where Isaiah was sawed asunder. I asked a Greek priest to show me the passage, in my pocket Bible, where Isaiah was sawed at all. As he couldn't read English, he showed it to me in his Greek Breviary. But as I couldn't read Greek, I didn't see it, and I don't believe it is there. The other tree is a tremendously old and withered fig tree, on the hill top, south of the valley of Hinnom, where they say Judas hanged himself. I asked the guide what Judas it was? He said *Iscariot.* I asked him how long since Iscariot hung himself? He said he would enquire of the priest and let me know. He said nobody ever asked him such questions before. The fact is, the pilgrims never ask the guides *any questions.* The guides show them things. They kiss the things and then go on to see the next things. One man told me he had seen more than three hundred miraculous things in one morning. I told him that was nothing at all. The Armenians, also, show the building in which our Saviour washed the disciples' feet. They say that Mary was born there.

Around the Holy Sepulchre, outside, you can get as many stories told you as you choose to write down. They say there that when our Saviour was crucified, His face was turned to the *west*, but when He was buried, His feet were pointed to the *east;* that the waves of Noah's flood tore up the body of Adam from the grave, in which it had been buried, seven hundred and twenty-six years before, and swept it to this spot, where it sunk in the soft mud, and when the hole for the cross was made, they found Adam's skull there; that the Apostles, the night our Saviour was betrayed, hid themselves in what is now called the Tomb of St. James, but between His Crucifixion and Resurrection, in the tombs above the valley of Hinnom; that the sacred fire was concealed in the bottom of the Well En-Rogel, at the time Nebuchadnezzar destroyed the Temple, and was brought to light again when Zerubbabel re-built the Temple; that near the Damascus Gate, Christ gave to the Apostles the Holy Ghost and the Apostles' Creed; that the spot where Jesus "stooped down and, with His finger, wrote on the ground" (John viii : 6), can still be pointed out; that the place where He wrote the Lord's Prayer, in Hebrew, has been discovered on the side of Mount Olivet, and a rich French woman is building a church over it; that the Tomb of Eve, stands by the Red Sea, and is a hundred feet long; the Tomb of Joshua is on the Bosphorus, ninety feet long; that of Noah is on Mount Lebanon, eighty-five feet long; that of Abel is close by Noah's, thirty feet long; that the window is still standing at which Pilate brought Jesus forth, and said, "Behold the man;" (John xix : 5) and that pieces of the true cross are still preserved in different parts of the world. An unbelieving sailor swore horribly, in my hearing, that he had seen enough of that true cross to make a jib-boom of, and the same of the old Connecticut Charter-oak. They say, also, that a writer in the year A. D. 400, was bold enough to claim that the sacred cross has inherent powers of re-production; take away a portion and it is immediately re-produced; that every year a fire descends from heaven, in the Holy Sepulchre, and lights their candles for them; that in the palace of the Syrian bishop, near the Holy Sepulchre, is the silver font in which St. Mark was baptised; also a portrait of the Virgin Mary, painted by St. Luke; that the houses in which the rich man and Lazarus lived can still be shown; that in France, in the fourteenth century, they had part of our Saviour's crown of thorns and one of the nails which fastened His hands to the palm wood beam; and the spear head which the Roman centurian thrust into his bleeding side; while at Constantinople, they had the sponge, the seamless coat, one of the nails, and some of the cross; that in old times rain never used to fall into the Tomb of Mary, near Gethsemane, though it had no roof on it; that in the eighth century they showed, at Jerusalem, the holy grail, the sponge, the centurian's lance, broken in two pieces, and other relics equally curious; that the bodies of Nicodemus, Abido, Stephen the martyr, and Gamaliel, were buried on Mount Zion; that the tree out of which our Saviour's cross was made, grew on a spot west of Jerusalem, where they have built a fine church; that the marks of our Saviour's fingers may still be seen in the rock in Gethsemane; that the water in the spring, at Cana, of Galilee, will make a man drunk to drink it; that in old times the Tower of Hippicus was so high you could see, from the top of it, *Mount Sinai*, on the south, and *Mount Herman*, on the north. But these are stories enough for one day.

JOHN'S DIARY.

CAMP OF THE ASSYRIANS, Friday, 6 P. M.

To-day, Mr. Fountain advised Harriet and myself to stroll hither and thither at random, and take in such miscellaneous objects of interest as may accidentally fall in our way. Our first four days were spent upon systematic research. Elliot, poor fellow, is lame, to-day, with an ankle sprained by the exploit of jumping some twenty feet down a limestone ledge. The lad found that if this Jerusalem stone was *soft* enough for Peter's shoulders to make a hole in it, A. D. 33, it is *hard* enough, A. D. 1869, to damage the most elastic ankles. He will be well, however, in a day or two.

What a splendid outburst of architectural intelligence followed the outbreak of the Crusaders, in the eleventh and twelfth centuries; here, at Jerusalem, as well as all over this country, they left indelible marks of the chisel under the unerring hand of genius. At the entrance of the old Hospital of the Knights of St. John, is a splendid Gothic archway on which the carving of a lamb is seen. I make a drawing of it:

Passing through that once magnificent archway, and into an open area once a grand hospital, that contained three hundred beds, we found it a mass of ruins, encumbered with abominable filth and garbage. The ruins are so commingled, that refectory, oratory, and church, can only be separated by the skill of the architect. Over St. Stephen's Gate are four lions' heads carved in stone, similar to that which I purchased last week, and plainly referable to this period. It was while examining those, that we met the first *Discalced*

Carmelite, as Herbert calls the barefooted Carmelite friars, who are somewhat scarce here, as the Franciscans outnumber them ten to one.

Calling at the palace of the Greek Patriarch, near the Holy Sepulchre, we were most politely welcomed by that "old public functionary," (as Mr. Buchanan used to call himself,) who, with his suite, were dressed in black robes, edged with fur. They all wore the high, square and extremely comical and homely cap peculiar to the Greek Church. I asked the "pub. func." if he was going to attend the Œucumenical Council that the Pope had summoned to meet next fall, at Rome? He soon let me know, and with a show of indignation, too, that *his* branch of the Holy Catholic Church was vastly *older*, and far better established in history and tradition, than the feeble sect at Rome; and that none of *his* clergy would ever be found paying homage at the Vatican. I told him that, in the United States, what little we know of the Greek Church, is more favorable to its antiquity and purity of doctrine than the other. And so we parted, mutually pleased. The Greek Church has at Jerusalem, eleven convents for men, four for women, two boys' schools, one girls school, and a college.

A witty gentleman, who was present, came out with me and thanked me for my compliment to the Greek Church. He said the present Pope seems to believe, not that he is the vicegerent of *Christ*, on earth, but that Christ is *his* vicegerent in heaven! He gave me this sentence for my diary:

"Since the time of St. Peter, there have been two hundred and ninety-seven popes, including one female pontiff. Of these, thirty-one were declared usurpers, and banished from Rome, and of the two hundred and sixty-six legitimate wearers of the triple crown, sixty-four experienced violent deaths. Out of the whole number, one hundred and fifty-three, or more than half, showed themselves unfit for the office; six, in spite of their vows, had children. The successor of Leo IV., it is said, was a woman, and died in childbirth; *perperit papissa papillam*, said his cotemporaries. Urban V. confessed his fallibility, and submitted to the censures of a council, and two others confessed they had sinned. On the whole, the history of Christ's vicars shows frequent and lamentable absences of the influences of the Holy Spirit in their conduct, and makes a rather strong argument for Pio Nono to meet in his scheme for the declaration of infallibility."

We have always had such genial receptions from the Armenian patriarch, that we have called on him again and again. He presented each of us with his photograph, and asked ours in return. He showed us portraits of Mr. Bidwell and Dr. Morris, two American gentlemen whose acquaintance he had formed, and asked about them. He is one of the handsomest men I ever saw. In his convent, on Mount Zion, a type foundry and printing office are kept up for printing in the Armenian language. A magazine is printed there, of which several copies were given us. We found here, a young gentleman of whom we had heard much, both at Joppa and Jerusalem, Mr. Serapion J. Murad. At the age of twenty years, he is expert in speaking and writing the Armenian, English, French, German, Arabic, Turkish, Italian, Persian and Greek languages! What a memory of words such a linquist must possess. He reminded us of what we had forgotten, that the Crimean War, with its untold bloodshed and horrors, grew out of the simple question whether the Greek or Latin sects should have control of the Holy Sepulchre, here.

Among the ruins of the Hospital of the Knights of St. John, I climbed up to a ragged projection, and was interested to see the great number of sparrows and small birds with which Jerusalem is filled. They had quite choked up the cavities in the turrets, with their building materials. Great numbers of these are caught in nets, roasted, strung on skewers and eaten as a *bonne bouche*, by the people in the markets.

We purchased a terra-cotta lamp that had been taken from recent excavations in the valley of Hinnom, and have made drawings of it from two points of view:

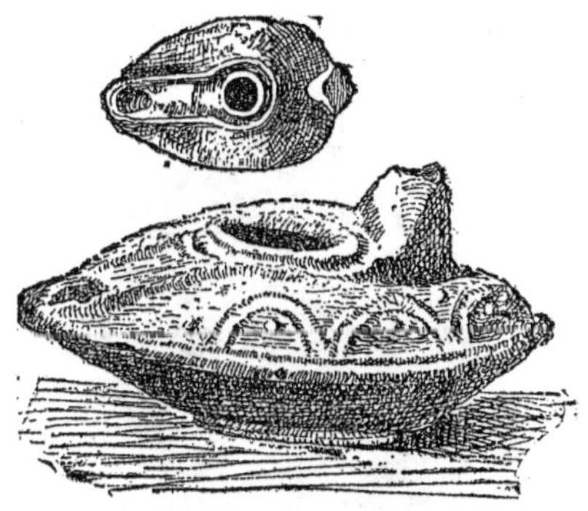

Specimens of Roman lamps, in the European museums, of silver, bronze and terra-cotta, are very highly valued. Does not the small size of this one throw light upon a passage in the parable of the ten virgins, where it was made necessary to bring oil with them in their vessels! One of our large American hand lamps will burn *all night*, while one of these will scarcely burn *two hours* without replenishing.

Talking with Hassan, I asked him how a man of his age and experience in life, could consent to act as a mere companion to a boy, and upon such wages as one hundred piastres a month? He answered, as the Orientals are prone to answer questions, by an Eastern adage, "a man will go anywhere who has lost his purse."

We hired an Arab to carry to our tents a carved stone we had purchased near the old Judas tree, on the Mount of Evil Counsel, and to hurry back, so as to meet us at another point. In exact imitation of the Jewish custom, he "girded up his loins," then, following the example of the ancient Romans, he "tucked up his toga," before starting. No wonder, with such absurd dresses these people are so lazy. Exertion to them is an unmitigated evil. How the Romans ever conquered the world, in flowing pantalettes, is a marvel. The saying amongst these Arabs is, "never stand up when you can sit down; never walk when you can ride; never sit down when you can lie down." Good counsel, and faithfully followed.

The custom, practiced by Eastern women of *coloring the eyes* black or blue, is a continuation of the Roman practice, as theirs was of the Egyptian. It enables us to see the eyes through the *yishmah*, or veil, which, by the way, is being made thinner and thinner every year, as the doctrine of "woman's rights" is making its way from the west to the east.

It is curious how a mere tradition, entirely unfounded, and in itself absurd, can influence people through a long succession of periods. We were reminded of this in visiting the old Potter's Field, or Akeldama, (field of blood) and remembering that many vessel loads of the earth have been carried from this place to Europe under the delusive belief that it will consume dead bodies in the space of twenty-four hours. As far back as A. D. 1218, the Campo Santo, at Pisa, in Italy, was covered with earth from this place.

At the Prussian consulate, we formed the acquaintance of the good Dr. the Rev. Hendrick Peterman, and I have begged of him the loan of a photograph long enough to make a pen and ink sketch of it:

REV. H. PETERMAN,
Chancellor of the Prussian Consulate, Jerusalem.

This venerable gentleman, now more than seventy years of age, has been engaged in the employment of his government, at the different Oriental consulates, for nearly half a century.

As Jerusalem is a city without trade or manufactures, and the country in the vicinity is but poorly cultivated, the support of the different classes, who live here, has been amusingly summed up in this manner: The Roman Catholics live by contributions, chiefly from Spain; the Greeks and Armenians, by alms from the pilgrims; the Jews from collections made annually among their own people, the world over; while the Turks exact money from all, indiscriminately.

The only thrifty palm tree we have noticed, in Jerusalem, is near the Jew's quarter, a fitting place, seeing that the palm tree was the time-honored emblem of Judæa, at the Roman period. The old belief, that the presence of petrified palms in certain strata, indicated a *warm climate*, in the days when those deposits were formed, would scarcely be sustained by the fact that this palm tree, as I am assured by natives, is often covered for weeks together with snow and frozen rain, destructive to orange trees and other shrubbery. We venture to dedicate this solitary palm to Henry Ward Beecher. Its grand fronds, like his doctrines, are spread out from a celestial altitude, equally to the north and the south, the east and the west.

In one of the smaller Catholic churches, here, we were pleased to see our American *kerosene oil* supplying the place of the traditional olive oil of the sanctuary, though the lamp was made, as nearly as possible, like the old ones. The Catholic church is slow upon innovations. I used to laugh to see, in the New York papal churches, the gas lights burning from the tops of imitation wax candles, so much the simon pure, that it required some smartness to detect the cheat.

Dr. J. T. Barclay once told us that the richest place around Jerusalem, for ancient coins, was on the south side of Mount Moriah, near the southeast corner. Hundreds of them have been found there by the native children, who search after rains have furrowed the soil. Harriet and myself spent an hour there, to-day, and succeeded in finding three. Here they are:

Mr. Fountain requests me to embody these relics in a—

STORY OF THE COIN.

"I was minted in the reign of Augustus Cæsar, at a time when the temple of Janus was closed, because all the world was at *peace*. Then Jesus was born at Bethlehem, 'Coming to His own, though His own knew Him not.' When the apostles and disciples of the new dispensation, moved swiftly over these hills, telling the wondrous story of the cross and the crucified, I passed more than once into their hands, secretly given them by some, in whose hearts the fire of Jesus' love glowed, but 'secretly for fear of the Jews.' In this manner, I have been fingered by Peter, and John, and Paul, whom I saw entering the towns and villages; delivering their divine messages; hurrying away to the next. Thus, I beheld the Christian church increasing, spite of opposition or hatred, of persecution, even to the fire and the tree, until within less than three centuries after Golgotha and its tragedy, the religion of the despised Nazarine was the religion of the Roman Empire, the state religion of the now whole world.

"Three hundred years more, and the invasions of the new religionists overthrew all that had been done here; and amidst the dust and debris of the crushed city, I was lost, and only now, twelve centuries later, have come forth to the light to rehearse my story of the coin."

HARRIET'S DIARY.

CAMP ASSYRIAN, Friday, 6 P. M.

Our brave little boy has met with an accident that incapacitates him from pursuing active researches, to-day. It seems, by Hassan's report, though Elliot is not at all proud of the fact, and makes no entry thereof in his diary,—that the keeper of Jeremiah's Cave, upon some pretext, refused him admittance. Whereupon the hardy little man climbed over the wall, explored the inside of the grotto in spite of the noisy protestations of the hermit, and in returning to the light of day, jumped from the roof of the wall to the ground, and so sprained his ankle. I offered to sit with him, to-day, but he will not listen to it. Mr. Fountain says the whole thing will be forgotten in a day or two. His two faithful servants took him in their arms into the city, exciting much comment on the way, and moved him from place to place as he desired.

Our visit to the Jew's quarter has been one of our most unpleasant experiences; and this, not only because that portion of the city is the filthiest, but as implying such degradation among the once-favored people. All the time I was there, the words of Isaiah were ringing in my ears: "Woe to Ariel, to Ariel, the city where David dwelt." (xxix : 1.) How forcibly the poet has written the condition of these people—

"A proverb to most, and a moral to all;
And a lamp unto others, though sitting in gloom.
He seems like a mute in a festival-hall,
And is still looking forward for *that which hath come;*
Like the children of Eblis, he hideth his mart,
And walks through the world with his hand on his heart."

I saw a paragraph, in a New York paper, recently, to the effect that there are more Jews in New York and Cincinnati, than in the Holy Land. "Lo, I will command and I will sift the house of Israel among all nations, like as corn is sifted in a sieve." (Amos ix : 9.)

The Judaism of the United States is of a mild tolerant type, but that of this country is an exclusive one. They are a hated and hating class. The necessity of separate slaughter houses requires them not to eat with the Christians but to separate themselves from general society. I asked one or them to-day, a fine looking Jew from Prussia, whether the Gentile would be allowed to live in the Holy Land, in case "the redeemed of the Lord" should return to occupy it, as their faithful ones anticipate? He would not reply in direct terms for fear of paining me, but I saw the drift of his hope, which is, that alien and the stranger shall no more desecrate this sacred dust.

This Friday is the regular day for the Jews to visit the Wailing Place and touch the second row of its great stones with their foreheads, and mourn for the desolation of Zion, a practice begun by them, A. D. 362. The place selected for this purpose is the nearest point to the ancient Temple to which they are permitted to have access. It is on the west side of Mount Moriah, about five hundred feet from the southwest corner. For the privilege of coming here they are required to pay a tax. Here the Israelite appears as Jeremiah, in his Lamentations, conceived him. His thin, intellectual face, glittering teeth, and his black ringlets shading his pale cheek, will ever be associated in my mind with this place. Here they show that state of excitement, which, with them, is considered essential to the existence of true devotion. The modern Jew, by nature, is enthusiastic and superstitious to fanaticism, and their ordinary worship in Jerusalem is accompanied with as much agitation and gesticulation as though they would take heaven by storm. At the Wailing Place they weep; they rock their bodies to and fro; they read those portions of Scripture most expressive of spiritual woe; they simulate, and no doubt *feel*, deep mental anguish. But I must confess it appeared to me, upon the whole, a sort of dramatic representation, as much so as the worship of the Papist and the Greek.

At their festivals, the Jews make a more pleasing appearance. Their costume then is picturesque,—velvet caps with borders of fur, and robes lined with fur. But they enter upon their rejoicings in the same wild and extravagant manner as their expressions of grief.

There is an organization here called *The Hebrew Christian Mutual Aid Society, of Jerusalem*, that is doing something to ameliorate the condition of that race. Their Annual Report for 1867, showed collections and disbursements of about $1,000 (in *piastres* 23,438), nearly half of which was contributed by the Hebrew Christians themselves. The objects are to relieve those actually in want, and to assist meritorious workmen in procuring tools and materials. Such a society as this in this ancient city, carries the mind back to that early period described in Acts vi, when the infant Hebrew Church was compelled to choose deacons and stewards to attend to the temporal wants of Christ's poor.

Besides this, the *London Jews Missionary Society* employs three ordained ministers and six lay agents, and sustains a Depository at the Bible Depot. There is a Hospital and Dispensary connected with this enterprise, and a series of schools containing more than one hundred children.

We have frequently been told by acquaintances made here, that the political condition of the Jews is improving; and the fact is cited that in the City Council there is an Israelite, coupled with two Christians and four Turks. This is the Board of Aldermen. In another branch of the city government, there is also an Israelite. The number of Jews here is claimed to be nine thousand, having of all sects, twenty-two synagogues and thirty Medrashim, or studying places.

An hour with the venerable and beloved Bishop Gobat, of the Protestant Episcopal Church, is included to be treasured in memory. His Diocesan schools of both sexes, embrace more than one hundred children. The work of

13

the Prussian Deaconesses is one to elicit the prayers of all Christian souls. They have seventy pupils, a hospital and dispensary. The ladies give much attention to the preparation of the wild flowers of the vicinity, which they sell for the benefit of their Society. We were glad to invest some of our funds in this way. A neat little bouquet, embracing flowers from the Shepherd's Plain Rachel's Tomb, Mount Zion, Moriah, Olivet, Bethany, Valley of Hinnom, Tomb of Kings, Valley of Jehoshaphat and Gethsemane, combining a cluster of sacred associations that would fill a volume. There is, also, under Mr. Schneller, a Home for Orphans of the Damascus massacre of 1860.

"Tarry then till I come. These words shot through me. I felt them like an arrow in my heart. My brain whirled. My eyes grew dim. The troops, the priests, the populace, the world passed away from before my senses like phantoms."

These words from Croly's *Salathiel*, recurred to me this moment as I exchange salutations with a grave and solemn Rabbi, who has passed our tents. That singular work, Salathiel, was the first historical novel I ever read, and though I can now see how much extravagance there is in its descriptions, yet it is calculated, I think, to give the reader a taste for Oriental literature and research. This Rabbi, like many of his race, exhibits a sort of nobility that I do not see in any other men. Mr. Dickens, in "Our Mutual Friend," has delineated it most beautifully in the character of Mr. Riah. This class of Jews always recalls the words of Paul in Romans 9: to them pertain "the adoption, and the glory and the giving of the law;" and poor as they are in worldly things, they walk as if they felt their princely heritage. They seem to linger here in their paternal country, anxious to be present when Messiah shall come or to be buried near by in case he shall still tarry. I am told, however, that their Rabbis are the most dictatorial, often the most tyrannical of the cruel rulers of Jerusalem. They have almost princely power of their own people. They seem to revenge themselves for the insults that all other classes heap upon them, by putting their feet upon the necks of their own people.

When Jonas King was here, May 7th, 1823, he wrote these affecting words: "My feet now stand on that awful hill where our dear Lord and Saviour poured out His soul unto death and finished the work of man's redemption. Here the arms of everlasting love were extended on the cross, and here the meek and tender heart of the Son of God was pierced with a spear. Here flowed that precious blood in which our polluted souls must be cleansed or be lost forever."

Returning to our camp we came up the Valley of Jehosaphat, entered the Gate of St. Stephen, passed to the centre of the city, turned northward, went out at the Damascus Gate and so round the northwest corner of Jerusalem to camp. As we passed by a small church called St. James, just north of the Serai, or Governor's Palace, our ears were saluted with a familiar air from "Don Giovanni." Entering the church we found the people at vespers or evening service. An invisible choir, was singing, with Latin words, that most beautiful aria marked in the Opera "No. 27, Finale, allegretto." The music was almost celestial. I never could see why the composer put that solemn movement in so frivolous a work. It rang in my ears all night long, and I could only relieve myself by rising and throwing together these words to the air:

> " In those expansions, in His blest mansions,
> Every tie broken, He will restore;
> Father and mother, sister and brother,
> Round the Throne meeting, part nevermore."

From St. Stephen's Gate westward is the traditional *Via Dolorosa*, the *grievous way*, where " He, bearing His cross, went forth." (John xix: 17.) The street was crowded with pilgrims, each group under the guidance of a priest, visiting the traditional spots. I had learned them by heart years ago. Here they are: the house in which Christ was mocked and set at nought by the soldiers; the place where he was scourged; the Ecce Homo lattice; the first place where he fainted and fell; the second place; the third place; the spot where Simon assumed the weight of the cross; the spot where Mary sorrowed at the tragical spectacle; the spot where Veronica presented him her handkerchief to wipe his bleeding brow,——but enough.

And yet if *we* believed as these Greek and Catholic Christians do, we should do exactly as they. For they believe that all things forewritten and foretold of the Messiah were actually fulfilled upon this one little space of ground. And I do not so much differ in my veneration of the Holy Land from these people, except that I equally revere the whole country as the scope of my religious fervor, while they circumscribe it all within a little space where they deem their respectable frauds eternally safe.

In the services of Passion Week, to-day is called *Good Friday*. It embraces all the scenes in the Lord's earthly life, from His Agony in Gethsemane to His Death upon Golgotha. It is "the day of days" in the Christian calendar According to the writer of the article " Jesus Christ," in Smith's Dictionary of the Bible (the Archbishop of York), this event occurred on the 7th day of April, it being the 14th of the Jewish month *Nisan*.

THE OAK OF ABRAHAM, NEAR HEBRON.

CHAPTER XIII.

THE JEWISH SABBATH.

Barbarian manners—American song—Eating pork—Cedar cone—Stepping the city walls—Good measure—A valuable ring—Defenses of Jerusalem—Russian convent—Ancient bottle—Attempted cheat—Horns of the Ibex—Abraham's oak—Shape of the city—Great stones—Stone marks—London Palestine fund—Prof. Kiepert—History of Jerusalem—Telegram from Beyrout—Legend-mongers—Mosaic pavements—Telegram from New York—Native houses—Abd-el-Kader—Persian singer.

ELLIOT'S DIARY.

CAMP OF THE ASSYRIANS, Saturday, March 27th, 1869, 4 P. M.

WE are preparing to move our camp in an hour or two, and I will write out my diary for Saturday.

If I could have half the sport at witnessing the costumes and manners of these people that they do at witnessing *mine*, I should be a happy boy, indeed. This morning, a crowd of Arabs came round my tent and gazed at me as though I was some wild animal. When I got out my tooth brush and used it, they raised a hoot that made the oak leaves quiver overhead. If I hadn't got used to this sort of intrusion, I should hardly stand it so patiently. But I suppose if an Arab boy were to go through the streets of New York, dressed in his native garb, and practicing his native customs, we should stare at him quite as impolitely as they do at me. I soon took their attention away from my outlandish garments by setting the music box in motion. This never fails to give delight.

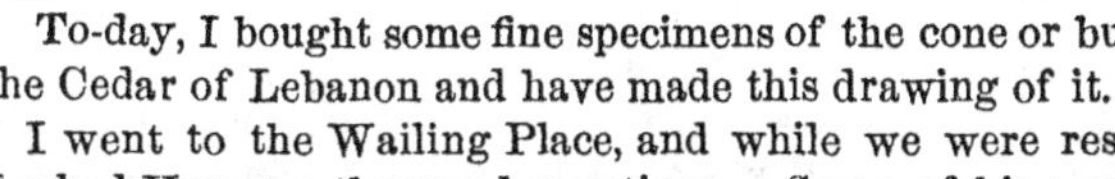

Cone of the Cedar of Lebanon.

To-day, I bought some fine specimens of the cone or burr of the Cedar of Lebanon and have made this drawing of it.

I went to the Wailing Place, and while we were resting, I asked Hassan a thousand questions. Some of his answers are very funny. I have got them all down in short hand. He says the reason why the Jews and the Mohammedans don't eat *pork* is because the hog is the brother of a man, and it would be cannibalism. I asked him how he knew this. He couldn't tell. Thought it was in the Koran, but I have looked there for it, and it isn't. He says when you kill anything for food you must say *Bismillah* over it. That means, *in the name of God*. I asked him, suppose you were dumb and couldn't speak! There I I got him. I showed him where it says in the Koran if a man is starving, he may eat pork. He never saw *that* before.

As I am too lame to do it, I got John to *step* the distance around Jerusalem to-day, and let me enter it in my diary. Here it is:

From our camp at the northwest corner to the Joppa Gate.................300 paces.
To southwest corner..468 "

That is for the *west* side, 768 paces.

To Zion Gate...195 paces.
To bend in south wall..295 "
To Mograbbin Gate...244 "
To southeast corner...415 "

That is for the *south* side, 1,149 paces.

To the Golden Gate..353 paces.
To St. Stephen's Gate...230 paces.
To northeast corner..360 "

That is for the *east* side, 943 paces.

To Herod's Gate...359 paces.
To the Bend...250 "
To Damascus Gate...150 "
To northwest corner..660 "

That is for the *north* side, 1,419 paces.

The total is 4,279, which, allowing 5 paces to the rod, gives 856 rods, or about two miles and two-thirds for the circumference of the city.

A man came round and offered to sing me an American song, to-day, for a piastre. I gave it to him and promised him another one if it was genuine. Now here is exactly the song he sung:

"I look inside of heaven,
And dar I saw King Jesus a comin,
Wid a a white cater nappen tied round he wais,
Moses and children wid de lamb."

Where on earth he ever learned such a mess of nonsense, I can't imagine. I gave him his other piastre, for I'm sure the song is both *American* and *genuine.* I suppose some frolicsome young men taught it to him. He considered it one of the standard religious hymns of our country, and it is odd if he don't push it through the hills here as a substitute for native music.

I saw a man, to-day, measuring beans. As fast as he filled the measure he whirled it rapidly round and then heaped on as much as would lie on top. This reminded me of the passage: "Pressed down, and shaken together, and running over." (Luke vi : 38.)

Hassan says he has seen a ring on the finger of a Hadji that has such magic power that if a wall was ready to be pulled down and tottering, only touch it with that ring, and it will stand a hundred years longer. I asked him how he knew that? but he never can answer such questions as that. It is enough for him to *know* it without having to *tell how* he knows it.

The walls and gates of Jerusalem, look to me now, like old acquaintances In A. D. 1178, subscription papers were passed through Europe, soliciting seven annual payments, to re-build the then dilapidated walls. But these proved small obstacles against Saladin. So under the modern system of warfare, the planting of even a single twelve-pounder upon the slope of Mount Olivet, would lead to the immediate surrender of the city. A good artillerist there could hit any edifice in the place with unerring precision. The gates are usually double-arched, and quite Oriental in character. Towers around each afford guard-houses and apartments for soldiers' quarters.

To-day, I had an opportunity to visit this great Russian convent, near which we are encamped. They call it here the *New Jerusalem*, it is so large. The buildings are truly immense, including a college, pilgrims' home, and church. It is quite a town by itself. The Russian consul lives there, also the Russian bishop, who, for his singularly attractive manner and appearance, is said to be a universal favorite. The view from the terrace of the main building is fine. The fittings of the church are gorgeous. They were all executed at Moscow. The panels of the organ loft and screen are painted with full-length pictures of saints, on a gold ground, and the oak carvings are extraordinary. The lamps, too, are objects of great admiration. In the strife of European governments to secure the strongest foothold at Jerusalem, the Russians have certainly succeeded in erecting the most costly buildings.

From some excavations in the valley of Hinnom, a fine, ancient bottle of glass, holding about three quarts, has been obtained, and Mr. Fountain bought it for me. The first glass ever made, was made of the sands of Belus, near Tyre, and this one looks old enough to have come from there. The glass is very iridescent and not at all clear. It is the thinnest and lightest glass I ever saw. Here is my drawing of it:

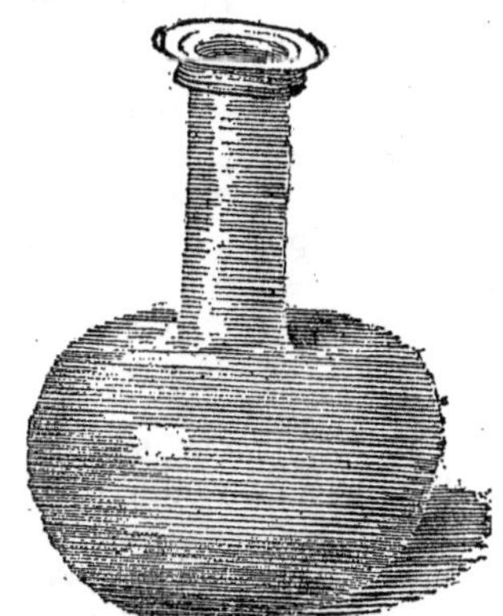

TYRIAN BOTTLE.

In the fifteenth century, the island of Murano, near Venice, was renowned for its glass manufactures.

While I was standing in the court yard, at the entrance to the Church of the Holy Sepulchre, looking at the trafficing that was going on there, in toys and emblems, I was reminded of the time when our Saviour made a scourge of small cords, and drove from the temple just another such a gang of petty rogues as these. (John ii : 15 and Matthew xxi : 12.) Among these sacred pedlars, was a priest, who offered me a piece of limestone, grey, streaked with red, which is nothing but oxide of iron in the stone. He said it came from the place where St. Stephen was stoned to death, and that these red streaks are some of his blood. (Acts vii : 59.) I told him if he would guarentee that the stone was a piece of one of the stones thrown at Stephen, I would give him a dollar for it. He said he thought *it was*, but he was *sure* the red streaks were the good deacon's blood. Then I lold him I had been traveling over just such rocks as that with the soft, pink hue, and weather-stained, exactly in that way, for nearly a week; and that what he called the Sepulchre of Christ, was of the same stone. Then I let him know I was from New York, and a Protestant boy, and couldn't be fooled any how. He praised my smartness and asked me for *backsheesh.*

I bought, to-day, a beautiful pair of the horns of the ibex, and am going to examine the books for a description of the animal. These horns are elegantly shaped. They came from the wilderness of Judæa, near the Dead Sea. I gave *medjeedy* for them—that is ninety-five cents.

CAMP OF THE OLIVE TREE, 8 P. M.

We have removed our camp to a place about two-thirds the way up Mount Olivet to a point northeast of Jerusalem. It is near a large olive tree, having a stone wall around it, and so we name the place the "Camp of the Olive Tree."

JOHN'S DIARY.

CAMP OF THE OLIVE TREE, Saturday, 7 P. M.

In sketching the noble oak tree, which stood near our tents all the week, in full glory with its shining green leaves, I find a close resemblance between it and the celebrated Abraham's Oak, near Hebron.*

This tree, botanically reckoned up, is a holm-tree, the *quercus pseudo-coc cifera,* and the finest one, by universal consent, in Southern Palestine. The natives call it *scindiarn.* Its trunk is sound, twenty-two feet in circumference. A common name for it here is *baloota.* It is an evergreen. It shades a space more than ninety feet in circumference.

I have paid more than ordinary attention, to-day, to making a map of Jerusalem. In shape the city is a square, or rather a rhomboid. The northeast and southwest angles are *acute,* the other two *obtuse.* The east wall, for the whole length, is nearly straight. On the north and south sides, the wall bends *out,* and on the west side bends *in.* It is nearly an *octagon* in shape.

Measuring some of the great stones in the walls of Mount Moriah, I note down the fact that in the granite quarries of Monson, Massachusetts, a block was recently quarried that would have done credit to the builders of King Solomon. It was three hundred and fifty feet long, eleven wide, and four thick. It weighed one thousand two hundred and eighty-three tons, reckoning granite at one hundred and sixty pounds to the cubic foot.

To-day, I have enjoyed the uninterrupted attentions of Lieutenant Charles Warren, who has, all the week, been extremely kind to our party. He took me through his excavations, so far as they remain open, and showed me his drafts, finished and unfinished. He allowed me to copy from his notes, these marks by which the ancient stone masons designated and identified their work:

---

* See the drawing of the famous oak, facing Chapter Thirteenth.

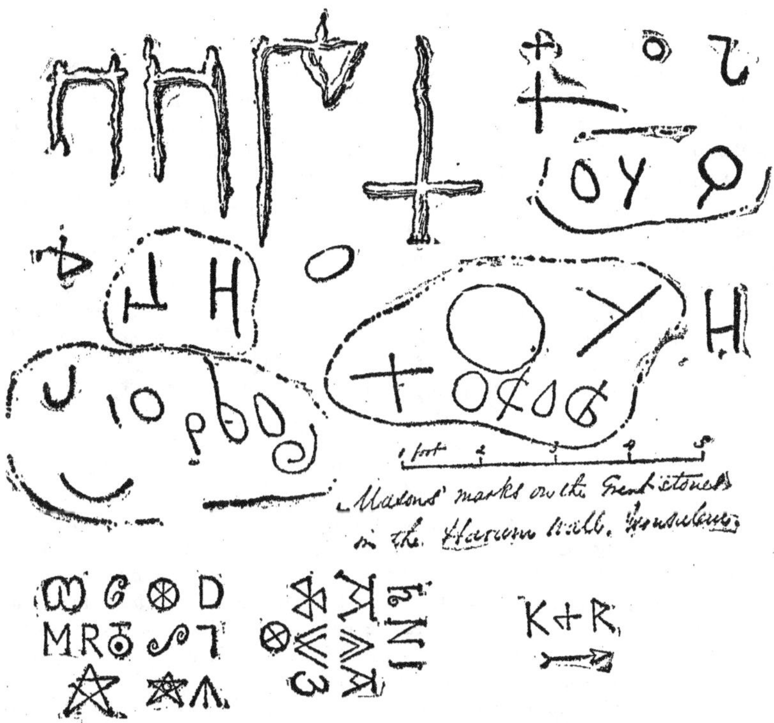

Lieutenant Warren says that the great curiosity of Christendom can never be fully satisfied, so long as a separate square mile in the Holy Land remains unsurveyed, or a mound of ruins, in any part consecrated to Bible history, remains unexcavated. Oh, that I could give five or ten years to this work! How cheerfully I would devote all my energy to the correct description of the lilies and cedars, the lions, eagles, foxes and ravens of the Bible.

The Society, represented by Lieutenant Warren, is known by the rather insignificant title of *The London Palestine Fund.* It was organized by the best Biblical scholars of Great Britain, in 1865. The first person sent here by the Society, was Captain C. W. Wilson, who had already conducted an ordance survey of Jerusalem, at the expense of a wealthy English lady, Miss Coutts, for the purpose of supplying the city with water. They have engineered and mapped a large part of the Holy Land on both sides of the Jordan. For the last two years, Lieutenant Warren has had the sole charge, and is giving his principal care to the development of antiquities at Jerusalem.

It is reported here that the great Prussian geographer, Professor Kiepert, has been deputed, by his government, to give a year of his valuable observations to this city.

Under the lead of the skillful and industrious Warren, I was enabled to stand upon the ancient causeway, but now buried one hundred feet under the earth, upon which the Apostle Peter probably stood, when he delivered that soul-stirring discourse recorded in Acts ii.

In the partial opening of ancient Jerusalem, it may be compared to a beautiful person whom we have not seen for many years, who has passed through a great variety of changes and misfortunes, which have caused the rose on her cheeks to fade, her flesh to consume away, and her skin to become dry and withered, and covered her face with the wrinkles of age, but who still retains some general features by which we recognize her as the person who used to be the delight of the circle in which she moved.

This city, Jerusalem, first appears on the sacred page about B. C. 1910, in the affecting account of the meeting between Abram and Melchizadek. A few years later, the faithful obedience of Abram was commemorated at Mount Moriah, an outlying spur of the hills of Jerusalem. We hear no more of it until B. C. 1400, when the soldiers of Judah and Simeon took it from the Jebusites, and burned it. (Judges i : 8.) It reverted back, however, to the hands of the original proprietors, and so remained for 354 years. B. C. 1046, David took it by assault, at the head of two hundred and eighty thousand troops, choice warriors of the flower of Israel, (1 Chr. xii) and made it the capital of his kingdom. Solomon gave it great celebrity, by erecting here his magnificent temple. Under the weak rule of his successor, Rehoboam, it was captured B. C. 970, by Shishak, King of Egypt, and the treasures of the temple and palace carried off. (2 Chr. xii.) About B. C. 887, under the detestable King Jehoram, the city was captured by the Arabians and Philistines, and plundered. This was its fourth siege. (2 Chr. xxi.) About 830 B. C., Jerusalem, under King Amaziah, was captured by Joash, King of Israel; again pillaged, and much of its walls thrown down.

About 711 B. C., it is supposed that the city, under Hezekiah, was besieged by the Assyrian armies of Sennacherib; if so, it was not captured. It was, however, taken by the Assyrians, about B. C. 690, and King Mannasseh carried captive to Babylon. B. C. 608, the Egyptians took it and sent King Jehoahaz, captive, to Egypt. Twice, perhaps three times, it was taken by Nebuchadnezzar, King of the Chaldeans, during the successive reigns of Eliakim and Zedekiah, each of whom was sent, in turn, captives to Babylon. The last capture resulted in the total destruction of the city and nation, B. C. 586.

Being re-built from B. C. 532, a new lease of life to the renowned city began. It surrendered peaceably to Alexander, B. C. 331: B. C. 320 it was taken by the Egyptian King, Ptolemy Soter; B. C. 203, by Antiochus, the Syrian; B. C. 199, re-taken by Scopas, the Egyptian; B. C. 198, re-taken by Antiochus; B. C. 165, the Machabees rescued it from the enemies of their country; B. C. the Romans, under Pompey, took it; A. D. 66, the Romans were driven out; A. D. 70, it was finally taken and destroyed by Titus.

A. D. 136, the Roman Emperor, Hadrian, re-built it under the name of Aelia Capitolina; A. D. 326, it became a Christian city, under Constantine the Great, and resumed its original name; A. D. 614, the Persians, under Chosroes II, captured it and inflicted much devastation; A. D. 634, the Saracens, under Omar, took it and made it a Mohammedan city; A. D. 1099, the Crusaders captured it with horrible slaughter, and held it until A. D. 1187, when the Sultan, Saladin, restored it to the Mohammedan power. During the next century the Christians once or twice held a brief and feeble possession of it, since which it has ever remained in the hands of the Moslems.

From Joshua to Titus, fifteen centuries, it was seventeen times besieged. Twice it was razed to the ground. Twice more its walls were leveled. Such is the history of the beloved site to which the Jewish rabbins affectionately refer in these words. "The world is like an eye: the *white* of the eye is the ocean surrounding the world; the *black* is the world itself; the *pupil* is Jerusalem; the *image* in the pupil is the Temple!"

We have just received a telegram from our excellent consul-general, Mr. J. A. Johnson, at Beyrout. He is son-in-law of father's old friend, Dr. J. T. Barclay, whose book, "The City of the Great King," is so much better than any other on this subject. Miss Barclay wrote that sprightly book, "The Howadji in Syria." The telegram cost us one medjidia, or ninety-five cents, for twenty words. In counting words in despatches, these people count the names both of the sender and receiver. They turned the telegram into Arabic, at Beyrout, but gave it to us in English, at Jerusalem. This makes some queer changes in the grammatical construction of the despatch, but does not affect the sense. When General Grant was elected President, last November, the telegram announcing it read in this way: "General Grant has been named President, and Head of the Sheikhs. And Aclafoks has been named Second President." I think Mrs. Colfax must have marveled at her husband's name when she saw it turned into *Aclafoks*.

Elliot is getting pretty sharp with these legend-mongers. They have told him so many lies, and contradicted themselves so often, that he scarcely shows patience with any of them. A Greek priest, who undertook, to-day, to point out the rock on which the cock crowed that recalled Peter to penitence, was dumb founded by Elliot asking him if he had ever heard of Peter the Great sailing across the Dead Sea, in a lead coffin, with his head under his arm! The best policy for a visitor to Jerusalem, is one that Dr. Robinson adopted; that is, to give no attention to such stories or the narrators of them.

I wonder that more has not been said by travelers, especially those who, like De Vogue, have made ancient architecture a specialty, in relation to the great quantity of *tesseræ*, parts of mosaic floors, that are found all around Jerusalem. On Mount Zion, oustide of the walls, I discovered them in such great profusion, that I set some native boys at work to collect them, and within the four days that I limited them, they had more than as many thousands. Thus far, I have not found in any instance, enough *tesseræ* remaining cemented together, to enable me to detect a pattern or device. I saw in Westminster Abbey, in Henry III division, that the *tesseræ* are of jasper, porphyry, alabaster, lapis lazuli, and other varieties of rare stone, arrayed in stars, circles, squares, wedges, lozenges, etc., from one-half inch to four inches long. These in my possession are all of native stone. I hope to see near Tyre the splendid pavement that Kenan discovered there in 1860, of which I have his drawings. Roman history intimates that Sylla, B.C. 80, introduced this ornament into the palaces in Roman architecture. It became extremely common there, afterwards, and now the Italian workmen are famed throughout the world for their skill in mosaic handwork. In the great Armenian church, on Mount Zion, the mosaic pavement resembles that of St. Mark's, at Venice.

Yesterday we sent our second telegram home, and to-day, have received reply. We said:

"Safely arrived on Monday. All well. Making great improvement. A happy expedition."

The answer is—

"All well here. Our hearts are with you. Improve as fast as you can.*"

The Armenians live around their great convent on Mount Zion. The Greeks and Catholics north of them in the northwestern quarter of the city. The Jews live in the dust, between Zion and Moriah; the Turks in the northeast ern quarter of the city.

Mosks are on each side the Holy Sepulchre, like the two thieves on the right and left of our Lord.

All the country houses we have seen, from Joppa to Jerusalem, are alike. They are stone walls plastered inside and out with mud; a roof of long poplar poles laid across, flat, having brush wood piled and woven together upon them, and the whole covered with mud and gravel. The house has but one room. The floor is the earth, pounded hard and smoothed over. No windows. In one corner a fire is sometimes made, but there is no opening for the smoke. However, fuel is too costly to permit the luxury of fire, save for cooking, so this is of less importance. In front of these low and miserable huts you often see one or two handsome arches thrown over the entrance. It is the only thing in which the native builders excel—*raising arches.* With a few poles and a lot of brush wood for a framework, they will fashion an arch of artistic shape and spring that is really beautiful. Mr. Fountain says the only arch he has ever known to *fall*, in this country, was in the Protestant church, last year, at Beyrout. In that accident, several workmen were killed.

I cannot conceive a greater contrast between the splendid and magnificent structures erected in this country, first by the Jews, afterwards by the Romans and Crusaders, and the low, filthy shebangs in which the present population exists.

HARRIET'S DIARY.

CAMP OF THE OLIVE TREE, Saturday, 7 P. M.

We esteem ourselves, indeed fortunate, in finding, among the visitors to Jerusalem, the Arab ex-Sultan, Emir Abd-el-Kader. He was very kind last year to Mr. Fountain, and expressed a desire to see us also. In our short call we had but little opportunity to converse with him, yet were impressed with his lofty and commanding manner and Oriental style. He is a genuine Abraham, an Oriental pattern, a prince in the land. With large possessions, he has a numerous retinue, and is distinguished throughout the east for his integrity,

---

* In April, 1870, the rates of telegraphic business has been so greatly reduced that a message of twenty words can now be sent from New York to Bombay, nearly twice the distance to Jerusalem, for $17.50.

hospitality and generosity. Desiring to compliment him, I could think of nothing better than to say that a city in Iowa has been named after him, *Elkader;* at this he expressed his satisfaction. As an instance of his sententious style, he said to us when we told him we were endeavoring to make *Nature* bear testimony to the truth of the Holy Scriptures: "God created the world full of variety, and all nature teaches wisdom, and abundant illustrations can be drawn therefrom. The world is full of wisdom, but like rich ore, deep down into the depths of the earth—it must be toiled and striven for."

I make this pen and ink sketch of General Kader, from a cabinet photograph:

ABD EL KADER.

We had heard much of a Persian singer and reader of Oriental verse, who is giving readings in Jerusalem, from the poems of Hafiz and Firdousi, and others, and at my request, Mr. Fountain brought him this afternoon to our tent. The man exhibits but little outward show of a poet. The absence of his front teeth, his short, upper lip, a sickly smile stereotyped upon his countenance, and a harsh, cracked voice, such as I have observed in street-singers, at home, prepossessed me unfavorably towards him, while John, in his rapid way, condemned him as a mere boot black on Parnassus.

The bard was low of stature, slightly built and thin, even to a skeleton. His eyes were small, black and piercing, shadowed by thick brows, which, like his beard, were red. His lips were livid pale, the nails of his skinny hands long as talons. His head was closely shaven above the temples and covered with the *tarboush*, over which was the *kafeeah*, a coarse cotton handkerchief, triangularly folded, with broad stripes of white and yellow, the ends ornamented with a plaited fringe, hung on each side of the face down to the shoulders, and confined over the *tarboush* by two bands of a roughly-twisted black cord of camel's hair. An *abah*, or narrow cloak made of camel's hair of extremely coarse texture, broadly striped white and brown, and fashioned like the Syrian *bournoose*, or horseman's cloak, hung negligently about his person. Beneath the *abah* he wore a long, loose cotton shirt, confined at the waist by a narrow leather belt. A pair of faded red buskins, very sharp at the toes, completed his costume. His instrument was the Rebakeh, or violin of one string.

Such was the unprepossessing appearance of the celebrated Persian poet, musician and *improvisatore*. Yet he showed one evidence of genius. He proved that he belonged to the *genus irritabile uatum*, or irritable race of poets, by declaring that unless our dog and donkey were removed further from the tent he couldn't exhibit. I admired his taste in this, though Elliot did not.

When I had offered him the conventional dish of sweetmeats and the fingan of coffee, his poor dull eye kindled up with an inspiration I was not prepared for. He broke forth into an inspiring strain in a manner that I can no more describe, than imitate. The peculiarity of Persian verse is a measured, musical utterance, filled with recurring sounds. Even their prose is interspersed with rhyme, balanced clauses and pairs of jingling names. Instead of Cain and Abel, for instance, they say *Abel and Kabel*, and so of most of the traditional names.

His first piece was a religious poem, heart-rending and lugubrious in accent, but quite consolatory in sentiment. His next piece was the Arabic story of Moatzim and his pied horse, after which he discoursed of Antar, of Haroun al-Raschid and all the heroes of Oriental romance until the hour was exhausted, and we were obliged to dismiss him.

We notice a peculiar wailing or screaming of females here that is strictly Oriental. It is nearly the same at weddings, funerals and family mournings. In making it they let their voices die away into a low murmur, then gradually increase the sound until the whole womanhood present exert themselves to the top of their voices. The noise resembles the tremulous tones of the screech owl, only much louder, and, until we get accustomed to it, more disagreeable.

The Oriental character of the Scriptural books causes them to abound in metaphors and symbols taken from the common life of the time. They take the wildest range, the barren precipitous rocks, alternating with the green and fertile valleys,—the trees, flowers and herbage,—the creeping things of the earth,—the fishes of the sea,—the birds of the air,—and all the beings which abide with man or dwell in deserts.

The gait of the women here is ungraceful and shuffling, caused, probably, by the use of loose slippers, which require a peculiar stiffness of the foot to keep them on.

The better classes go to the graveyards wholly enveloped in what seems to be a large sheet, falling in folds to the ground as if thrown over a statue to conceal it or protect it from the dirt. As the sun went down, these groups of women broke up, and wrapped in their snow-white vestments, looked like so many lengthened lines of vestal virgins ascending from the Pool of Gihon to the gate.

Elliot's acquisition of Arabic words and phrases is remarkable. Already he can repeat the current phrases of travelers and bazaar merchants. He can hold quite a conversation with Hassan in Arabic and is adding to his vocabulary every hour. The worst effect of catching the sounds from the lower classes is to give him an inelegant pronunciation, which may be seen in his manner of spelling the Arabic words in his diary. But this cannot be avoided.

In the services of Passion Week, this is called *Easter Eve.* During this day, a seal was set by the Jews, and a Roman guard stationed at the door of the sepulchre in which the Lord's body had been lain. It was the Jewish Sabbath, and the city, resting from the passions and turbulence of the preceding day, lay calm and serene under the blue April sky.

VIEW OF JERUSALEM FROM OLIVET.

CHAPTER XIV.

THE CHRISTIAN SABBATH.

Ostrich eggs—Palm tree broom—Loaded donkeys; their music—Dominoes—Idle women—Collecting taxes—Public whipping—Street music—Goats—Water supply—Squashes—Negro belle—Heretico—Coin helmet—Jerusalem stories—Jews—Mohammedan prayers—Song of backsheesh—Valley of Jehoshaphat—Collecting relics—Franciscans—Protestants—Brief tarrying—The English party—Golgotha—Protestant burying ground—Opthalmia—Leprosy—Communion service—Conversion of the Jews—Protestant Sunday School—A night within the walls of Jerusalem—Summing up.

ELLIOT'S DIARY.

CAMP OF THE OLIVE TREE, Sunday, March 28th, 1869, 6 P. M.

I HAVE been too lame to-day to walk about, so I have spent the time making notes. This is a beautiful place to see Jerusalem from. As I was obliged to sit still a good deal, I have written up all the notes of the week's work that I didn't have time to copy before.

In one hour's time that I sat at the corner of the street in Jerusalem, yesterday, I saw a great many things:

A street pedlar with six ostrich eggs for sale. I would have bought them, only we are to wait till we get to Damascus, where they are plentier and cheaper. His eggs were small and poor, and he wanted four piastres apiece for them. I saw some very fine ostrich eggs used for lamps in the Church of the Holy Sepulchre; also in the Armenian Church of St. James. The pedlar also had rosaries for sale, made of jasper, agate, and sweet-scented woods, but his prices were too high.

A servant sweeping out the entrance of a passage way with a palm leaf, such as I cut off the tree at Joppa. It makes a good broom, but not equal to broom corn.

Nine donkeys in a row, all loaded with building stones. Hassan says the stone comes from Anatta, two or three miles northeast of Jerusalem. It is white and soft, with red streaks. I shouldn't think it would last well; but he says it gets harder and harder and never wears out. But I don't believe that.

While the donkeys were going by, one of them raised his tail and brayed. Then the other eight raised their tails and brayed. I never *did* hear such a noise. So much donkey braying in this country affects people's way of talking; and may be that's the reason they talk so guttural. They say that Mohammed talked Arabic that was music to the ear; but he lived at Mecca where, I suppose, there were no donkeys. Hassan says if you tie a stone to the tail of a donkey he never will bray. Says he can't bray till he raises his tail.

14

Each donkey in this row has a string of shells around his neck to keep off the evil eye. Hassan doesn't seem to know what the evil eye is, but he says the shells keep it off. The donkey drivers always wear these shells, but then *their* eyes are already so evil that it is too late to help *them* much.

A group of men playing dominoes, They enjoy that silly game better than ever I could. They fairly scream with joy when one of them makes a double; and when the big one-eyed fellow matches his last domino, while the little one-eyed fellow has a whole handfull left, they laughed so loud that a woman overhead opens her lattice window to see what's the matter. But when she sees me drawing her picture, she pulls it in very quickly. She is right; for her hair hasn't been combed and she looks ugly.

A group of six idle women are looking at the sore-eyed dirty baby of a seventh idle woman. These folks enjoy their own ignorance better than other people's wisdom.

A couple of men going by chained together. A soldier guards them. This is the way St. Paul left this city once. (Acts xxiii: 31.) Hassan says they came from Bethel, eleven miles north of here, and that they haven't paid their taxes this year. He says this is the way government collects taxes here. Says their friends will come to-morrow with the money and pay them out. But they will have to lie in the dungeon near the Joppa Gate, to-night, and a horrible place it is.

The soldier was polite to me. I gave him a cigarette and he let me ask the prisoners questions. He didn't know anything about the case himself, as they were only put in his hands at the Damascus Gate to bring through the city.

One of the men told me he owed fourteen *herresh*, that is *piastres*. The other one owed forty herresh. They said they didn't want anything to eat, but they wanted a smoke. So I gave them a bunch of cigarettes. They kissed my hand and went off cheerful. They were fairly alive with fleas and lice, and some of the fleas hopped on my clothes while they were kissing my hand. In this country a man may be kept *forever* in jail if he owes the government. But if he only owes *another person*, he can swear out as an insolvent as soon as he pleases, by taking the benefit of the Bankrupt Law.

A man was whipped by the officers. The soldiers laid him on the ground, face downward, each foot and hand being held separately. Two soldiers then whipped him alternately on his bare back, thirty blows, with thongs of leather. How he halloed. The soldiers laughed and so did the spectators.

No merchant here sells more than one kind of goods. The stock of each one is very small; five hundred dollars will set up the best Jerusalem trader I have seen.

A street itinerant musician who has an instrument that is turned with a handle like a handorgan, but sounds like a diseased melodeon. I can't understand the Italian what he calls his instrument, and Hassan can't understand him either. But as I don't want to hear him play I gave him *backsheesh* to move on. He also blows on a sort of double reed, music almost as disagreeable to me as the Scotch bagpipe.

A drove of she goats under charge of a woman, a funny little dried-up woman in mannish trowsers. She makes a goaty noise, and when people open their doors, she stops,—milks a goat,—takes their money and travels on. The rest of the goats lie down and sleep while she is milking. I shouldn't like to drink *that* milk after seeing her milk it. A boy walks with her who has a pair of trowsers made of chintz, the large pattern used for settees. The pattern is green parrots and he has a whole green parrot behind him.

A man with a skin of water under his arm, peddling it out like lemonade. I took a cupfull and paid eight paras for it. That is nearly a cent. It wasn't good. Tasted as if it had soap in it. Was hairy and muddy. When I handed it back the fellow poured it in again with the rest. And yet they say they rank good water here among the best gifts of nature.

A boy with a lot of long green crooked squashes. People eat them here raw, like watermelons. I tried a few mouthfulls and it was quite good.

A fat negro woman riding by, man-fashion, on a mule. Has enormously large rings on her hands, a green glass breastpin and earrings. A gay embroidered belt goes round and round her waist. String of amber beads as big as sparrow eggs round her neck. Ragged piece of white lace round her head. Is eating a handfull of *particcio*, a sort of candy which people here are very fond of.

Parcel of Greek sailors mounted on donkeys. Each donkey has a boy running behind to punch the donkey up. Most of these sailors are drunk. The rest are fast getting drunk, for they drink as they ride. One of them shied his bottle at me as he went past, and called me *heretico*. That made Kosroo madder than I ever saw him before. I believe he would have given his bayonet to the sailor if I had let him. The poor drunken papist was glad enough to ride on peaceably and let Heretico alone.

Some women from Bethlehem. They wear strings of coins of gold, silver and copper in a sort of a helmet around their heads. Hassan says they would rather die than lose these queer ornaments. They look homely enough for them to want to die to *get rid* of them. These strings of coins are handed down from mother to daughter for hundreds of years. He says nobody ever steals them. I asked one of the women what she would take for hers? She answered *Al insarn laho aahl amma al baheema fala.* That means, "*men* have got sense, but *beasts* haven't." That was not complimentary to me! These women were dressed in bright blue petticoats with scarlet bodices and snowy white head dresses. They looked more like American women than any other females I have seen in this country. They live close by the place where our Saviour was born. Mother told me always to notice how women dress in this country, so that I could describe them to her. The most of them only wear one dress apiece, a kind of blue chemise.

Surely there never was a place so full of stories as Jerusalem. I don't know which tells the most, or the biggest ones, the *Jews*, the Christians, or the Mohammedans. I don't believe there is a stone around this city, big as my head, that hasn't got a story about it. I don't believe there is a thing named in the Bible about Jerusalem, but what you can find somebody who will show you right where it happened. All the accounts, of old travelers here, are made up of these stories, and these mostly copied from each other. Upon the whole, I had rather hear the Jews tell *their* stories. They are older than the rest, whether truer or not. One of them showed me in an English newspaper a paragraph copied from the New York *Times*, that Rabbi Iverson had called on our Secretary of State and appealed to him to have the "stars and stripes" raised over the Jewish part of Jerusalem, so as to protect them. That would be glorious. The old man hugged me after he read it. I didn't like that part of the performance. He said *harthar assibi mohabbab ilyna jiddan.* That means we love this boy, dearly. I answered *tyeeb.* That means good.

The Turks pray a great deal. Each one of them has a string of one hundred beads around his left wrist, and he keeps slipping them along, one at a time, with his right hand, repeating the names of God. Here is the list, as I copied it, from the "History of Mohammedanism:"

O Compassionate, O Merciful, O King, O Holy One, O Saviour, O Protector, O Defender, O Glorious, O Absolute Sovereign, O Magnificent, O Creator, O Author of Nature, O Maker of the Universe, O Thou Who Forgivest Sins, O Conqueror, O Truly Generous, O Preserver, O Victorious, O Omniscient, O Omnipotent, O Boundless, O Humbler of the Proud, O Elevator of the Humble, O Author of all Honor, O Author of all Humiliation, O Thou Who Hearest, O Thou Who Seest, O Judge, O Just, O Thou Worthy of Love, O Truly Wise, O Great, O Gracious, O Rewarder of Thy Servants, O Most Mighty, O Most High, O Guardian, O Thou Who Affordest Nourishment, O Avenger, O Sublime, O Beneficent, O Observer of Actions, O Hearer of Prayer, O Boundless, O Source of Knowledge, O Source of Glory, O Thou That Lovest Us, O Cause of all Causes, O Witness, O Truth, O Governor, O Strong, O Permanent, O Master, O Object of all Our Praises, O Thou That Calledst Being From Nothing, O Calculator, O Author of the Resurrection, O Giver of Life, O Giver of Death, O Living One, O Enduring, O Source of Discovery, O Worthy of all Honor, O Thou Only One, O Immortal, O Powerful, O Thou to Whom Nothing is Impossible, O Thou Who Existest Before all Ages, O Thou Who Existest After all Time, O First of Beings, O Ancient of Days, O Eternal, O Invisible, O Manifest, O Our Patron, O Our Benefactor, O Thou Who Dost Accept Our Repentance, O Thou Who Dost Justify Us, O Thou Who Dost Punish, O Benign, O Sovereign of Nature, O Possessor of Glory and Majesty, O Equitable, O Thou Who Wilt Re-assemble Us at the Day of Judgment, O Rich, O Source of Riches, O Lord, O Thou Who Dost Deliver Us From Evil, O Thou Who Dost Permit Evil to Come, O Author of all Good, O Illuminator, O Guide, O Marvellous, O Unchangeable, O Thou Whose Inheritance is the Universe, O Director, O Patient, O Mild, O God.

In the Arabic language each of these expressions is made up of only one word. But in English, some of them must make a whole sentence.

JOHN'S DIARY.

CAMP OF THE OLIVE TREE, Sunday, 6 P. M.

Yesterday we removed our encampment to a place about three-quarters of a mile eastward of the Camp of the Assyrians, as Harriet wished to complete her sketches of Jerusalem, from this point, it is near the traditional spot where David paused in his flight from Absalom, and ordered the ark-bearers to return to the city with their sacred deposit.

Just below us, in the valley of Jehoshaphat, in which both Jew and Mohammedan locate the awful tragedy of the judgment-day. How appropriate these tremendous words from *Dies Iræ:*

> Tuba mirum spargens sonum,
> Per sepulchra regionum,
> Coget omnes, ante Thronum.

Among the very large collections of specimens we have made here, I enumerate: rosaries of olive-seeds, dried and strung neatly; ancient coins, more than one thousand two hundred, representing periods from Alexander the Great (B. C. 333) to the era of the Crusades; (A. D. 1180) ink stands made of the bitumen stone of the Dead Sea; carved shells from the Red Sea, wrought at Bethlehem; models of the so-called Holy Sepulchre; dried flowers from sacred places; elegant specimens of calc-spar and the various calcarous and silicious stones of this vicinity; bottles of the waters of Siloam, En-Rogel, the Fountain in the Great Quarry, and other water pools; specimens of the earth, from Akeldama, Gethsemane, and other noted localities; photographs made here of all the striking points, costumes, and of Jerusalem; models of the Tomb of the Kings, Tomb of Lazarus, and other ancient tombs; and many other things. To take to Joppa, the numerous and ponderous boxes in which these these are packed, Mr. Fountain has employed a *camelier*, with five camels.

Among the sects of Roman Catholics that abound here, the *Franciscans* have most attracted our attention. They are styled "Fathers Minors of the *ab observentia*." The order was first established by St. Francis, in 1209. Webster's dictionary defines them, "pious laymen, who devote themselves to useful works, such as manual labor schools, etc." All the sacred places in Palestine are under their care, and have been since their founder received from the Sultan of Turkey, this right to him and his order in perpetuity. For more than six hundred years they have maintained their place, often amidst great trials and sufferings. Their general-guardian resides here; he is always an Italian, and is elected for three years. He has fourteen convents subject to him in the Holy Land, employing one hundred and fifty monks. The convents at Joppa and Ramleh, and the Garden of Gethsemane, are under the care of Franciscans. Their convents, I understand, are always denoted by the emblem of "the crossed and stigmated hands," representing the pierced hands of Jesus.

The Protestants have two places of worship, a church on Mount Zion, the property of the London Jew's Society, in which services are conducted in Hebrew, daily, at six A. M., during the summer, at seven, in the winter. English service on Sundays, at ten A. M., and during Lent; also, an evening service at half-past seven. German service at four P. M., in summer, and three P. M., in winter. In the adjoining school room, a service in Judeo-Spanish, on Sundays, at half-past seven A. M., and a German service on Wednesdays, at seven P. M. The Arabic chapel is a commodious building, leased by the Church Missionary Society, in which the Rev. F. A. Klein officiates, in Arabic, every Sunday morning, at ten o'clock. United prayer meetings are held in the chapel every Tuesday and Friday, at half-past four P. M., and on the first Wednesday in the month, a missionary meeting is held at seven P. M.

Elliot was afraid that a *week* was not long enough for our party to explore Jerusalem, but he now sees that with three of us, so actively employed from daylight till dark, after having studied so much of the investigations of other travelers, a week is *amply sufficient*, and he already wants to be off, over the hills. Looking over the books of Palestine travel, last summer, I was surprised to see how short a time each explorer gave to this interesting country. Dr. Robinson, who wrote so many books of Holy Land travel, so full of good sense, was here only two months and five days, in 1838; and three months and three weeks, in 1852. Dr. Bellows, last year, spent here about two months; the most of tourists only stay ten days!

We have met, almost every day, the English party who left us at Joppa. They are very polite to us, and extend to us every sort of courtesy. How these English win upon an American's affections! After all, are they not our relatives? This party is busily engaged in verifying all the statements in "Murray's Hand Book" in regard to Jerusalem. Being nearly through, they will soon be off "to fresh fields and pastures new." Health, happiness, and plenty of pale ale go with them!

Somewhere, in yon northwestern part of the city, was probably the Golgotha, the *place of a skull*, where the cross stood. Not in the centre of the city where the "Holy Sepulchre" stands. That is incredible. If now, when Jerusalem is reduced to one-third its ancient limits, that location is still so far *within the city*, how much less likely is it that in the palmy days of Jerusalem, the spot could have been *outside* the walls! Jesus was crucified "without the gate." "Jesus, also, that He might sanctify the people with His own blood, suffered without the gate." (Hebrews xiii : 12.) We do not know *which gate.* Dr. Barclay thinks it was the one now called St. Stephen's Gate, but the common opinion is that somewhere in the northwestern part of the city was Calvary, and somewhere, not far off, was "the garden," (John xix : 41) and in the garden "a new sepulchre which was hewn out of the rock." (Mark xv : 46.) The "own new tomb," of Joseph (Matt. xxvii : 60; "wherein never man before was laid." (Luke xxiii : 53.) From this place, then, He arose on the third day; "very early in the morning;" "as it began to dawn;" "when it was yet dark." So here I hastened to interrupt my sleep, that on this "first day of the week," consecrated as a Sabbath day, in perpetual memory of the resurrection of Jesus, I may commune for a sweet morning hour with the spirit of the place. "Then He arose." How often has that Easter Anthem rung in our happy parlor at home!

"Then first humanity triumphant passed the crystal ports of light."

Then it might have been said that "truth sprung out of the earth; righteousness looked down from heaven; mercy and truth met together; righteousness and peace kissed each other." (Psalms lxxxv.)

Nor must I forget that according to the received opinion of the Christian world *this is Easter Day*, the day of Christ's resurrection. The city yonder has been all astir with the celebration. Always early risers, the natives and the pilgrims vied with each other, this morning, which should earliest forsake their slumbers and engage in what they deemed the most pious duty of their lives.

HARRIET'S DIARY.

CAMP OF THE OLIVE TREE, Sunday, 5 P. M.

Among the sacred walks of this holy day, the most affecting one to me is to the Protestant burying-ground on Mount Zion. For here in this little cemetery lies a woman, whose story, as related once at our house by Dr. Van Dyke, is one of the most affecting ones in the history of missions. This was Mrs. Eliza N. Thomson, first wife of Dr. Wm. M. Thomson, author of "The Land and the Book," whose acquaintance we hope to form in Beyrout. This lady came here with her husband, in May, 1834. They secured a house in connection with Rev. Mr. Nicolayson, of the London Jews Mission, near the castle at the Joppa Gate. Having left his household effects at Joppa, Mr. Thomson started after them May 20th, but owing to the civil wars then raging throughout Syria he was unable to return to his family until July 11th, although but a day's ride distant. The experience of this dear lady, left thus for more than two long months in a strange city, is one of the most affecting recitals I ever heard. Scarcely had her husband departed when the rebels closed in around the city, and at once shut out all communication from the coast. Cannons were mounted upon the walls and the city prepared for resistance. May 24th, a terrible earthquake rent Jerusalem almost to pieces. The houses occupied by the mission suffered fearfully and threatened to bury all within the ruins. The weather was intensely hot and sultry, and there was a *Khamsin* or Sirocco wind which gave a painful dryness to the air.

For several days they were compelled to sleep in the garden. By this time the rebels had commenced to fire into the city. The return fire from the castle was so directed that their dwelling places stood between the two fires and were greatly torn up by cannon shot. Then the rebels entered the city and murdered many of the people, drove the missionaries back to their doubly shattered tenements and plundered them of nearly all their effects. Famine then afflicted the suffering ones, and but for the fact that the other missionary stations in Jerusalem kindly shared of their supplies, the worst consequences would have followed. Following upon this came the plague, which nearly depopulated the city of what war and the earthquake had spared.

On the 11th of July, her husband returned to find that his brave wife, overcame by the heat and the excitement through which she had passed, was suffering from violent opthalmia and in a high inflammatory fever. She lingered eleven days and died on the 22d of July. In her last hours she calmly sent messages to near friends, spoke of her dear babe with emotion, but resigned him to Him that gave. Strangers bore her to the grave. Her sleeping dust, here on the top of Zion, near the sepulchre of David, lies awaiting in hope the joyful morning of the resurrection.

I spent many tears musing at the head of this precious grave. Oh, that I were worthy to participate in the crown bestowed upon this sainted creature! How truly has it been said that the blood of martyrs is the seed of the Church!

To-day we were again compelled to notice the prevalence of sore eyes, worse here than at Joppa. Scarcely a native we have met has good sound eyes or eyelids. Opthalmia is the great epidemic of the Orient. One native traveler (Ali Bey) gives his opinion that this disease is produced here entirely by the irritation of the fine grains of sand and the rubbing of the hand which the itching compels. This will scarcely explain the phenomena. The disease is plainly infectious; the flies that cluster around the children's eyelids, carry the poison from one to the other. Nothing but cleanliness, good diet, and proper care of the infected can ever eradicate it. How affecting to me it was to read the petition of blind Bartimeus: "Lord, that I might receive my sight!"

Jerusalem is also sadly conspicuous for the great number of its lepers and the desperate character of the disease as seen here. The law of Moses, which forbade the leper to approach a person, is so far regarded by this Mohammedan government, that the lepers are obliged to reside at night in a portion of the city by themselves. They form an isolated collection of huts just within the Zion Gate, from which every morning they spread themselves over the city to beg. People are generally kind to them and many of them accumulate considerable money from alms. They form a distinct class, being only allowed to marry among themselves, and will probably die out in a generation or two. I could not form an idea how long this leper colony had existed here.

We attended service, to-day, at the church of Bishop Gobat. It being Easter Sunday, the communion was spread, of which Mr. Fountain, John and myself, partook. I dare not record the overwhelming feelings with which we received, at such a place, on such a day, the emblems of the broken body and the shed blood of the God-man.

We also attended a meeting held by the missionaries in view of the conversion of the Jews. There were about forty present, mostly enquirers, a few converts. German, Hebrew, and English, were alternately spoken in the readings, in discussions that followed. The chanting of David's Psalms was the finest thing of the sort I ever heard. That of Psalm iii, which was done in Hebrew, was absolutely thrilling. How it rang, between those thick stone walls of the dwelling house where we were sitting. How rich, full and strong is the Hebrew voice. There was an indescribable pathos and power in it, sung upon Mount Zion at the close of the Jewish Sabbath. I copy the first verse or two, giving the English sounds:

Solo—Halleluyah, Odeh Adonai!
Chorus—B'col layvav:
Solo—B'sod yesharim.
Chorus—Vayadar Odeh Adonai, b'col layvav,
Bsode yesharim, vayadah:
Halleluyah, Halleluyah.

Nor must I forget to speak of the Protestant Sunday school, in which, among other pleasing exercises, the children sung to our own familiar tune—"There is a Happy Land," a pretty Arab hymn, of which I copied one verse:

Li manzilum bead
Fouka el samma;
Killon amran saied
Haza et hana.

Time and again we have visited the more interesting spots, and repeated our observations from every point of view. Three times we have deliberately "walked around Jerusalem," on the outside of the walls. Seven times we have clumb the steep, western slope of Olivet, and taken the great panorama of Jerusalem from thence, morning, noon and evening. We have descended to the Pool of Siloam, so often, that even the dull inhabitants of filthy *Silwarn*, opposite, have learned to recognize our party. In our programmes of daily researches, we have included the mountains, the valleys, the pools, the tombs, all that was needed to fill up our outlines of Jerusalem.

Even the sacred shows, painfully uninteresting as they are to our Protestant minds, have been so often and soberly viewed as the most rigid Papist or Greek could desire, and our examinations have but confirmed our opinion that they are the works of mistaken piety, credulous imposition or pious frauds.

Of our dear friend, Mr. Fountain, and his attentions to us in our journey, it is impossible to say too much. As wise as he is zealous, as laborious as he is fervent,—as honest, and faithful, and pious, as he is loving and friendly,—as sincere and single-eyed as he is calm and decided,—we must esteem it the greatest of all the blessings connected with this pilgrimage to the Holy Land that we have had his undivided thoughts and care during our whole journey.

I could not bear the thought that I should not spend one night *in the city of Jerusalem.* So Mr. Fountain made arrangements for my accommodations at the house of the Prussian Mission of the Knights of St. John, adjoining the Prussian Consulate. It is a cleanly, comfortable mansion, all of stone and cement, as all the houses in Jerusalem are, and the furniture extremely neat and appropriate. It is a charitable establishment, all Protestants being admitted, so far as the capacity of the house admits, whether they can pay or not. Those who pay are charged five francs a day, each. The managers, with their charming infant of two years old, and their plain, domestic ways, make me feel quite at home here.

From the level housetop of this mansion, I look right down upon the open area of thirty-six acres, in which the Temple of Solomon stood. The topmost crescent of the Mosk of Omar, which is seventy feet high, is about on the level of my eye. From this point all the details of the ancient Temple, and its gorgeous service, must have been visible.

And now, before retiring to sleep, let me enjoy from this housetop, the matchless glory of the Oriental heavens. Upon a housetop, in this very city, the Royal Psalmist, too, looked above and around him, three thousand years ago, and saw what I do now. The scene inspired him. He burst forth into words almost as sparkling, almost as sublime, as the astral imagery that called them forth. "When I consider The heavens, the work of Thy fingers, the moon and the stars, which Thou hast ordained, what is *man* that Thou art mindful of him? and the son of man that Thou visitest him?" (Psalms viii: 3.) "The heavens declare the glory of God, and the firmament showeth forth His handiwork." (Psalms xix : 1.)

The milky way shines with a lustre so far exceeding that which it has along its northern semicircle, that I cannot help thinking heaven is nearer Palestine than New York.

The Jews believed the heavens to be an immense crystalline dome, studded with stars, this dome resting upon the horizon, and separating the waters above from the waters below. Such a faith seems scarcely out of place here.

As I gaze, a brilliant meteor goes gleaming down the valley of the Kedron, to the southeast, and points the way which we are to take, to-morrow, when we visit the Dead Sea and the Jordan.

MR. FOUNTAIN'S DIARY.

CAMP OF THE OLIVE TREE, Sunday, 8 A. M.

And now it is left to me to sum up the diaries of the second week. All has gone well, save that Elliot somewhat injured his ankle and this has kept him more than ordinarily quiet for two or three days. But he will be well to-morrow.

In all their busy course, the young people have ever kept pencil in hand, noting first in phonographic character, afterwards elaborating in their diaries the best incidents of the way. These diaries I have examined every evening and corrected, but only so far as as *positive mistakes were made*, leaving the young writers to give, generally, in their own words and style, the impressions made by the country and its inhabitants upon their minds. I think no such vivid, original and entertaining series of observations was ever before penned concerning this thrice hallowed land.

In the margin of their pocket Bibles, they write, first with *pencil*, afterwards with *ink*, the *time and place* where each chapter is read. Our Bibles being in flexible covers and protected by oil-cloth, will not be frayed by this usage, or injured by wet, and they promise to preserve them for sacred memorials as long as they live.

I have not taken such careful notes of the hymns sung and Scriptures read as I did the preceding week; yet in no instance have we neglected to open the labors of the day without a goodly portion of the precious Book, a hymn and prayer. In partaking of the communion to-day, Harriet and John appeared more impressed than I had ever seen them before.

All is ready now for our departure to-morrow to the Dead Sea and the Jordan. With a good stock of Arab words, my pupils are competent now to converse upon many topics with the natives. Elliot, particularly, has made wonderful improvement in that direction.

As members of *The Scholars' Holy Land Exploration* of the United States, we have all paid attention to the proper *objects* of collection, the *modes* of collection and the *cost.* We trust, through the influences of that Society, that ere many years every Sunday School in our own dear Protestant country will be supplied with illustrative objects from the Holy Land.

As a fitting close of the week's diaries, Harriet has given me her beautiful sketch of Joppa.*

---

* See the drawing which closes this chapter.

JOPPA.

INDEX.

This Index is prepared in so simple a manner that the youthful reader can easily find any subject in the book.

1st. If the word looked for is the name of an insect, see *Insects;* if a bird, see *Birds;* if a tree, see *Trees;* if a flower, see *Flowers.* The rule applies to a majority of the subjeets.

2d. Every place visited by the party is found in the Index; also, every noted person met upon the journey.

3d. For religious matters, see *Religions, Prayers, Churches,* and headings of a similar character.

4th. For items of expense, and the values of money, see *Money, Revenue,* etc.

A.

B.

C.

T.

V.

W.

Z.

www.ingramcontent.com/pod-product-compliance
Lightning Source LLC
LaVergne TN
LVHW050531100826
845148LV00002B/517

* 9 7 8 1 4 2 5 5 1 9 1 4 8 *